LUKE

Other books by the author:

Matthew: Spirituality for the 80's and 90's
The Lay Centered Church
John Paul II and the Laity

LUKE

The Perennial Spirituality

Leonard Doohan

Bear & Company
Santa Fe, New Mexico

Acknowledgement

I thank my wife, Helen, for her constant encouragement and support who, along with Eve-Anne, our daughter, made time for me to study. I also express my thanks to Ms. Catherine Rosa for her help in preparing the manuscript.

ISBN 0-939680-24-6

Library of Congress Card Number 85-071858

Bear & Company, Inc.
P.O. Drawer 2860
Santa Fe, NM 87504

Cover Design: William Field, Santa Fe
Photo by Patrice Ceisel
Typography: Copygraphics, Santa Fe
Printed in the United States by BookCrafters, Inc.

With love and gratitude
I dedicate this book
to my wife Helen.

Contents

Introduction
SPIRITUALITY AND THE NEW TESTAMENT

The decade which followed the Second Vatican Council was a time of enthusiasm, excitement, and rediscovered baptismal freedom. It was also a period of individual and community experimentation in lifestyles, prayer, ministry, and worship. The spiritual reawakening of the '70s has been followed by a period of frustration and tension, provoked by differences of understanding in the search for authentic and relevant forms of Christian life in the '80s. While desiring a fresh presentation of the Christian message, Christians in all walks of life also want a modern spirituality, one rooted in the essential challenges of Jesus' message. This search for today's Christian identity manifests a tension between the desires for relevance to the present day, and faithfulness to Jesus' original and unchanging word. The challenge for many Christians today focuses on which parts of Christ's message are changeable, which permanent. This reflection on the writings of Luke is an attempt to contribute to this search for the authentic roots of Christian life, since Luke, more than any other New Testament writer, offers us the components of a perennial spirituality.

Christian spirituality. Spirituality studies the incarnation of the perennial values of Christian life. It is a hard and complex theological discipline, a knife-edge with sentimental devotionalism on one side, and cold, unchallenging theological principles on the other. Spirituality is a theoretical and practical discipline based upon revealed principles and a deep knowledge of the human person. It studies the progress and development of Christian life. Both science and art, the methodology of spirituality is complex. It deals with "a living synthesis of human and evangelical elements. Spirituality is really the structuring of an adult personality in faith according to one's proper genius, vocation, and charismatic gifts, on the one hand, and according to the laws of the universal Christian mystery on the other."[1] A "living synthesis of human and evangelical elements" is not easy, in theology or in life. When human conditions change, syntheses change, and evangelical elements are interpreted and applied differently. However, what was proclaimed by Jesus as spirit and life can still be so today.

Spirituality is also a practical discipline through which one can study the vital activities leading to the growth and maturity of Christian life. Spirituality is concerned with the stages of commitment and development, and with the means that will help in directing others to the goal of union with God. Christian life is constantly evolving; the integration of the elements of spirituality is never complete. As our notions of God, person, and the Church develop, so does our definition of spirituality. Notions of God and Church are demythologized as we mature, and are gradually adapted into personal living and spirituality. Simply put, there is a time lag in popular piety, before new levels of understanding in Christian lifestyles are generally attained.

The relationship between spirituality and scripture is profound and vital, complex and delicate. The two are in constant tension; a tension that can lead to life or death in spiritual relevance and growth. The process needs to be fed by a good grasp of Christian source teaching, and stimulated and challenged by day-to-day living. Spirituality is "a general science that cuts across all the rest and bridges all subjects relevant to theology. Always directly flowing from the font of revelation in Christ, it brings all such subjects into the life of the individual. Therefore it naturally arranges the other disciplines according to their bearing on actual Christian existence."[2]

The success of spirituality depends on its ability to integrate Jesus' past with the Christian's present. Any lasting synthesis must be open to future change because of the tension of an ideal spirituality with what is inadequately expressed in the static concepts of any age. This tension already appears in New Testament times. The New Testament is therefore a direct source of material for the contemplation of the dynamic of ideal spirituality, provided we realize that it finds expression in the static concepts of the times in which Jesus lived.

Christianity is a religion rooted in the events and teachings of Jesus. He did not present us with an elaborate and systematic spirituality, but, through the inspiration of the Spirit, the saving events of Jesus' life and ministry are embodied in Scripture. Scripture has become the Word of God for us, "the principal witness of the life and teachings of the Incarnate Word, our Savior," and we are reminded by St. Jerome that "Ignorance of the Scriptures is ignorance of Christ."[3] Scripture is not to be identified with the Word of God or with revelation; rather, it is a testimony to the Word of God, a prolongation of the word of revelation.[4]

There is an unbreakable bond between the Bible and spirituality. The Bible is the source of spirituality, and Christian life must be penetrated by its teachings.[5] But life is not simply an attempt to repeat what is contained in scripture. Rather, in the Bible, we find events that as Christians we must relive, reshare, recelebrate, and reincarnate. Furthermore, we meet other disciples who lived these events in their own time, and with whom we can identify. The Bible is a retelling of the events of Jesus' life with the interpretations of those times. It directs us to the revelation of God by offering with those interpretations, their adaptation and application by believers. The Bible comes to us through the Church, the community of believers. God reveals his call to us through scripture, which provides "the authoritative and definitive word that continues to shape and enliven the Church."[6] But this word is in process, it is a combination of Jesus' message and the New Testament communities' interpretations and living of it. Our understanding and appreciation of the canon constantly grows, and it should be read with an awareness of post-biblical traditions, and with a complementary consideration of the history of spirituality.[7]

The Bible and spirituality. What is the relationship between the Bible and spirituality? Scripture is a source, but this could lead to fundamentalism without interpretation. Before being a source of teachings, the Bible is simply a source of inspiration and edification. The believer finds in it a feeling for faith, a sense of scripture's priorities, and resonance with disciples of another time. When read in faith, the scriptures give us accounts of the discoveries of God, of the reader's own potentials, and of a shared mission in God's plan. In some respects our reading highlights attitudes, not concrete situations. We discover a biblical mentality or perspective which can be lived out in new situations, unforeseen by biblical writers.[8]

Scripture is also an inspired synthesis and vision of what discipleship was understood to be during the period of Jesus and the early Church. This synthesis has been referred to as biblical spirituality, but is so restrictive as to be useless.[9] The revealed synthesis was essential in its own time, but more is required of us. The Bible, then, becomes for us an occasion for our spirituality, and the Church's preaching of the Bible becomes the word of God. Because of today's technological lifestyle, immediate and natural contact with the Bible is rare. Often the text simply does not speak to contemporary people, who then read their "simple faith" into the text. This can be devotionally helpful, but seldom results in biblical spirituality.

The Bible is the yardstick for measuring authentic spirituality, but is usually reduced to mere support of the doctrinal positions of the times. It should be *the* standard for measuring the authenticity of the spiritual teachings and practice of the times.

The relationship between the Bible and spirituality is one of constant dialogue between the unchanging Word and the changing situations of disciples. Biblical spirituality results when the dialogue is complete, Christian life re-emerging to echo the biblical message.[10] It has been suggested that, today, biblical spirituality is not found in the Bible, but in those people who live the Bible's message.

The Bible is not a blueprint; it calls to new life. It is a means for growth in life, a synthesis of Christian vision. It is an occasion for new proclamation, a norm for evaluation, a point of dialogue, a means to discover a perennial spirituality. The Bible, then, calls forth many spiritualities, and we really do not have a biblical spirituality. The Bible deals with real people in concrete situations, people faced with real choices: the challenge faced by Matthew's community when tempted to return to Jamnian Phariseism; or Mark's calling of his persecuted community to a spirituality which emphasizes imitation of the suffering Jesus. There is no singular New Testament spirituality; we should avoid attempts to systematize Christian life. Each New Testament author has his own spirituality, his own attempt to apply the message of Jesus to the concrete circumstances of his own Church. In accepting the canon of scripture, we trust that God works through the interpretations and applications of each author.

Biblical criticism has made it possible to discern the real life situations from which teachings in the early Church first arose, but contexts may differ from those envisioned by the authors. It is even possible, at times, to identify the circumstances which called forth a particular teaching from Jesus. Then we actually have the components of spirituality as understood in the times of the author, his Church, and Jesus. Spirituality, one and unique in Christ, evolves and is incarnated in a variety of ways in local Churches and disciples. Spirituality is rooted in the life, example, teachings, and mission of Jesus, but each author brings to this the problems and experiences of his own Church. Jesus' challenge is permanent, the spiritualities transitory.

When new life responses are verified in the essence of Jesus' call, new spiritualities emerge. Each must be viewed with reverence, but never absolutized, lest the result be frozen revelation and the creation of new blocks to fresh interpretation and openness. If we are to be inspired by the unique spirituality of Jesus today, we must be guided by an evolving awareness of how the spiritualities of the early Church emerged from their own appreciations of the relevance of Jesus. It is we who must now reformulate and reincarnate the call of Jesus, as did the early Christians in their times.

Spirituality in the Lucan writings. In the following chapters we will be studying spirituality in the Lucan writings. Luke, so systematic in his presentation of the development of Christian life, is unquestionably a spiritual theologian. He represents the kerygma as "good news," and pursues its application to pastoral life. He verifies the challenge of the origins of Jesus, and shows how that unique spirituality is to be lived in Lucan times and circumstances. He then recommends courageous interpretations and an openness to the newness of God's call.

As we reflect on Luke-Acts, we must avoid absolutizing Luke's spiritual message. We must be aware that the spirituality we find in the context of Luke's times is provisional and transitory. In that sense, Luke's writing must be seen as revelatory, and focusing on his insights must not lead to fragmentation of the biblical message. His challenge must always be open to the rest of scripture.

We will attempt to get close to the meaning of the text, not just to the interpretations of scholars. However, we will also use the invaluble tools of biblical criticism, with the understanding that such critical methods do not answer all the issues. We also need to get to know Luke's writings in depth. Identifying directly with them, we can be open to the call, experiencing the life within the text. The message we find may not be new or different, but the call from Luke may challenge us again.

Chapter One
A MODEL CHRISTIAN

Many have undertaken to compile a narrative of the events which have been fulfilled in our midst, precisely as those events were transmitted to us by the original eyewitnesses and ministers of the word. I too have carefully traced the whole sequence of events from the beginning, and have decided to set it in writing to you, Theophilus, so that Your Excellency may see how reliable the instruction was that you received. (Luke 1:1-4)

Luke is an exciting person. He embodies the best of what we look for in an integrated Christian today. He approaches the critical issues of his own day with the insight that comes from reflection on, and conviction about, the Christian message and its perennial relevance. In looking over the history of Christian spirituality, and the great figures who have incarnated its challenges, I find none comparable to Luke himself. He is a model of Christian life and a personal embodiment of the perennial values of Jesus' call.

Luke centers on the person Jesus. The focus of his revelation is Jesus Christ, not a veneration of outward forms or propositional statements of a religion. Harnack called him "an enthusiast for Christ," and so he is. Luke presents Jesus as the center of history, the answer to all the hopes of humankind. He sees Jesus as the embodiment of our calling in life and as a revelation for every stage of human history. This leads Luke into a theological freedom and newness grounded in true conviction and faith. He brings Jesus and his message to bear on critical life issues with the awareness that nothing is alien to Jesus. Luke is a genuine prophet, so motivated by a living faith that he can handle new and difficult issues at the turning points in history.

Luke courageously portrays Jesus for different cultural groupings, interpreting the message with a spirit of discovery and confident openness. His approach to the traditions he receives is not fundamentalist; rather, he reincarnates the revelation for people accustomed to thinking quite differently than Jesus' original Palestinian followers. Therefore his message has special vitality for today.

Reflections And Traditions

Traditions of the early Church. Who was Luke? Early Church traditions identify him as a traveling missionary companion of Paul. In Colossians 4:14, written possibly as early as 61-63 during Paul's first imprisonment in Rome, Paul says: "Luke, our dear physician, sends you greetings." Around the same time, Paul wrote to Philemon, who also lived in Colossae, again adding Luke's greetings (v. 24). A third Pauline reference to Luke is found in 2 Tm 4:11, which the early Church presumed was written by Paul possibly during his last imprisonment in Rome in 67. In this, Paul's last will and testament, we read the sad acknowledgement of a lonely prisoner: "I have no one with me but Luke."

The person we know as the author of Luke and Acts is, for the early Church, Luke the physician and traveling companion of Paul. In fact, in Acts 16:10-17; 20:5-15; 21:1-18; 27:1 - 28:16, we get the impression that the writer accompanies Paul on that part of the missionary journey. The narrative begins just after Timothy joins the group, a fact that could confirm their friendship (2 Tm 4:11), and continues to Rome. Early traditions and writings confirm the identity of this Luke with that of the author of the Third Gospel and Acts.[1] Eusebius, Jerome, and the Anti-Marcionite Prologue add the information that Luke is from Antioch.[2]

From the mid-second century on, there is general agreement that Paul's companion authored both works. It was thought unlikely that the Church would ascribe the two works to such a secondary figure of the early Church unless he had actually written them. If we were dealing merely with the ascription of the works to an apostolic figure, surely someone of greater historic and foundational stature would have been chosen. That Luke was Paul's colleague was supported, it was thought, by the epistolary references and the "we" sections of Acts. The constant and intelligent use of medical language confirmed his status of physician,[3] and his awareness, appreciation, and documentation of the development of the Antiochean Church indicated clearly his association with that city.[4]

Critical questions since the 17th and 18th centuries. With the development of critical methods for studying scripture in the 17th and 18th centuries, this presentation of the early Church has been seriously questioned. It did seem that the few incidental references to Luke in the New Testament had solid support and confirmation in the early records and history of Christianity. However, it now appears more likely that these records are not confirmations, but repetitions or quotes of New Testament information. They actually tell us nothing more than what is in the New Testament texts.[5] It is presumed throughout that the Luke referred to is the same Luke who authored the two-volume work.

Some commentators still feel that "it is quite unnecessary to discuss the early Christian traditions of New Testament authorship as being without question or validity. It is safer to accept the traditions and ask whether in the written sources there is any supporting testimony and, if so, what value can be placed upon it."[6] This seems reasonable and still leads some to reaffirm the early traditions.[7]

However, I agree with those who conclude that the internal evidence of the Lucan writings points to an author who could not have been the companion of Paul, his secretary and physician. As Ernst Haenchen, commentator on the book of Acts, put it: "When all indications converge as they do in the book of Acts, and when they all speak against the author's having been an eyewitness, we must not blindfold ourselves."[8] An examination of Luke-Acts does not support the idea that the author is Paul's companion. He may have been devoted to Paul, but not as a companion. He is intelligent and cultured — even above average — in his use of medical language, but this is insufficient reason to conclude that he was a physician. His research and documentation is sound, giving a concrete picture of local churches, but this too is insufficient evidence from which to conclude that he was an Antiochean.

When we examine the internal evidence, what sort of portrait of the author emerges? The common ideas, theology, language, and particularly the structure of Luke-Acts convince most that we are dealing with two volumes of a single work. Both seem planned, organized, and structured before a word was written. He deliberately selects from his sources those episodes which portrayed the religious and theological themes he wove together. He was a second or even third generation Christian (Lk 1:1-4), who had ample opportunity to associate with reliable sources of the traditions to which he was committed. His language, his interests, even his omissions convince commentators that he is a Gentile. He claims to be a historian, and, provided we judge him by the standards of his day, we find much in support of that claim.

In the rest of this chapter, we examine Luke's style and interests, his development of content and theology, the needs of his audience, and the local situation which he addresses. Each of these add a little more to a fuller portrait of the man.

Style And Interests

The author's personality emerges in his use of language, in the methods, structures and forms of his work, and in his compositional and editorial attitudes. An author's qualities of mind, heart, and conviction are also revealed in the atmosphere created in his work. So, too, much is revealed of his interests, which consistently surface throughout the writings.

Culture. Luke is the educated and cultured figure of New Testament times. The idea that early Christianity appealed only to the uneducated masses falls apart here. Equally is contradicted the belief that all Christians fled the world and its cultural offerings, since Luke itself is a sign of the dialogue in faith between early Christianity and the world of that time. He makes the Christian message available to the intelligentsia of his day. Scholars agree that Luke-Acts is the finest literary work of the New Testament.

Luke's vocabulary is the most extensive of all New Testament writers, including Paul. His writings contain 732 words not found anywhere else in the New Testament. Comparing Luke with other writers of his time, Haenchen concludes that his vocabulary far surpasses that of many contemporaries.[9]

Conzelmann singles out Luke as "the first Christian author who consciously tries to conform to the standards of Hellenistic literature," and sees this as symptomatic of a Church wishing to come to terms with the world it must, with the delay of the

Second Coming, live in for some time.[10] Luke is a master of classical Greek, of vernacular or koine Greek, and of the biblical Greek of the Septuagint. He moves skillfully and deliberately from one kind of Greek to another as context demands. The classical Greek and legal format used in the prologue (Lk 1:1-4) readily convey to Theophilus an important secondary aim, namely, the defense of Christianity. The biblical Septuagintal style of much of the infancy narratives gives them a suitable Palestinian flavor, helping to focus the author's intention to write in continuity with the sacred records of Jewish/Christian salvation history.[11] Luke is well aware of the religious and secular interests of the Hellenistic world. On the other hand, he is more appreciative of the social and religious background of Judaism than any other New Testament writer.[12] The first impression on reading Luke is that of an historical writing. Not history as we understand it today, to be sure, but history as understood by his contemporaries.[13] Historians in Luke's time did not concentrate on the day-by-day record of events, but rather described typical reactions and beliefs of the people of their day. Such descriptions were based on fact, but not always identical with it. Luke does this as well. He also gives accurate accounts of the characteristic features of the early Church's life, vision, and hopes, even though he cannot always be relied on as an accurate chronicler of the specific, or even actual, events of those years.

Structure. Luke-Acts are structured carefully, with great emphasis on parallelism and the balance of narratives.[14] This structure relates to Luke's own faith, life, and convictions. For example, the balance and parallelism between gospel and Acts mirrors the unity and continuity between Jesus and the Church. Luke balances the life of Paul with the life of Jesus, and the beginnings of the Church with that of Jesus' ministry. In each, his stylistic methods convey convictions of faith.

Luke presents the message in ways interesting and relevant to his audience. Jews read hymns very much like their own psalms, appreciating the dialogue between the Christian message and their own liturgical celebrations, such as Pentecost. For a Hellenistic world accustomed to the Aeneid and the Odyssey, the latter part of Jesus' ministry is portrayed as a journey to Jerusalem, Paul's final journey as a voyage on dangerous seas.

Tradition. Luke is no mere compiler, chronicler, or secretary. He is unquestionably one of the greatest figures of New Testament times, placing his talents of culture and education at the service of a reincarnation of the gospel message. The major quality of Luke is his sense of responsibility for the message of Christ: he is a steward of the tradition. This does not lead him to slavishly repeat that tradition; rather, he is an artist, a genuine author who tells the message of Jesus in a new way for peoples Jesus never knew. He dares to discover new religious concepts to describe Jesus; to enter into dialogue with the world, the empire, the philosophies and beliefs of his day.

As we shall see in chapter two, Luke displays considerable liberty in his editorial work. With tenderness and sensitivity, realizing that his message appeals in different ways to different people, he finds nothing confusing in including different impressions in the same work. He is a fascinating writer who takes a Palestinian-based tradition, discerns the essential for Christians, forms a new strategy and structure, utilizes the methods of his day, and retells the message of Jesus to another world.

Atmosphere. Luke creates an atmosphere conducive to the reception of the message. In the early part of the gospel, the reader is drawn into a spirit of expectancy, then led to participate in the sense of realization and fulfillment permeating the infancy accounts. It is a time of passive appreciation of the interventions of God, and of acknowledgement that the unfolding of the divine plan is always Spirit-filled. During the ministry of Jesus, Luke constantly identifies the psychological reactions of the crowds. We are consistently told that even unbelievers are impressed with Jesus (Lk 4:32; 8:26-37; 13:17; 23:8-9; 23:47-48). Those who follow Him are opened to the mysterious, miraculous, and supernatural in their midst, and even the reader is led to awe. Luke skillfully shows every major moment in Jesus' life as filled with prayer. Prayer is the atmosphere of the realization and unfolding of the message. In Acts, when the Church begins to spread the message, Luke uses refrains to show how the reception of the message brings peace and joy to believers, how their enthusiasm leads to the growth and expansion of the Church.

So consistent are these editorial modifications that they must be considered deliberate descriptions of those attitudes Luke considers necessary for the reception and growth of faith. He is convinced that reverence, reflection, and awe are needed for faith, and that peace and joy result from it.[15] Luke shows us the atmosphere in which faith grows, and the attitudes found in people of living faith. Even before we examine the content of his presentation, the very atmosphere he creates produces a raising of religious consciousness and a deepening ecclesial awareness.

Interests. While concentrating in his work on the systematic exposition of the message, Luke still weaves in a multiplicity of secondary interests. No other scripture writer shows such a breadth of interests.

He is intrigued with the kingship of Christ, underlining this in spite of the difficulties and possible conflict with Roman Caesars. The great parables of the lost sheep, lost coin, and prodigal son, together with the Lucan slant to the beatitudes and the Sermon on the Plain, earn for Luke's work the title of the Gospel of Mercy, or the Gospel of the Great Pardons. He is concerned for underprivileged groups: Gentiles, women, and the poor. He focuses on the quality of Christian life, emphasizing the absolute and radical character of discipleship, and the constant need for prayer. The Third Gospel also preeminently qualifies as the Gospel of the Holy Spirit.

Although, as we shall see, Luke writes at a time of crisis for the Church, he is not fearful or reactionary. Rather, he optimistically and faithfully gives a picture of Christianity as interesting, fulfilling, and vitally relevant to our world.

Content And Companions

Luke and Paul. A major contribution to our growing picture of Luke is his relationship to Paul. Tradition has generally considered Luke to be the physician companion to Paul, and there is much to support this position. Paul is a real person in Acts, not a creation, and his letters confirm many personal characteristics. In both Luke-Acts and Paul's letters, Paul is a leader, a special figure alongside the Twelve. Skilled in Judaism, Paul feels particularly dedicated to his own people, but is aware of a call to serve the Gentiles. He is convinced of being specially chosen (Acts 22:14; 26:16; Rm 1:1-2), and wants to be all things to everyone (Acts 13:47; 1 Co 9:19-23). He acknowledges Peter's prime role (Acts 15:1-29; Ga 1:18; 2:7), but contests his positions when disagreements arise (Ga 2:11-14). He is a key figure in the early Church, but meets with serious problems in relation to the Jews and his own Church.

That Luke knew Paul is supported by the section in Acts which identifies the writer as a traveling companion of Paul (Acts 16:10-17; 20:515; 21:1-18; 27:1 - 28:16). It has been suggested that these "we" passages, written in a style distinguishable from the rest of the book, consequently belong to a different source, possibly the travel diary of another companion of Paul's. Luke, however, generally careful in his editorial work, would have tidied up this first person plural if it belonged exclusively to his sources. He seems to have rewritten everything else; why not this? The natural conclusion seems to be that the author of the "we" passages is the author of the two volumes and journeyed with Paul from Troas to Philippi, from Philippi to Jerusalem, and from Caesarea to Rome.[16]

The conclusion arrived at by many commentators is that Luke knew Paul, traveled with him, personally observed much of what he wrote, but, given the distance from the events, adapted his material to fit a changed world.[17] Difficulties exist, but the most likely historical explanation, they believe, is that the author of Luke-Acts knew Paul.

The Lucan Paul and the Pauline Paul. Many commentators, particularly German but some American, today find unacceptable the position that Luke knew Paul. There is a certain similarity between the Paul of the Letters and the Paul of Acts, but the theological convictions and positions of the Pauline Paul are so different from those of the Lucan Paul that they do not seem those of the same person. These German and American scholars conclude that Luke did not personally know Paul.

The first time we meet Saul, he is portrayed as presiding over and approving the stoning of Stephen (Acts 8:1). We have no confirmation of this; it could be a literary device of Luke to provide contrast for the first account of the conversion experience. Saul goes to Damascus, authorized by the High Priest to persecute followers of the Way (Acts 9:1-2), but such an authorization was not within the jurisdiction of the High Priest and Council.[18] After his conversion, Paul goes twice to Jerusalem (Acts 9:26; 11:27-30), but in Galatians emphatically denies that this implies dependence on Peter (Ga 2:1), since he is concerned to establish his authority from Jesus Himself.[19] Once Paul's missionary work begins, Luke presents him as a great orator (Acts 17:22-34; 21:40; 22:1-21; 24:10-21), but Paul says the Corinthians consider him no preacher at all (2 Co 10:10). In Acts, Paul works miracles (Acts 13:4-12; 14:8-10; 19:11-12), but in his letters claims that God's power is seen only in his own weakness (2 Co 12:10). Again in Acts, the mission to the Gentiles is authorized and supported (Acts 10:1 - 11:18), but Paul in his Letters claims he had to defend it (Ga 2:1-10). At the Council of Jerusalem, the participants agreed on four prescriptions to be observed by the Gentiles, entrusting Paul with conveying these requirements (Acts 15:22-29), but Paul never refers to them in his letters. In fact, he issues teachings contrary to them (1 Co 10:23-30).

Acts sees Paul as a Jewish Christian utterly loyal to the law (Acts 16:1-3; 21:23-26), but in his Letter to the Galatians he considers as slanderous the very idea that he circumcise anyone (Ga 5:11-12). Acts shows Paul as a disciple of Gamaliel (Acts 22:3; 23:6), but Paul himself never claims this, even in Philippians (Ph 3:2-7). Paul claims Roman citizenship in Acts (Acts 22:22-29), but never in the Letters. For all, and particularly for the Gentiles, Paul claims to be an apostle, emphatically using the title (Ga 2:8; 1 Co 15:5-8; 1 Co 1:1), but Luke never grants him this position.[20] When eventually brought to trial in Acts, it is because of his belief in the resurrection. Other apostles taught this, however, and the Pharisees believed it. The Letters constantly give the impression that Paul's problems with Jewish authorities stemmed from his teachings on the law.

These inconsistencies in the two portraits of Paul are heightened by the comparison of Paul's teachings in his Letters and the teachings ascribed to him in Acts. There are major differences in the teachings on natural theology, law, and justification by faith, Christology, and eschatology as found in the two sources, differences that seem irreconcilable.[21]

Moreover, Luke never quoted Paul's Letters. If he had known Paul and traveled with him, surely he would have mentioned the fact that Paul continued his missionary work through the Letters. Since the Pauline letter corpus must have been in its final stages of composition when Luke-Acts were written, it seems unbelievable that Luke would not know and quote Paul's letters, if, indeed, he was the companion of Paul.

This second picture of Paul and Luke leads to important conclusions. The personality, ministry, and theological positions of Paul in Luke are different from the Paul of the letters. It has been suggested that Acts is pre-Pauline in Christology, and post-Pauline in natural theology, the concept of law, and eschatology.[22] In fact, Luke has kept little specifically Pauline. He certainly admires Paul and appreciates his universality, but he does not know, or understand, or disagrees with, or chooses to ignore, crucial Pauline theological positions. The portraits are so different that serious questions can be raised on the historical reliability of Acts' presentation of Paul. What then is to be done with the "we" passages? In this second position, the "we" passages are a literary device used by Luke, an imitation of techniques by which Hellenistic and Roman authors of historiography, tried, by the use of the first person plural, to heighten the reader's involvement, at the same time creating the impression that the author was personally there.[23]

Companion or disciple? The question we must now ask is whether there is any possible reconciliation of these two positions, and if so, what is the picture of Luke that emerges?

The contrast between Luke and Paul has been overemphasized. The fact that opposing positions are identified with national groupings or schools of interpretation is not convincing. Differences often rest on weak methodological foundations, while impressive agreements are passed over,[24] on the other hand, major theological differences are ignored or forced into agreement.

It is not necessary that Paul be consistent and uniform in his presentation. Theologians and pastors of every generation are full of contradictions, often giving different recommendations to different people with the same problem. If they were one hundred percent consistent, we would probably criticize them as doctrinaire and dogmatic. Moreover, we sometimes demand of Luke an accuracy of history and detail that secular historians would not demand of his contemporaries.

Admittedly, the crucial differences are the theological positions of Paul in his letters and those of Luke in his Acts. These differences, however, are not now seen to be as great before. Exegesis of Paul's writings is showing more and more that the existentialist interpretations supported by many German schools are not found in Paul, but read into him. "It is Paul, interpreted existentially, who is so sharply set against Luke as the great but dangerous corrupter of the Pauline gospel. But the existentially interpreted Paul is not the historical Paul."[25] Once this unacceptable filtering of Paul's thought is removed and his concepts compared to Luke's, there remains a difference, but one not as great.

Luke writes about twenty years after Paul. Circumstances have changed. Some issues crucial to Paul are now peacefully accepted. Other topics, possibly not dealt with by Paul, are now of great importance. After all, the bulk of the traditions on Jesus were accessible not to Paul, but to Luke. Luke admires Paul, tries to immerse himself in his thought, but does not absolutize him as have some modern writers. Luke had no scruples in changing Mark or "Q", as we shall see, nor did he hesitate in changing Paul. Conzelmann suggested that Luke "understands himself to be the steward of tradition. He does not limit himself to handing it on, but he reflects on the nature of the tradition by defining his own standpoint in the chain of tradition."[26] This is precisely his attitude toward Paul. Had Luke not changed Paul, he would have been irresponsible. By the time Luke writes about his hero some of the topics Paul had dealt with in his letters would have seemed irrelevant to Luke's audience, and so Luke presents him as involved in the crucial issues of Luke's own day. Pauline theology becomes the presupposition for Lucan theology,[27] but Luke comes to grips with the vision and attitudes of Paul, reinterprets them, and applies them to new situations. The Paul of Acts emerges as "the real Paul, seen in retrospect through the eyes of a friend and admirer, whose own religious experience was different from Paul's and who wrote for another public and purpose than Paul had in view when writing his letters."[28]

Had Luke been Paul's companion, he would have been more factually accurate in details, clearly identifying himself as involved with Paul's work. Luke is a second or third generation Christian who sees Paul as the embodiment of the Christian vision and ideals. The questions and answers of Paul's past are not, however, the questions and answers of Luke's present. In fact, Paul is only a part of that past, and Luke now has a broader picture of the Jesus tradition than Paul ever had. Luke's careful study of Paul, and the traditions concerning him (Lk 1:1-4) has given us a portrait that, in general, is as accurate as it needs to be. Luke uses Paul to portray what it means to be a Christian in Luke's time, since that is precisely what Paul had done in his own. The suggestion that Luke's portrayal of Paul is inferior to the Paul of the Letters is unwarranted.[29]

Audience And Conditioning Situation

What motivated Luke to write? Why write a gospel when the Church already had Mark's? More particularly, why write Acts? Is Luke indeed an exceptional person who, with great insight, discerns new needs in Christianity and responds to them? What are those needs, and whose are they? When does he write? If we can answer these questions, we can gain a little more insight into who Luke is.

We now turn to the opinions of commentators about when and for whom Luke wrote. We shall then look at some of Luke's answers, and try to see what are the unstated needs and questions of his audience.

The earliest possible date. The traditional Christian view of Luke-Acts is that the author was writing a history. His account is accurate and reliable and, since it ends before Paul's martyrdom, both volumes can be dated before the year 64, generally considered the earliest possible date for Paul's death. Acts, completed before this date, does not deal with the events of that time, and the Third Gospel is, in turn, written before Acts (Acts 1:1).[30] This position was generally accepted before the critical period of biblical scholarship, and has proponents today. There are several considerations which suggest this early dating of the Lucan writings.

The prominent position of Paul in the writings suggests an early date, since he did not occupy such a key place at the turn of the century. Yet Acts ends abruptly, with no mention of Paul's death. Since Luke was so skillful in paralleling Jesus and Peter and then Jesus and Paul, he would surely have dealt with Paul's passion as a culminating imitation of his master. After all, he had prophesied it three times, as he had in Jesus' case (Acts 23:11; 25:10; 27:24). The suspense the writer builds in his audience would have been thwarted unnecessarily had no mention been made of such an event. If, on the other hand, we presume that Acts was written later, after Paul had actually been released, again it seems reasonable that Luke would have mentioned it. Paul's release could have been the climax of Luke's political apologetic of Rome. Whatever the ending, death or release, it would have been excellent material for Luke's editorial contributions. The fact that neither is dealt with leads to the conclusion that the writings antedate Paul's death. Moreover, the absence of any reference to the Pauline corpus is due, according to this position, to the fact that the Lucan writings antedate the collation of the corpus.

An examination of Christianity's relationship to the empire also leads, it is believed, to a dating of Luke-Acts in the '60s. The geographical, historical, and political information Luke gives is detailed, accurate, and, it is thought, reflects a contemporary author. Moreover, to give so much support to Christianity as a *religio licita* would be futile after 64, when Nero had definitely withdrawn this privilege.[31] The positive approach to the empire, which Luke constantly stresses, would surely have been modified after the bitter persecutions. Yet, not only are the persecutions not mentioned, but the two volumes are quite optimistic in their hopes for the Church/State relationship. This would seem to indicate a date before 64. Finally, there are no hints of the Jewish War or the fall of Jerusalem.

Even when we look at the themes which seem special to Luke, such as the admission of the Gentiles, they are important only before the fall, and irrelevant afterwards.

These reasons convince many that Luke-Acts was written toward the end of Paul's two-year detention in Rome.[32]

A late date for Luke-Acts. Any dating of these books will reflect what is already thought about them. One of the first results of the critical approach to the New Testament was a late dating of Luke-Acts. Baur's application of the Hegelian dialectic of history to developments in early Christianity led him to the conclusion that Luke-Acts was the reconciling synthesis of the interaction between the Judaizing thesis and the Pauline antithesis. This development would need many years, pushing the date for Luke-Acts past 130.

If Luke-Acts are seen primarily as history, the dates given them are likely to be early. However, some scholars consider the general impression given by a reading of Luke-Acts to be one of looking back over an extended period of time. The concerns of primitive Christianity are no longer present, and any disagreements between Peter and Paul are long reconciled. Early beliefs in the immediacy of the Second Coming of Jesus have been reinterpreted, and the Church is an organized institution settling down to a dialogue with the world of its day. There is now a looking back to the traditions, a reflection on early history, a searching for roots. This is not early.

One proponent of this late dating of Luke-Acts is J. C. O'Neill.[33] Studying the Lucan writings, he tried to identify the general theological environment in which they were written. He researched early Christian writings for a similar theological milieu, and was convinced he had found it in the apologist Justin. Like Justin's dialogue with Trypho, Luke's writings are an explanation that Christianity is the natural outgrowth of Judaism. According to O'Neill, Luke writes apologetics and must be dated at the same time as the apologists, certainly not before 115.[34]

John Knox also supports a late dating of Luke-Acts, placing it around 125. Acccording to Knox, Acts in particular was written after Marcion, who lived around 150. This early heretic had rejected everything about the Old Testament and formulated a canon of scripture consisting only of Paul's writings and Luke's gospel, which Marcion saw as dependent on Paul. He rejected everything else. Acts was then written to show Marcion the close connections between his great hero, Paul, and the Twelve, and between Paul and Judaism.[35]

In general, this late dating of Luke-Acts has not obtained much support from scholars.

A date around 80-90. Most commentators today place Luke-Acts around 80-90. It cannot be earlier than 80 since the gospel is dependent on Mark, and the general consensus is that Mark was written ca. 70. Any suggestion that it is later than the turn of the century has gained little support. Luke himself says he is not among the eyewitnesses nor among the ministers of the word (Lk 1:1-4). Rather, he comes later, and, after reflecting on the traditions, gives us "an ordered account." Are there any indications in this account which can give us an idea of its audience and date of composition?

Luke's readers. We have already seen that Luke's structures and forms presume some cultural sophistication. The implications of his many parallelisms demand serious reflection. His length, content, and style presume an audience with the leisure to undertake the task.

Luke fosters in his readers a sense of mystery, awe, and wonder by his constant emphasis on the supernatural and the miraculous. He certainly emphasizes the importance of prayer, challenging his readers to a life of poverty. He strongly portrays the Lordship of

Jesus and the need for radical and total commitment in his disciples. He stresses the areas of needed growth for the Christian in his journey through life. Finally, in a period of acknowledged delay in Jesus' return, Luke offers meaning and new ideals for the present life of the Church.

Luke presents an already structured and institutionalized Church, one big enough to be world-minded, and distant enough from its beginnings to be interested in its own traditions and its roots. It is a Church that needed to be reminded of the importance of minorities and the underprivileged. In general, it is a Church called to social justice, to dialogue with the world.[36]

The individual and institutional attitudes Luke presumes in his readers, or calls them to, are descriptive of an audience that has reflected deeply on the implications of the delay of the Second Coming and must be challenged to meet the future. They must be reminded of their roots in the past, called back to spiritual values lost with the fervor of early times. Luke's audience has "found a place in the sun and the leisure to make the celebration of its own existence a basic ingredient of its theology. At worst this is bourgeois in a complacent sense. At best it finds the intersection of God and man in the world around, in Church and family life and the whole process of human history."[37] Writing of Jesus, Luke identifies for his audience the spiritual implications of their commitment. Luke's work is neither primitive proclamation nor the systematic reflection and philosophical apologetic dialogue of the apostolic fathers. Luke is a preacher and a prophet, the spiritual theologian at his best.

The Spirituality of Luke

In this first chapter, we have tried to gain some preliminary ideas on the person Luke. This portrait will be enlarged as we proceed. So far we have examined the information of tradition as well as the internal evidence of critical analysis. We have looked at Luke's education, culture, and interests. We have reviewed his relationship to Paul and the personal, creative responsibility that Luke shows towards the tradition he has received. Finally, we have seen Luke giving leadership to the Church in a time of transition. We are now challenged to study and reflect prayerfully on his writings, identifying their content and their affects on our lives. This is the concern of the following chapters. At this early stage, however, it is useful to confront not only Luke's content, but also his attitudes, life vision, convictions, sense of responsibility, and dedication. He teaches both by what he says and who he is. We are accustomed to seeing the content as revelation, but the revelatory value of Luke's attitudes and approaches to life are also important. It is often difficult to identify biblical spirituality in the writings of the New Testament, for in them we find a variety of spiritualities. The choice, commitment, and incarnation of these spiritualities are still to be effected. Biblical spirituality is best seen in concrete living models in which are integrated the manifold challenges of the scriptures. In this sense, Luke is a model of the perennial values of Christian life.

Luke is entirely dedicated to Christ. He belongs not to the chosen people, but to the Gentiles; he, like us, had to make a positive decision for Christ. He is a second or third generation Christian, and did not witness the events in the life of the person to whom he now gives himself in faith. Nor was he a companion of Paul, or a member of those enthusiastic early Church communities. Rather, he must dedicate himself to building community. Part of his contribution is to write two volumes: one on the life of Jesus, the other on that of the Church. He dedicates himself to carefully tracing his present convictions, rooting them in the traditions of Christian origins. He is not a chronicler of the specific events of those times, but accurately presents us with a typical history of them. He has obviously reflected on the mystery of God in Jesus, and its impact on every aspect of our lives. With Luke, we reach a deeper level of awareness regarding the place which Jesus must have in our lives and in our world.

Luke uses all his talents in his service of the Word. One of the most educated and cultured figures of the New Testament, he is a master of Greek and conforms to the standards of Hellenistic literature. He knows the forms, styles, and interests of his day, and integrates them into his presentation. More than any other writer of the New Testament, he takes the message and courageously incarnates it in new ways to show its perennial relevance, skillfully winnowing from the kernel of the message its cultural chaff.

Luke is not a secretary to Paul, but is himself a steward of the tradition, responsible for making that past of Christ ever present and fresh today. Confronted with the delay of the Second Coming, Luke more than anyone else faces the crucial issues of the day. The way Luke faces these tensions gives birth to new insights into the meaning of Christian life, showing how to anticipate the future while retaining the values rooted in our past. He makes the connection between justification in faith and living now in hope. We are pilgrims, but not in opposition to life. Life deserves to be lived, and in the way we journey, we can build up this life and this world (Lk 8:13-15).

Luke's message is the most challenging retelling of the Jesus event we have. We are Luke's new audience, and he is in some ways our spiritual director, showing us how life evolves to fullness in Christ. For Luke, the past of the Church was not to be slavishly repeated, but to live on in new ideals, new vision, and present relevance rooted in the past. The call is radical and has personal, institutional, and world implications.

The interests and concerns of Luke are ours as well. We need his attitudes today. As we search for Christian identity in the '80s and '90s, Luke identifies the Lord's perennial values, indicating even the interpretation of those values. We shall examine his teachings more closely in the chapters ahead, but the keys to Luke's spirituality are his own life, example, and attitudes.

Chapter Two
SOURCES OF FAITH

He said to him, "Do you really grasp what you are reading?" "How can I," the man replied, "unless someeone explains it to me?" (Acts 8:30-31)

Jesus began his public ministry around the year 27, and for three years he preached and taught. Around the year 30, he was crucified. Twenty years later, Paul wrote his first letter to the Thessalonians, beginning seventeen years of epistolary evangelization. Mark wrote his gospel ca. 70, and it was not until ca. 80-90 that Luke wrote the Third Gospel and Acts. There is a period of over sixty years between Jesus' public teaching and Luke's account of it, and some twenty years between the last episode recorded in Acts and Luke's account of it.

Luke's audience was very different from Jesus'. People's interests were different; what appealed to, called, and motivated them had changed. Even the ten to fifteen years separating Mark and Luke had witnessed a move from possible extermination by way of persecution to renewed growth and consolidation.

It has been suggested that Luke's response was an entirely creative work betraying the initial eschatological call and preaching of Jesus. Others claim that he changed the traditions to suit his own theological prejudices. Still others feel he was ignorant of Paul's thought, or did not fully appreciate the theological implications of Paul's teachings.[1] The Third Gospel is, however, a legitimate response to important changes in circumstance.

Luke is a model Christian of vision, commitment, world view, and life, a model for the Church today in dealing with the sources and traditions of our faith. In the selection and editing of his sources, in his careful refocusing and delineation of theological interests, Luke shows us the spiritual qualities needed to handle responsibly the sources of faith. In its final form, his is a work of inspiration, in which he discerns the essential in the Christian message, refocusing its challenge and spirituality.

Christian life evolves with our notions of God, people, Church, the sacred and profane. Christian spirituality differs individually and institutionally in successive generations. The incarnate Lord is born anew in each generation. We have an evolution of lifestyle and an evolution of what it means to be Church in changed situations. The result is the evolution of our notions of spirituality.

Luke is an outstanding example of how to use the sources of our faith-life in each new generation. We betray the call of Jesus by passing over substantial aspects of his message. We also betray his message by fossilizing it, thus assuring its irrelevance. The way we relate to and use the sources of our faith authenticates our living of it. Luke's writing is an example of the best attitudes for authentic spirituality today.

This chapter examines Luke's sources and his use of them. It analyzes his compositional contributions and theological interests, and synthesizes the attitudes Luke deems necessary for interpretation in faith.

Luke's Sources In Gospel And Acts

Sources of the Third Gospel. There is no consensus regarding Luke's sources for either his gospel or Acts, though several opinions have emerged. Regarding the sources of the Third Gospel, many agree that Luke used material unique to him, material not available to the other evangelists. This we call "L", understood by some as one source, by others as a Lucan collection from several sources. This accounts for half of the Third Gospel and contains some of the best-known stories of the New Testament: the Good Samaritan, the Prodigal Son, and the Widow of Nain. It is also a source of major theological and spiritual clarifications of earlier gospel traditions regarding prayer, poverty, the place of women in God's plan, and so on. L is where we find positions and interests specific to Luke. Some scholars have noted in L similarities with the Fourth Gospel, and have suggested some influence. However, the similarities do not seem strong enough to merit interrelationship, and can be easily explained by their common origins in the oral traditions which preceded all formulations of the New Testament.[2]

A second point of substantial agreement is that a quarter of Luke's gospel is similar to a third of Matthew's. This has given rise to the theory that Luke and Matthew had access to a common source. Their retelling of the traditional content of this source is so close, even in word usage, that many believe this common source to have been written. I would personally support this. This common tradition of Luke and Matthew is known as "Q," an abbreviation of the German *Quelle*, meaning fountain or source. This common source may have originated in Antioch about the year 50. The positing of Q as a part of the answer to the synoptic problem was one of the great achievements of source criticism, but it has always had its opponents. Some commentators consider it an unnecessary hypothesis, preferring to believe that the material shared by Luke and Matthew stems from Luke's use of Matthew. This seems unlikely.[3]

The third source of Luke, accepted by the vast majority of commentators today, is Mark.[4] This gospel, the first, was completed around the year 70. It consists of about 661 verses. Matthew, writing about fifteen years later, uses approximately 600 of these, giving the impression that Mark was already considered special, even canonical. Luke uses about half of Mark, considerably changing even that half for stylistic and theological reasons, as we shall see. Luke retains about fifty percent of Mark's actual words. While Mark is a major source for Luke, we can already see that he treats it with greater editorial freedom than did Matthew.

How are these sources combined? These three sources, together with Luke's editorial work, account for the Third Gospel. The next question is how the author combined them.

It is apparent that the Marcan sections in Luke can be separated from the non-Marcan. The remaining sections are combinations of Q and L. This is so generally the case that Luke's combining of Q with L is considered independent of Q and L combined with Mark. Which came first? Were the Q and L sources added to Mark, or was Mark added to an already existing mini-gospel of Q and L?

Some commentators claim that Q and L existed first. This, they hypothesize, was the original, shorter version of Luke's gospel. Later he came in contact with Mark's gospel, interpolating it into his own. They refer to this prior, shorter Lucan gospel of Q and L as the "Proto-Luke".[5]

Other writers are more impressed with the fact that Mark's gospel provides the general plan of Luke's own. Without Mark, the Q and L combinations lack the development of the gospel as we know it. Q's arrangement is considered topical, not ministerial. I would also hold that Luke, like Matthew, has expanded Mark's basic outline with material available to himself.

Mark is generally thought to have been written in Rome. The content of Q so reflects the Syrian region that it may have been composed under the influence of the Antiochean Church. Luke's own source, like much of his material in Acts, is thought to reflect Caesarea. Luke's final presentation may thus reflect the traditions of at least three of the great centers of early Christianity.

Sources in Acts. As for the sources of Acts, Dom Jacques Dupont, after extensive study, concluded: "It has not been possible to define any of the sources used by the author of Acts in a way which will meet with widespread agreement among the critics."[6] When considering the sources of Acts, the obvious problem is that we do not have as many Acts as gospels — there is only one. Consequently, it is not possible to draw conclusions from comparison. Acts can be studied only through internal evidence.

We know from gospel comparisions that Luke gave all his source material his own personal imprint, skillfully molding distinct sources into a unity. We should expect the same of Acts. It is difficult to distinguish sources stylistically in such a well written, homogeneous work. It would be incorrect to conclude, however, that Luke's unified presentation in Acts is a creative work independent of sources. There is a series of techniques available that can reveal indications of the possible multiple sources of Acts.[7]

The two major sections of Acts are the early developments of Christianity in Palestine and the missionary journeys of Paul. They are almost two separate books. This could suggest one source for Paul's journey narrative, another for the early developments of the Church. Some see sources of each of these, based on specific places or people. For the first part, we have suggestions of a Jerusalem (Mark) source, a Caesarean (Philip) source, an Antiochean (Luke) source, and a Samaritan (Stephen) source. In Paul's journey section, commentators have identified at least three: the "we" source, a source for the speeches, and the itinerary source.

Other commentators have noted two ascension stories and two

visits of Paul to Jerusalem, and are convinced that elsewhere they have identified different Christologies: two approaches to Jesus as Messiah (in Ch 2 and 3), and two understandings of Jesus as Son (in Ch 3 and 4). In addition, they see two strands of tradition in the Pentecost story, the account of Stephen's martyrdom, the story of the visit of Peter to Cornelius, and the report of the Council of Jerusalem. These commentators believe that this shows double or parallel sources for several elements of the early tradition.

Luke used material to which the communities had already given fixed forms. This is not the case in Acts. The second volume unquestionably shows Luke working with less formed material. As Dupont said, it is difficult to present sources on which critics can agree. However, critics generally do agree that Luke used sources for Acts, even though there is no agreement on what, precisely, these sources might be.

In the next section we examine Luke's use of his sources. Even at this stage, there are valuable conclusions for our own positions in faith. In his gospel and Acts, Luke uses material from several of the great centers of early Christianity: Jerusalem, Antioch, Rome, Caesarea, and elsewhere. He reworks the material, but grounds his ideas in the consensus of the Church. His work is not simply creative, divorced from its roots. Rather, he respectfully associates himself with a consensus of opinion that guarantees the authenticity of his presentation. His editorial work is thorough, but original sources and ideas are still discernible. Luke's own understanding and interpretation, though clear, are not imposed in such way as to replace earlier traditions. In general, Luke is respectful of the fixed traditions of the early Church, particularly that of Mark, which seems to have special community acceptance. Yet Luke feels free to rework, reinterpret, and modify the unformed and fluid traditions that come to him from individuals, whoever they may be.

Luke's Use of His Sources

Luke's sources in both his gospel and Acts — their language, religious concepts, and cultural and historical background — were clearly Palestinian. The characters in the stories were Palestinian, the issues debated reflected local color, and the content often challenged current Palestinian theological issues. Jesus' message, incarnated in Palestine, reflected the history, culture, religious concepts, and life values of the day.

Openness and flexibility in adaptation of sources. Luke shows great openness and flexibility in adapting this Jewish-based tradition to his own audience, who were mainly Gentiles living outside of Palestine and the influence of its culture, history, religion, and values. He subjects the traditions to stylistic, cultural, and theological revision. He values the content and perennial message of the tradition while feeling free to change its form. His audience was not expecting the immediate return of the Lord; they were people who valued this world and its cultural and literary achievements. Mark's rough presentation and Q's disjointed topical arrangement needed much reworking to make them appealing to Luke's intelligent audience.

Polished style. Whether it be clumsy wording (Mk 10:29 and Lk 18:29b), unnecessary doubling (Mk 10:24,26 and Lk 18:24-26), or tautology (Mk 1:32 and Lk 4:40), Luke first of all polishes the style of his sources. Mark's abrupt introductions are smoothed over (Mk 8:14 and Lk 12:1), and his monotonous and purposeless repetition is substantially trimmed (Mk 4:14 and Lk 8:11; Mk 4:21 and Lk 8:16). The longwinded presentations of Mark (Mk 4:1-9 and Lk 8:4-8; or Mk 5:1-20 and Lk 8:26-39) and possibly Q (Mt 5:13-16 and Lk 14:34-35) are made more succinct, or, when their purpose is not clear (Mk 8:14-21 and Lk 12:1), omitted entirely.

Clarity. Luke clarifies sections of his sources where not clear themselves (Lk 4:42-43 and Mk 1:35-38), expands a section where the teaching seems abbreviated (Lk 9:30-36 and Mk 9:4-8), and suggests a possible context of a story when Matthew or Mark omit it (Lk 15:1-7 and Mt 18:12-14).

Adaptation to the needs of his audience. Luke adapts his sources to the needs and experiences of his audience. This is done even in simple ways. The Palestinian roof of Mark and Matthew becomes a tiled roof for Luke's audience (Mk 2:4 and Lk 5:19). Mark's "King Herod" becomes Luke's Roman tetrarch (Mk 6:14 and Lk 9:7), Matthew's "king who gave a banquet" becomes Luke's "man. . .who invited many" (Mt 22:2 and Lk 14:16). Mark's scribes, and Matthew's Pharisees and Sadducees, in Luke become "a lawyer" (Mk 12:28, Mt 22:34 and Lk 10:25). Luke does not deal with concepts alien to his audience. Stories of ritual purity are omitted (Mk 7:1-23 and Mt 15:1-20), as is the episode of ethnic difference between Jews and Gentiles (Mk 7:24-30 and Mt 15:21-28).

Awareness of cultural differences and the need to present a meaningful message challenges Luke's creativity to find appropriate presentations for his new audience while remaining faithful to the content of the traditions. Luke's Gentile world did not link sickness with demonic possession. Thus, when Mark and Matthew tell us of those "who were possessed with demons" (Mk 1:32; Mt 8:16), Luke has those "that were sick with various diseases" (Lk 4:40). Again, an "unclean spirit" (Mk 1:23) is now described as "a spirit of an unclean demon" (Lk 4:33).

When Jesus is questioned as to whether he is the Christ, the Son of Man (Mk 14:61; Mt 26:63), Luke indicates to his non-Jewish audience that this is as much as asking "Are you the Son of God, then?" (Lk 22:70) Earlier, when Peter confesses his belief in Jesus as the Messiah (Mk 8:29), Luke finds another concept for his audience in Peter's recognition of Jesus as the "anointed of God" (Lk 9:20).

Use of the Old Testament. Another special quality of Luke's style is his extensive use of the Old Testament. Franklin says of Luke that "he must have been one who was influenced supremely by the Jewish faith, one who loved 'our nation,' who was moved by its law and captivated by its scriptures."[8] Although writing for the Gentile world, Luke has a superb knowledge of the Old Testament, the rabbinical teachings, and the liturgical readings of the Jewish feasts.[9] Elizabeth is presented as another Hannah (1:5-24), Mary is paralleled with the Ark (1:34-35, 43), Jesus is shown as another Elijah and Elisha, and so on. Jesus' exaltation is compared to Moses' ascent of Sinai (Acts 2:33), the Twelve are the Patriarchs (Acts 1:15-26), and the early Church is the eschatological community foreseen by Moses (Acts 4:32-34; Deuteronomy 15:4-11). Luke uses the Old Testament to highlight the fruitfulness of the new era. Rather than using the texts as proofs, he meditates and homilizes on them.

Order and structure. While integrating source material into his final document, Luke makes judgments on their uniqueness. He dislikes useless repetition, omitting it where he finds it. In the Third Gospel we have only one account each of the multiplication of the loaves (9:12-17), the cursing of the fig tree (13:6-9), Jesus' return to the sleeping disciples in Gethsemane (22:39-46), and the trial before the Jewish authorities (22:66-71). This economy of narrative is found not only in entire episodes, but, "when a word, even the name of an object, occurs too often in his narrative, Luke either by omission or by the use of a synonym secures variety of phrase."[10]

In spite of his dislike of useless repetition, Luke gives an interesting slant to an episode by a technique which Danker calls "echo-diction": the purposeful repetition of a word within a section. While remaining faithful to his sources, Luke adds new dimensions to a story by the constant echoing and re-echoing of the same word.[11]

Transposition and rearrangement of the tradition. Finally, in the gospel or Acts, Luke transposes, rearranges, and reorders his sources.[12] Even the basic outline of Mark is not sacrosanct. Jesus' sermon in Nazareth in the middle of his ministry (Mk 6:1-6a) becomes the inaugural address of Jesus for Luke (4:16:30); the call of Simon, early in Mark (1:16-20) and Matthew (4:18-22), is delayed until after the catch of fish in Luke (5:1-11). The call of the Twelve, preceding the Sermon on the Plain in Luke, follows most of the Sermon on the Mount in Matthew and the brief references to it in Mark. These displacements are generally made for theological reasons, but they sometimes give strategic importance to key points. Thus the second and third temptations are changed, from Mark and Matthew, to give emphasis to Jerusalem. Two episodes in Q which deal with "entering" are removed from their original contexts (Mt 7:13-14; 25:10b-12) to the eve of Jesus' entry into Jerusalem (Lk 13:22-30).

Luke feels free to polish the styles, and clarify the meanings of his sources, adapting them to his audience and their cultural experiences and religious notions. He homilizes on the Old Testament as he integrates its stories, types, and hopes into his proclamation. While disliking repetition, he can still use "echo-diction" in his retelling of the traditions. He values his sources, using them with respect, but feels no guilt in rearranging the material for the benefit of his audience.

Luke's Major Compositional Contributions

We are accustomed today to reading the works of different theologians in the knowledge that they write from their own styles, interests, and pastoral concerns. Even when dealing with the same source-document, their aims, audiences, and the needs they address are often different. Their understandings of events vary, as do their talents and abilities to express them. These same factors are present in the evangelists as they retell the events of Jesus' life, proclaim his message, and highlight its meaning and importance for their different audiences.

Luke modifies and adapts his sources, imprinting on them his own pastoral and spiritual concerns. The forms he uses, the atmosphere he creates, the structure he gives his work, and his strategy are teachings in themselves. He redirects Jesus' teaching, giving us a portrait of him unquestionably more suitable and spiritually challenging for Christianity's new audience. In all this work he is inspired.

In this section, we reflect on Luke's editorial contribution. In reshaping his material he is convinced that his contributions are themselves faithful representations of elements of early Church traditions not contained in the writings which preceded him.

Gentile literary conventions. Apart from the general Hellenization of his sources, Luke major compositional contribution is the adoption of the methods and literary forms of his own Gentile culture. "The complexity of the sentences, the acknowledgement of predecessors in the field, the expression of purpose by the writer, and the address to the patron are all part of the literary conventions of the time. Luke is making a bid to have his books regarded seriously by the literarily, perhaps even the intellectually, sophisticated of his day."[13]

The prefaces, letters, and speeches of the Third Gospel and Acts contain oratorical and epistolary features common to the Greco-Roman world and are indicative of his very purpose for writing.[14] His travel narratives of Jesus in the Gospel and of Paul in Acts show Luke to be an intelligent participant in the literary life of his Mediterranean world. Jesus' joining the travelers to Emmaus and Philip's appearance to the eunuch reflect classical themes. We find a philosophical dialogue with the Stoics and Epicureans, an ideal description of the early Church communities reminiscent of Plato's Republic, and so on. This assimilation of literary forms in Luke's redactional activity is not merely for artistic effect. The prefaces and speeches, with their legal language, show Luke's apologetic determination; the travel narratives highlight the Christians' need to pilgrimage through life; the stories of the "divine tramp" convey his conviction of our need of Jesus in our own journeys through life. The redactional work itself teaches; we shall see more details of this in the chapters ahead.

The atmosphere of faith. As mentioned in the previous chapter, Luke is skillful in creating an atmosphere in which his story can be appreciated. This is done by his editorial contributions. Often, before a block of source material or after it, he gives a short summary statement in the imperfect tense. These descriptions set the scene for the following section, or are typical descriptions of Christian life, creating an atmosphere for subsequent events or portraying the atmosphere resulting from the preceding missionary work (Lk 4:14-15; 19:47-48; Acts 2:43-47; 4:32-37; 5:12-16; 9:31).

Similar to the summaries is Luke's constant use of refrains. He frequently makes his readers pause while he briefly speaks of the peace and joy of the early Church (Acts 8:8, 39; 13:48, 52; 16:34), or of the constant praise and thanksgiving of the believers, or the increase in numbers and expansion of the missionary endeavors of the first communities (Acts 4:31; 28:31). Repeated often and briefly, these choruses or refrains color the narratives. No matter what the content of the chapter, Luke, by this simple but skillful editorial contribution, creates an atmosphere of peaceful, joyful expansion for the Church.

His deliberate adoption of the Septuagint and, more importantly, the Septuagintal style of large sections of his work, give the flavor of sacred history to his presentation.

We shall see later that much of Luke's two volumes are placed in a prayerful, meditative context. Digressions into the miraculous and the supernatural are more common than in the other gospels, as are pious, religious interpretations of traditions.[15]

These contributions create an atmosphere for Luke's retelling of the Jesus story, and constitute new insights into the message which he identifies and verifies in his sources of the oral tradition. He describes an ideal vision of the Church, suggests attitudes of hope, fosters an awareness of the Church's place in history, and calls us to a reflective appreciation of all this.

Elements of structure and strategy. The redaction critic's discernment of patterns and structures is invariably subjective. However, there is general agreement that Luke balances narratives not only for artistic purposes, but to convey theological convictions as well. Episodes in the life of Jesus are paralleled in the experiences of the early Church, thereby showing how Jesus' life and message live on faithfully in his Church. We read of the baptisms of Jesus and the Church (Lk 3:21-22; Acts 2:1-4), the inaugural speeches of Jesus and Peter (Lk 4:14-20; Acts 2:14-41), the cures wrought by Jesus and their counterpart in the power of God as it lives on in the early Church (Lk 5:17-20; Acts 9:32-35).

Elsewhere we see the balance of narratives between Peter and Paul, highlighting the continuation, in Paul, of the post-resurrectional ministry of the Church seen in Peter; this for the benefit of the Gentile mission. Peter's first sermon is paralleled with Paul's (Acts 2:14-41; 13:16-41); their power to cure is the same, their ministries similar (Acts 3:1-10; 14:8-10). At the end, Luke summarizes the achievements of each (Acts 5:15-16; 19:11-12).

Are we dealing with actual history or presentations found in Luke's sources? Could it be that his constant literary balancing between Jesus and his Church, between Peter and Paul, is unconscious stereotyping? These structural features are conscious, deliberate, editorial contributions. They are readily identifiable and theologically significant literary devices.

Even when Luke retells short episodes, he arranges the narratives in such a way that their strategic relationship is itself significant. This constant balance of narratives, or "law of two," is a stylistic characteristic of Luke. He relates two stories by placing them side-by-side, or by introducing them with the same question, or by the use of key words, or by content. The stories are then seen to complement each other (complementary parallelism); or one story prepares for the second, the theological climax (climactic parallelism); or they are placed close together for contrast (antithetical parallelism).

We notice that stories about a man are complemented with stories about a woman, thereby showing their equality before God.[16] Jesus is twice asked, "What must I do to have eternal life?" and his two answers are complementary (Lk 10:25-27; 18:18-22). We are given two parts to the teaching on the Ascension (Lk 24:50-53; Acts 1:9-11), and two complementary views of the end times (Lk 17:22-37; 21:5-36). Each time, Luke approaches the material in two phases, and, unless we know this and take the material together, we find only a partial answer.

Luke redactionally presents us with the annunciations of John (Lk 1:5-25) and Jesus (Lk 1:26-38), followed by their births

(Lk 1:57-80; 2:1-21). Each time, John's is preparatory to Jesus', the latter's thus emphasizing superiority before his stories are presented. The mission of the Twelve (Lk 9:1-6) and the mission of the seventy-two (Lk 10:1-20) are juxtaposed so as to highlight the importance of the new Israel's cosmic ministry. This climactic structure is also seen in Lukes positioning of the reactions of a doubting crowd and the clear, decisive belief of Jesus' close disciples.

Final examples of the "law of two" are stories which highlight Christian values by editorially introduced contrasts: the doubting of Zachariah and the acceptance of Mary (Lk 1:18, 34), Jesus' rejection in Nazareth and his acceptance in Capernaum (Lk 4:16-32), the four beatitudes and the four woes (Lk 6:20-26), Simon the Pharisee and the woman sinner (Lk 7:36-50), the priest-Levite and the Samaritan (Lk 10:29-37), the rich man and Lazarus (Lk 16:19-31), and the two thieves at the crucifixion (Lk 23:39-43). In these examples of balanced narrative, we deal not with accidental connections, but with connections made because of Luke's theological concerns.

These structural features are generally found in short episodes. In the second chapter of his major work on structural analysis, C. H. Talbert believes he can identify a detailed structure common to both the Third Gospel and Acts. General paralleling has been recognized for some time, but the details documented by Talbert are amazing.

A final structural element is Luke's reworking of his source material into two volumes of a consecutive history of Jesus and the Church. No other gospel writer set himself such a task.

Other structural features will be identified in the following chapters. Those we have seen are unquestionably editorial, and bring intuitions and insights into the message. Without Luke, that message would have been lost.

Luke's New Theological Directions

In this chapter we are concerned with Luke's sources and his use of them. We have seen that he modifies his sources for stylistic reasons, clarifies them where there are doubts, adapts them for a new audience and a different culture, maintains their roots in the Old Testament past, avoids repetition, and even rearranges the material where he sees fit.

Besides these secondary editorial modifications, we have seen that Luke contributes new elements to the gospel tradition by means of his own composition. These include the adoption of the literary conventions of his day, a new atmosphere created for the presentation and reception of the message, and the structures and strategies employed.

These editorial and compositional contributions give the message new vitality and relevance for Luke's audience. However, something more is taking place. When Luke has completed his editorial task of reworking his formed sources and introducing material special to him, new theological directions can be discerned in the finished books, the new structure and framework itself creating its own message and meaning. It is possible not only to interpret the meaning of each episode of the New Testament, but also to interpret the meaning of the structure and framework adopted. Into the finished composition Luke has integrated at least four new theological directions and concerns. He takes new directions in ecclesiology, apologetics, pastoral theology, and spiritual theology.

Ecclesiology. Since the time of Rudolph Bultman, Luke has been criticized for having replaced primitive Christian eschatology with salvation history. Bultmann and his followers have consistently held that Luke, moved by his Church's anxiety over the continued delay of the Second Coming, reinterpreted primitive eschatology, in doing so betraying the message of Jesus and surrendering to organizational religion. By the time Luke writes, he is convinced that the end will not come immediately. He then modifies some of his Marcan material and explicitly states that we have no idea when the end will come (Lk 19:11, Acts 1:7).[17] This final stage, after Jesus' departure, is viewed by Luke as a major stage of redemptive history, and is for Luke the period of the Church.[18] Recent research has not supported these positions of Bultmann and his followers, notably Conzelmann.[19] Their critics identify many references to the imminent end, both in Luke's sources, which he neither rejects nor modifies, and in other references added by Luke alone. "There has been widespread agreement that an expectation of the imminent end is found in Luke-Acts."[20] Luke definitely has new concerns, but they do not need to be justified only because of his concern at the delay of the Second Coming, nor must they necessarily be interpreted as a decadent phase of early Church history. This biased reading is erroneous.

Luke's creative contribution is not so much a systematic reinterpretation of primitive eschatology, but a reflection on how we should live in this period of expectation. We are reading more of an ecclesiology than a theology of history. Critics of Conzelmann agree that while Luke is concerned with living now, his approach still includes hope for an imminent end. Luke's is not a deliberate historicizing of the primitive message, but a pastoral concern for the quality of life as we together await the coming of the Lord. This shared waiting is our life as Church, the gathering of those who have had an interior change with visible results and are now followers of the "Way."[21] Those followers are the people of God, the eschatological community. Moreover, as we shall see in the chapter on Church, Luke's redactional contributions and theological concerns indicate constant interest in community and discipleship, and only secondarily in the structured aspects of this community. The recommendations he makes are not new to the New Testament witness; rather, they are syntheses of ideas referred to throughout the New Testament.

We shall deal later with the ecclesiology of Luke. It is sufficient now to point out that serious interest in how this community ought to live, as together it awaits the Lord, is a new direction introduced by Luke into the believer's awareness. Paul had already given advice, but Luke systematizes and synthesizes what it means to be Church. This is a deliberate compositional contribution.

The apologetic approach to faith. J. C. O'Neill dated Luke's writings around 130. As we have already seen, this date is unacceptable. However, O'Neill's reasons for giving this date are interesting: he considers Luke's concerns to be similar to those of the second century apologists. Although I disagree with O'Neill, he highlights a major secondary concern of Luke's, and one of his new theological directions: the apologetic approach to his faith. Matthew did this in relation to Jamnian Pharisaism. Luke is so convinced of his faith that he strongly defends its historical roots. He skillfully defends its fruitfulness in relation to Judaism, its positions and contributions to the Roman Empire, the life and attitudes of its great Gentile missionary, and its values before the cultural elite of the Hellenistic world. Apologetics is not Luke's primary purpose in writing, but he is convinced that his faith can withstand any critical examination. He seems to be saying to believers: "Do not be afraid to defend the values of your faith."

Much has been written about Luke as historian. There is a consensus among critical scholars today that Luke is primarily a theologian. However, his prologue constitutes a firm commitment to historically reliable information. His two volumes certainly give the impression that he wants to be taken seriously as a historian, although it is equally clear that history is not his major aim. There are inaccuracies in his presentation, digressions from his sources, symbolic use of geography, and forms imposed on his work which are clearly not historical, as, for example, the journey to Jerusalem in 9:51 to 19:27. Luke is not writing the first history of Christianity. He is an evangelist, a proclaimer of the Good News. The faith he calls us to, rooted in history, is the biblical idea of faith.[22]

Luke has clothed the kerygma in history because his sources confirm its roots in historical reality. This confirmation of the historical value of the teachings is typically biblical, which cannot be said of the existential interpretations of the Bultmannians. Because Luke "was a theologian, he had to be a historian. His view of theology led him to write history."[23] His historical form enables him to defend the reality of his faith.

Christianity is the eschatological community prophesied by Moses (Acts 2:42-47; Deuteronomy 15:4-11). Luke, convinced of this, is prepared to defend this understanding of his faith in dialogue with the Jews. Christianity is now the new Israel, built upon the Twelve, with a new gift of the law of the Spirit, a new Moses, and promised fidelity. Luke uses types from the history of Israel, their scriptures, and their liturgical celebrations to support his view. For Luke, Jesus is everything the Jews hoped for. "But if the Old Testament sheds light upon the Christ event, how much more light Christ sheds upon the Old Testament! Were not the texts used in the apostolic preaching all riddles before Jesus came to give them meaning? We may indeed wonder whether the ultimate significance of the Christian argumentation in Acts is not . . . [that it] is the Christ event which interprets those texts for us."[24] Dupont, here, synthesizes well Luke's own convictions.

Luke's defenses of Christianity and Paul before the Empire are so clear that some authors considered them Luke's major reasons for writing his two volumes. In both gospel and Acts, Luke consistently shows Christianity as no threat to Rome. John the Baptist does not undermine the role of the military (Lk 3:14), Jesus supports taxation (Lk 20:20-26), Paul is a proud citizen (Acts 22:25), and when the prison breaks open in an earthquake, he does not run away (Acts 16:25-40). Pilate finds no fault with Jesus (Lk 23:13-15), and Gallio is supportive of Paul (Acts 18:12-17). Festus finds no fault with Paul (Acts 25:1-12, 25), and Agrippa agrees with the Roman governor's decision (Acts 26:32).

Events of this kind are, for Luke, examples of the defense of Christianity by Rome. Rome's local representatives speak well of the religion, even asking for cures or baptism (Lk 7:1-10; Acts 10:1-43). In addition, both volumes are written to Theophilus, a Roman, to explain the objective goodness of the message, taught by Jesus and his followers (Lk 1:1-4). Moreoever, the language of the preface, together with that of the speeches, seems, even to contemporary scholars, to be a typical presentation of a legal brief in defense of Paul or Christianity.[25] I cannot support those commentators who conclude that Luke wrote exclusively to defend Christianity or Paul.[26] Luke, however, is not prepared to accept criticism of the faith, when historical facts prove otherwise.

This apologetical approach can also be seen in Luke's presentation of Christianity as defensible before the cultural and philosophical interests of the day. We will speak of this in a later chapter.

A pastoral theologian. Luke is one the first great pastoral theologians of the Church. He regards the contemporary situation as the summons of God to the Church, reminding it of its ever-new task of formulating and announcing the gospel of Jesus for human society in the here and now.[27]

Luke effectively considers the major issues facing the pastoral inventiveness of the Church in the last quarter of the first century. Other New Testament writers deal with one or another issue of the Church from time to time, but Luke systematically confronts these problems. He is a practical, realistic theologian.

With the death of the last apostles, Christians anxiously faced the problem of how to encounter the Lord. Luke suggests they do this in the study of scripture, hospitality, meals of friendship, the breaking of the bread, prayer, peace, and joy (Lk 24:13-53; Acts 2:42-47; 4:32-35). The community's disorientation at the delay of the Second Coming leads Luke to expound the need for quality living in the time of waiting. This leads to the problem of the relationship to the state, and, again, Luke deals with it. As the Church's missionary work expands and the Gentiles are welcomed into the faith, Luke grounds this practice in apostolic teaching, explaining his understanding of its relationship to the Father's plan. For a Church distant from Jesus, having lost its first fervor, Luke presents a gospel of absolute commitment and prayer, a gospel that challenges us to use all gifts, no matter how long the wait for the master's return.[28]

Luke systematically counteracts wrong beliefs in the Church. Attacks on marriage in the encratic heresy, found in most of the apocryphal Acts of the apostles, are not in Luke or Acts. Rather, he nurtures a positive valuing of marriage (Lk 16:18), indicates an appreciation of a wife (Lk 14:26), and shows married couples actively involved in the ministry of the early Church (Acts 18:26). Luke reacts against the false belief of those who think John the Baptist is the Messiah (Acts 19:1-7). He knows what problems Docetism can create, and documents his response. Finally, in times influenced by Gnoticism, the Church's most creative pastoral response comes largely from Luke (Lk 23:55; 24:3).[29]

As the Church expands, Luke shows the Lord's message to be for all: Gentiles, the underprivileged, the poor, and women.[30] As the initial fervor is lost, as sin and selfishness grow, Luke offers a two-fold answer: the Lord's is the gospel of mercy for all sinners (Lk 6:36-42; 7:36-50; 15; 19:1-10; 23:34-43), but is also one of absolute dedication (Lk 5:11; 9:23, 62; 12:33; 14:26), concern for all, and of life given to God.

A spiritual theologian. All New Testament writers call us to faith in and commitment to the teachings of Jesus. However, I would single out Luke as one of the first spiritual theologians of Christianity. Spiritual theology is a discipline which examines, studies, and teaches the evolution to fullness of Christian life. It is also an art of knowing and directing people in living. Luke takes the teachings of Jesus and presents them in a dynamic and progressive way. The disciples recognize Jesus, respond to his call, journey with him, and constantly listen to his teachings. This first happens during the Galilean ministry (Lk 4:14 - 9:50). Later, after a deeper recognition of who Jesus is, the call comes again for total commitment, and life's journey with Jesus begins. As we shall later see, it is not so much that this second journey is to different places, but that we all now journey in a different way (Lk 9:51). During the journey Jesus gives his major teaching on discipleship. The way leads to passion and death, but also to resurrection and the ever continuing journey of life (Lk 24:13-35; Acts 8:26-40). Luke's presentation is systematic, calling for progression, and identifies stages of growth.

As a good spiritual theologian, Luke identifies the essential elements of Christian conversion: a call to a person, under the shadow of the cross, in the light of the resurrection, and with the perspective of judgment.[31] These constants are present in Luke's teachings, and we shall see them in more detail in chapter six.

From the very first moment of God's call, Luke identifies what is needed psychologically and spiritually to move one to respond. His speeches and sermons in Acts manifest in the same constant structure the qualities he sees as necessary to move a person to conversion.

Luke's work, however, is not only systematized to facilitate progress, but shows sensitivity to people and their needs as well. He is an artist who understands psychological reactions and motivations (Lk 3:15; 4:14; 9:43; 11:1, 29; 13:1; 17:20; 18:19; 19:11). People are different; their needs and hopes vary. Here, too, Luke's two books succeed in highlighting the historical centrality and life-centrality of Jesus. The essential revelation of Christianity is a person, not teachings. Unfortunately, redaction criticism, highlighting as it does the content, composition, and theology of the writer, sometimes leads away from the fact that the object of belief is not primarily teachings but a person. Luke's presentation emphasizes the person of Jesus, and a person appeals to different people in different ways. Luke does not follow one interpretation of Jesus to the exclusion of others. There are different Christologies evident at the same time. Luke is not a systematic theologian who speculatively interprets the Christ event. Rather, he is a spiritual theologian for whom people's varied needs and reactions are a point of departure for his reflections. His contribution is pluralism in appreciation of Jesus.

These four new theological directions identifiable in Luke-Acts are editorial. We shall examine them in depth in a later section.

Luke's Recommended Attitudes

In this chapter we have seen Luke use a variety of sources in retelling the gospel story. He seems to tap the great centers of the early Church, and what he creatively gives us is built on the general consensus of the early Church.

He uses material with courage and freedom, respectful of his sources, but feeling free to omit sections when he judges them irrelevant. He adapts the Palestinian-based tradition to a new audience with different life experiences. As he reworks his material, he introduces new themes, new insights, and new challenges to meet the needs of his Church. He prophetically offers new theological directions while calling his people to be Church, to be convinced of their faith, to bring its relevant message to each new pastoral situation.

Pluralistic approaches in the Church. The Lucan writings show appreciation and positive support for a pluralistic approach in the Church. Attempts to integrate traditions go hand-in-hand with a willingness to let sources speak for themselves. Certain positions of Mark and Q, such as the Marcan messianic secret, or the primitive eschatology of Q, are readily identifiable, though not of major value to the Lucan position. In Acts, several movements or theologies co-exist. James, Peter, Paul, Stephen, and Philip can each be identified with theological and ecclesiological positions in the early Church.

Although a typically Lucan position is the main constituent, this is hardly the work of one creative mind. Rather, Luke re-expresses for his own contemporaries the theological patterns, traditions, and life values of a flourishing community.

Pastoral selection in the use of traditions. In his desire to respond to the needs of his time, Luke is pastorally selective in his use of traditions. He seems to have deliberately omitted much of what he must have known. Mark is valuable for him, but not all Mark's theology remains relevant to Luke's Church. "Luke can distinguish between those commands of the Lord which were meant only for the contemporary situation, . . . and those which are permanent."[32] This discernment of the essential, and the detachment from historically limited accidentals, are services needed by the Church at all times, not only in the last quarter of the first century. Luke wanted to serve the Church of his day, helping it to face its own difficulties and challenges. He has much to say to the contemporary Church and its understanding of doctrine and history.

Reincarnation of the message of faith. It is easy to make Luke "a dogmatician who must have self-consciously worked out his own doctrinal system, here intentionally rejecting a Marcan doctrine and there repudiating a Pauline conviction."[33] True, he seems in places to break with origins and traditions, but sometimes we must change in order to remain the same. The same teaching presented in the same way to two different cultures or generations can easily mean different things. Pastoral ability and spiritual leadership challenge missionaries of all times to present their messages in forms understandable and relevant to their audiences. Paul quotes the Old Testament to the Jews, but the pagan poets to the Athenians. Luke's courageous adaptation of tradition calls us to change and reincarnate the message of faith. Jesus' call was spirit and life for his audience, and must be that for every generation and every culture. Where it is not, we should confront our pastoral practice with the example of Luke.

Ecclesial responsibility. One outstanding quality of Luke is his ecclesial responsibility. The steward of tradition, he confronts his own presentation with the insights of those who were eyewitnesses and ministers of the word. He seeks the roots of his teachings in the scriptures of old, in the message of the Lord, in the authority of the Twelve, and in the lived experience of the early Church. He is so strongly convinced of the truth of the tradition he has received that he defends it against all attacks. He is equally convinced that his message challenges, personally and institutionally, the Church's organization and the unjust practices of the State. To both he delivers the challenge with clarity. At the same time he is willing to interpret the message for new situations in order to responsibly assure the perennial freshness of its call. When radically new circumstances develop, he moves with a sense of prophetic discovery motivated by faith and hope.

Luke's willingness to constantly confront present practice with the rooted traditions of faith, to courageously interpret the message for new situations, and to risk exploring in faith new ways of living Jesus' call, all show us the need for a constant demythological, hermeneutical, and heuristic approach to faith.

Chapter Three
THEOLOGY OF MINISTRY

The Lord appointed a further seventy-two and sent them in pairs before him to every town and place he intended to visit. He said to them: "The harvest is rich but the workers are few; therefore ask the harvest master to send workers to his harvest."(Lk 10:1-2)

We have studied so far the author, his sources, and personal contributions. In this chapter, we consider Luke's major purpose in writing the Third Gospel and Acts. What did he hope to achieve in writing these two volumes? What service did he perform for the Church of his times? How did these two volumes focus the attention of his audience on the perennial values of Christ's message?

We have already seen some of his many interests and identified several new theological directions in the work. We now ask whether one concern, more than any other, is the motivating force behind Luke's work. What was he hoping to accomplish?

A basic message was given in Mark. If Luke rewrote the message of Mark in order to interpret and apply it to a new culture, he did not write Acts for this reason. However, the Third Gospel and Acts are so intimately connected that we must seek Luke's purpose with both books in mind. What does Luke achieve by this two-part presentation? Over the centuries, various criteria have been used to discover this.

Some commentators have used criteria of literary analysis. They believe that in places Luke explicitly states his purpose (Lk 1:1-4; Acts 1:1-5). He writes to Theophilus to show the reliability of the instruction he has received. Moreover, he claims, as does no other New Testament writer, that he has carefully traced the whole sequence of events from the beginning, and offers an historically valuable record. This is the principal criterion used by F. F. Bruce. Cadbury, in his *Making of Luke-Acts*, prefers as the best criterion the general form of the work. Several other commentators, the most recent being Marshall, direct their attentions to Luke's distinctive word usage as the initial indicator of his aims and interests. Marshall concludes that Luke has special preference for salvation vocabulary, and that his major aim is the presentation of the theology of salvation. Some writers judge Luke's purpose by the quantity of material on any given topic.

With the aid of form criticism, scholars like Leaney, Caird, and Munck have sought an understanding of the nature of Hebrew and Hellenistic literary patterns and forms. The general style of Luke's work is believed by some to be juridical. The prefaces and speeches have the typical form of a legal work, and Luke's aim, according to these scholars, is the legal defense of Christianity or Paul.

Danker and Marshall have used general theological criteria to identify Luke's purpose. They seek a unifying theme, asking whether the content of the two volumes can be arranged around such a theme. Others try to highlight theological positions from Luke's specific portrait of Jesus.

Conzelmann was the first to use redactional criticism in identifying Luke's purpose. By comparing Luke with his sources, identifying textual modifications, studying the narrative atmosphere, and synthesizing his editorial contributions, Conzelmann concludes that Luke is deliberately writing salvation history. Since Conzelmann, redactional analysis has been extensively used to document Luke's presumed purpose for writing.

In analyzing Luke's compositional contributions, commentators have uncovered a structure which they believe deliberately given to the work, one which is indicative of his purpose. Dupont points out that at all key moments in the structure of the two volumes, Luke deals with Gentile salvation. Other structural features persuade some that Luke is interested in the journeys of Christianity's missionary expansion. More recently, Talbert has used architectonic analysis to show Luke's desire to document for his Church where true tradition can be found and in what it consists.

We have seen that commentators have used literary, form-oriented, theological, redactional, and structural criteria to discern Luke's purpose in writing. We shall first look at Luke's two volumes from a pastoral point of view, to identify the possible immediate reactions of his readers. Then, we shall examine structural features. These criteria will give us Luke's general aim. This purpose will need to be checked in the light of his own redactional work, and supported, if possible, by the new theological directions referred to in the previous chapter.

Purpose of Luke-Acts

The last quarter of the first century. We have seen that many criteria can be used to discern the purpose of Luke-Acts, some of them difficult to apply. Expounded by some of the best scholars in the world, these erudite and refined understandings of Luke's purpose seem out of place for the last quarter of the first century.

At that time, Luke was in touch with a Church which had already passed through the early enthusiasm of new beginnings, and was now threatened with mediocrity and stagnation. His Church, conscious of its emergence from Judaism, was now clearly separated from it. Its teachings were deliberate interpretations of the primitive Palestinian-based message of Jesus. Theologically, there had been movement from a Jewish to a Gentile emphasis, from primitive eschatology to revised eschatology, from local group consciousness to universal Church-consciousness. It was a time of problems, discouragement, disintegration, and a slackening of the missionary dedication of the earlier years. Paul Minear says that Luke "was more deeply concerned with all the social forces which were continuously and cumulatively casting doubt on 'the truth concerning the things of which you have been instructed,' forces which were undermining confidence in the future of the Way and were destructive of resilient morale within the church."[1]

The conflicts Luke faced generated new insights into his understanding of Christianity. His response was not abstract theology, but the call and challenge of a preacher and evangelist. Luke "has allowed his expression of God's saving action in Christ to pass into and determine the kind of response he hopes to elicit from his readers."[2] This is pastoral theology. He does not just restate the Christian message, but explains the way of salvation.

Jesus was not only obedient, but communicated to others the power gained by his obedience. Likewise, for Christians, a faith relationship implies *koinonia*, the deep union with others in common commitment. The vision Luke gives is attained through active participation. "Today" is the time, "now" the moment for our commitment to the message of Jesus.[3]

Pastoral criteria. Among the most important means for discerning Luke's major purpose must be pastoral criteria of immediate reactions. I find it unacceptable that his purpose can only be delineated with the aid of enormous literary machinery. What is the general form and content of the work? What are readers' immediate reactions to each part of the presentation? Are major themes readily conveyed by short sections?

The most striking feature of Luke's presentation is his linking of the stories of Jesus and the Church. He deliberately builds a bridge between the two periods, establishing literary and theological unity. The gospel tells us what Jesus began to do, and Acts shows us his effects following his visible departure. We are presented with a ministering Jesus in the gospel of Luke, a ministering Church in Acts. The gospel shows us Jesus ministering in Galilee, during the journey to and stay in Jerusalem, and Acts presents the early Church's ministry in Jerusalem, Samaria, around the seacoast, and during the great journeys.

Two periods of ministry and different geographical areas are evident in the structure of Luke-Acts. Luke-Acts differs from the other synoptics in its presentation of ministries: Mark gives us the message; Luke presents the ministry of the Word. Although Acts did not originally have a title, it is significant that the Church, reflecting its content, called the book "Acts of Apostles." "Acts" was a Hellenistic literary form describing the deeds of great heros. In other words, the book is recognized as describing the ministries of apostolic figures.[4] The two parts of Luke's work are not abstract statements, nor systematic, theoretical theology, but pastoral theology through ministry.

Ministry. Not only are periods and areas of ministry immediately evident in Luke's writings, but each small section, easily absorbed in one sitting, is a ministry with clearly delineated teaching and characteristics. Each ministry has the same major themes, and similar format and structure. The teaching of the whole is contained in the teaching of each part.

When Jesus begins his life-work in Nazareth, he outlines his future ministry (Lk 4:16-30). Questioned by the disciples of John the Baptist as to who he is, he answers by describing his ministry (Lk 7:22-23). At each stage of his work, he calls others to share his ministry, telling them what to *do*, not what to *say* (Lk 9:1-6; 10:1-20). After his own ministry of self-gift in the passion, he is raised and commissions his followers to continue the ministry (Lk 24:36-49). He says that not only were his own passion and death foretold by scripture, but so too was their ministry to the ends of the earth (Lk 24:46-48).

In Acts, we see a paralleling of ministries: Paul's with Peter's, and Peter's with Jesus'. A careful reading shows that each short section is a compact ministry. Moreover, as Jesus called forth others to ministry at each stage of his work, so too the Church calls forth others to minister as needs arise. We are witnessing the expansion of the message through the expansion of the call to ministry. The book of Acts ends with the detailed description of a minister's final paschal journey. The book is, in this way, unfinished, just as the Church's ministry will always be.

Luke's purpose may be summarized as follows: *As Jesus brought salvation through his ministry of calling to faith, so the Church brings salvation through the prolongation of Jesus' ministry of calling to faith.* The key call of Luke to his own Church is "renewal through ministry." Moreover, Luke's call to faith through ministry is relevant today. When the early Church showed signs of middle-class ease, lacking great leaders and in need of consolidation and vision for the future, Luke called for ministry. He showed successively Jesus, the Twelve, the seventy-two, outstanding Apostles, well-known disciples, lesser known apostolic figures, and unnamed Church leaders — all carrying on the Lord's ministering work. By the end of Acts, the question for Luke's Church and ours is: "Who next?" Luke seems to be repeating the Lord's words: "The harvest is rich but the workers are few; therefore, ask the harvest master to send workers to his harvest" (Lk 10:2).

General Outline Of Luke-Acts

The structure. As we read Luke-Acts, a clear sense of the two volumes as a series of ministries emerges. This is confirmed by a detailed study of the two volumes.

In the gospel of Luke we are given the ministry of Jesus:

Preface

I. Preparation for the ministry of Jesus

II. The ministries of Jesus
    In Galilee
    During the journey
    In Jerusalem

III. The essence of Jesus' ministry
    Anticipatory celebration of the event
    The saving events
    Post-resurrectional celebration of the event

In Acts, we see a remarkable paralleling of the ministry of the Church with the ministry of Jesus:

Preface

I. Preparation for the ministry of the Church

II. The ministries of the Church
    In Jerusalem
    In Samaria
    In the Antiochean region
    Around the Aegean Sea

III. The minister's self-gift in imitation of the saving event in Jesus' life

The outline of Acts mirrors the outline of the gospel, not only in major divisions, but also in the essential theological content of each section. This is verified in the two periods of preparation for ministry, whether Jesus' or the Church's. We witness in each the work of the Spirit preparing for new life. In both preparations, Luke shows the universal relevance of the message: it is presented in a sermon, received in baptism, confirmed by the reception of the Spirit, and results in a commitment to ministry.

A glance over the outlines of the ministries of Jesus shows, among other things, that he shares his ministry with others during each period of ministry. This sharing of ministry is a constant in each of the four periods of ministry in Acts. There is always some new development or need to which the Church responds with a sharing of ministry.

A further constant theme in the writings is opposition. Opposition crops up during every period of ministry. This is sometimes persecution, at others internal community problems or difficulties. However, the work of ministry to the Word continues through all trials.

In the third part of both presentations, Luke proclaims the essence of Jesus' own ministry as the saving event of his self-gift for others. The major stages in this sacrifical self-gift are relived in Acts by Paul, the model minister.

On the following pages is a detailed outline of Luke-Acts.

Detailed Outline of the Gospel of Luke

Preface: The work is dedicated to Theophilus and will deal with all that Jesus began to do and teach 1:1-4

PERIOD OF PREPARATION FOR THE MINISTRY OF JESUS

The gathering of Spirit-filled witnesses to the initiative of God. The child to be born will be filled with the Holy Spirit and will make a people ready for the Lord 1:5-25

The child will be Israel's Messiah 1:26-80

The birth of the son, the shepherd of the nations 2:1-52

Preparations for the coming ministry of the Lord — a sermon 3:1-20

Jesus praying at his baptism 3:21

The Holy Spirit descends on Jesus 3:22

The universality of Jesus' ministry explicitly stated 3:23-38

A clarification of the nature of Jesus' ministry — the temptations 4:1-13

THE MINISTRIES OF JESUS

Ministry in Galilee 4:14 - 9:27

Awareness of being commissioned for ministry 4:14-21

Some rejection to be expected 4:22-30

A ministry of preaching, teaching, and healing 4:31-5:32; 7;

Conflicts with religious leaders 5:33-6:11

The call of the Twelve 6:12-16

A major collection of Jesus' teachings begins the period of ministry 6:17-49

A sermon of directives for ministry 6:20-26

The ministry continues 8:1-18

True relatives of Jesus 8:19-21

Jesus shares his ministry with the Twelve 9:1-6

Herod, an example of false encounters 9:7-9

Ministers reaffirm their awareness of who Jesus is 9:18-22

Jesus reaffirms that there is no shared ministry without the cross 9:23-27

Ministry during the journey to Jerusalem

Awareness of being commissioned for ministry 9:28-36

Some rejection to be expected 9:52-56

A ministry of preaching, teaching, and healing 9:37-62

The call of the seventy-two 10:1-2

A sermon of directions for ministry 10:3-16
Jesus shares his ministry with the seventy-two 10:17-20
Ministry continues 10:21 - 11:36
True relatives of Jesus 11:27-28
Conflicts with religious leaders 11:37 - 12:3
Ministers' implicit reaffirmation of who Jesus is 12:41-48
Jesus reaffirms that there is no shared ministry without the cross 12:4-12
Herod and false encounters 13:31-35
A major collection of Jesus' teachings ends the period of ministry 14:1 - 19:27

Ministry in Jerusalem 19:28-21:38

Awareness of ministry 19:28-40
Some rejection to be expected 19:41-46
A ministry of preaching and teaching (but no healing in rejecting Jerusalem) 19:47-48
Conflicts with religious leaders 20:1-47
Jesus reaffirms the place of suffering in the disciple's life 21:1-36
Ministry continues 21:37

THE ESSENCE OF JESUS' MINISTRY 22:1 - 23:56

Anticipatory celebration of the event 22:1-38

The risk of Jesus' self-gift to others 22:1-6
Jesus' awareness 22:7-13
Ritual celebration of self-gift 22:14-23
Clarification of the nature of ministry — temptations 22:24-27
Sharing of mission with the disciples 22:28-38

The saving event 22:39 - 23:55

Prayer and discernment of ministry 22:39-46
Jesus' awareness 22:42
Jesus totally given to others 22:47-53
Temptations — people unclear as to the nature of Jesus' ministry 22:54 - 23:25
Rejected by Peter, his own disciple 22:54-62
Rejected by Jewish leaders 22:63-71
The state uninterested, uses religious issues for political purposes 23:1-7
Rejected by other political leaders 23:8-12
Rejected by Jewish crowds 23:13-25

A journey to death, including a sharing of mission with Simon of Cyrene 23:26-31
Jesus' self-gift in rejection 23:32-46
Appreciation of his ministry 23:47-55

POST-RESURRECTIONAL CELEBRATION OF THIS SAVING EVENT 24:1-53

Disciples seek Jesus 24:1-3
Awareness of who Jesus is 24:4-12
Indications of where to find Jesus and his message today 24:13-35
Jesus entrusts his ministry to the Church 24:36-49
The joy that results from this awareness 24:50-53

Detailed Outline of The Acts of the Apostles.

Preface: The work is dedicated to Theophilus and deals with what was done through the Holy Spirit by the apostles whom Jesus had chosen 1:1-5

PERIOD OF PREPARATION FOR THE MINISTRY OF THE CHURCH

The gathering of Spirit-filled witnesses to the initiative of God. The Church to be born will be filled with the Holy Spirit 1:6-14
The Church will be the new Israel 1:15-26
Birth of the Church, a community for all nations 2:1-36
Preparations for the coming ministry of the Lord — a sermon 2:37-41
The disciples pray as they await their baptism 1:14
The Spirit fills the disciples 2:1-4
The universality of the Church's ministry implied 2:5-13
A clarification of the nature of ministry — to be Church 2:42-47
The Church's ministry begins with a sermon, but the Sanhedrin arrests the apostles 3:1 - 4:22

MINISTRIES OF THE CHURCH

Each period in the Church's ministry presents similar characteristics. There is always a description of a call to ministry and an endowment with the power of the Spirit of God. The minister presents a Christ-centered proclamation which is always rejected by some of the audience. Although persecution inevitably follows, the Church's ministry continues to progress.

Ministry in Jerusalem 4:23 - 8:3

Peter and the Twelve 4:23 - 6:4
Stephen 6:5 - 8:3

Ministry in Samaria 8:4 - 11:18

Philip in Samaria and Gaza 8:4-40
Saul 9:1-31
Peter in Lydda, Joppa, and Caesarea 9:32 - 11:18

Ministry in the Antiochean region 11:19 - 15:35

The Church's ministry in Antioch 11:19-30
Barnabas and Saul on a first great journey 13: 1 - 15:35

Ministry around the Aegean Sea 15:36 - 21:3

Paul and Silas as far as Europe 16:1 - 17:15
Paul in Athens and Corinth 17:16 - 18:28
Paul in Ephesus and back to Caesarea 19:1 - 21:3

THE MINISTER'S SELF-GIFT: A Journey Ministry To Rome 21:4 - 28:30

Prayer 21:4-5
Awareness of what lies ahead 21:5-12
Paul's recommitment and self-gift 21:13-14
Temptations — people unclear on the nature of Paul's ministry 21:17 - 26:32
 Rejected by his own Church 21:17-40
 Rejected by the Jewish crowds 22:1-29
 Rejected by the Jewish leaders 22:30 - 23:11
 The state uninterested in the issue 23:23 - 25:12
 Rejected by other political leaders 25:13 - 26:32
A journey to death 27:1 - 28:22
Ministry ends in rejection 28:23-28
The Church's ministry continues 28:30

Theology of Ministry

The infancy narratives. I have suggested that a theology of ministry is Luke's key aim, and that this is the immediate reaction to his work. The simplest structuring of the two volumes is in terms of ministries. In this section, we deal with that compositional and editorial work of Luke's which confirms this position.

Since there are some similarities with Matthew's presentation of the infancy of Jesus, it is possible that both are dependent on material traditionally accepted by the early Church. However, the elaboration of these simple facts and beliefs into their present form in the Third Gospel is clearly the redactional work of Luke. These first three chapters are an elaborate editorial synthesis.

Conzelmann omitted the infancy narratives from his interpretation of the theology of Luke and, in general, has been criticized for it.[5] Whether we distinguish independent sources for these chapters or identify their markedly Hebraistic features, the fact remains that Luke used these sections to introduce his work. They are stylistically and thematically woven into the structure of the entire Lucan enterprise. Since their inclusion must be seen as Luke's deliberate decision, he must have thought they served his purpose and theological interests. In the dramatic presentation of these three chapters, Luke synthesizes the expectations of the Old Testament, identifies Jesus, gives a telescopic presentation of the whole of Luke-Acts, underlines the joy of these events, and anticipates briefly the future ministry of Jesus. A similar five-fold purpose is served by chapters one and two of Acts.

The style and form of the infancy narratives is Septuagintal.[6] The characters are the last leading figures of the Old Testament, reminding us of some of the great heroes of Israel's history.[7] Each is filled with the Holy Spirit, singing in psalms of the people's hopes, which each sees fulfilled in the child Jesus. Their convictions are confirmed by the statements of eight prophets in the course of these chapters. The general outpouring of the Spirit witnessed in these events further stresses the fact that the child is the fulfillment of hopes. He is called Great, the Son of the Most High, and the Son of David. He is addressed as Lord, Savior, and Christ. He is acknowledged as Salvation, the light of the Gentiles, and the glory of Israel. In describing Jesus in this way, the infancy narratives anticipate the Jesus of the resurrection. These titles will rarely be used in the Third Gospel, but here in the infancy narratives they anticipate the mature awareness of Jesus arrived at by the post-resurrection Church. It is possible to "view the birth in terms of the total activity of Jesus, and in such a way that the whole career is telescoped into one event. Because of this, the birth is itself described as the eschatological event."[8] The universality of salvation in Jesus is established, and the specific issue of Gentile entry into the Church is resolved before it arises. This salvation will cost the passion, but this too is anticipated and willingly accepted.[9] The result is joy among the representatives of the Old Testament, faithful observers of the law, attendants of the temple, and religiously and socially underprivileged groups. Into the infancy narratives is placed the story of the child Jesus in the temple. The story shows Jesus' piety and single-minded dedication, his wisdom, and his acceptance of the tension between this world's values and God, a tension that will be present throughout his ministry. This brief episode, a pre-ministry Christology, is another example of the synthetical presentation of Jesus' life and work in the infancy stories. "It is proleptically significant that 'the things of my Father' are going to bring Jesus back to the same city, and to the same temple (Lk 19:45)."[10]

The infancy narratives anticipate the major movements of the Third Gospel and Acts, and are an integral part of the Lucan statement. They form the period of preparation for the ministry of Jesus. The aims of his ministry are prophetically outlined and contrasted with the work of John the Baptist. We are shown that a new period is beginning, for God has remembered the people and is full of concern and graciousness. In his love, he gathers the people and brings salvation.[11] The agent in the ministry ahead is Jesus. Luke's prophetic synthesis is a preparation for ministry and a description of the nature of that ministry.

Jesus' Galilean ministry. Chapter three and the first half of chapter four continue Luke's presentation of preparations for Jesus' Galilean ministry. In fact, Luke is the only writer who explicitly refers to the work that begins as "a ministry" (Lk 3:23). This section is well structured. Luke 3:1-18 continues the contrasting parallelism between John the Baptist and Jesus, highlighting the qualitative difference of the latter's ministry by which the people's expectations are fulfilled. Moreover, the salvation established in Jesus will be universal. Luke 3:21-38 shows us the baptism and public presentation of Jesus as the servant of all humankind. Luke 4:1-15 deals with the temptations, but Luke's rearrangement of their order highlights the culminating role of the ministry of self-gift in Jerusalem. There follows, in Luke alone, the inaugural address of Jesus in the synagogue in Nazareth (Lk 4:16-30). This sermon is taken from chapter six of Mark. The episode in Nazareth is probably a composite account of three different visits of Jesus to his home town. Luke edits it in such a way as to encapsulate the ministry of Jesus, becoming the public anointing of Jesus by the Holy Spirit for his ministry (Lk 4:18-19; Acts 10:38). This episode puts all that follows in the context of ministry.

These four steps in the preparation are also interrelated: Jesus' ministry differs qualitatively from all others; the baptism is a religious experience implying commitment to ministry; the temptations clarify the nature of the ministry as one of service; and the Nazareth events are Jesus' anointing and commissioning for ministry. With the use of traditional material and some personal contributions, Luke gives us a theology of ministry.

Luke now omits the call of the first disciples (Mk 1:16-20) and proceeds to Jesus' preaching, healing, and teaching ministries in Capernaum. He clarifies Matthew's statement to show Jesus fully aware that his Father has sent him for ministry such as this (Lk 4:43). The whole section, up to Luke 6:19, follows Mark, with this notable exception; the solemn designation of the Twelve precedes the healing of the multitudes and the Sermon on the Plain in Luke, whereas it follows the sermon in Matthew (9:35 - 10:10) and the healings in Mark (6:6-13). As all other sections are parallel, this would seem to be deliberate. The only resulting difference is that the call to share Jesus' ministry precedes persuasive miracles and instruction. The call to share Jesus' ministry does not depend on the power of miracles, nor does it give the disciple knowledge of what lies ahead. This would seem to be a significant clarification for Luke's Church. There follows the collection of teachings held in common between Matthew and Luke.

Luke's continuation of the Galilean ministry (8:4 - 9:27) parallels the presentations of Mark (Mk 3:2 - 6:44) and Matthew (Mt 12:22 - 14:21). The later witnesses are assembled during this early ministry. In this first ministry, they observe Jesus; they will share his journey in the second, in Jerusalem they will weaken but then acknowledge him, and in Acts they will carry this faith to the ends of the earth. There follows the Marcan block (6:45 - 8:26) completely omitted by Luke. Nineham calls this section "Jesus' Gentile Mission," and Drury suggests that, since for Luke the since for "time of the Gentiles" is not yet here (Lk 21:24), the author of the Gentiles actually omits this section until the Church, later appreciating the importance of Gentile salvation, can then initiate large scale ministry as in Acts.[12] Together with Luke's dislike for repetition and his omission of exclusively Jewish concerns, this could well account for the Great Omission.

There follows Luke's special section (Lk 9:51- 19:27). Some of the content can be found in parts of Matthew, and the skeletal form of the section has traces in Mark 10:1-52. It is, however, basically Lucan. The teachings are unique to Luke, in places dealing with points of particular interest to him. More importantly, we are presented here with a second period of ministry for Jesus, one paralleling in general the development of the Galilean ministry. While the teaching is complex, as we shall see, there is an unquestionable clarification of issues relevant to the disciple/minister.

Jesus' ministry in Jerusalem. Beginning at 19:28, Luke describes Jesus' ministry in Jerusalem. He follows the leads of Matthew and Mark, but more briefly. With such short statements as 19:47-48, Luke skillfully gives the impression of an extended period of ministry. There are differences of detail in the passion narratives and modifications for explicit Lucan concerns, but the main units and order of the three synoptics are the same.

The post-resurrectional sections prepare for the ministries of the Church. Luke shows where Jesus can still be found, and places before the Church the final mandate of the Lord (Lk 24:44-49).

This final commissioning by the Lord (Lk 24:44-49) is repeated in the early verses of Acts (1:8). Not only the twelve apostles, but many other disciples who had accompanied Jesus in his ministry had been slowly prepared for this moment (Lk 9:18-23; 19:37-40). Jesus had called forth those who would be his witnesses from the early times in Galilee.[13] These constant companions could guarantee the authenticity of the events, since they had been eyewitnesses. The Acts will be structured on their ministries of testimony, their preaching of this Good News to the ends of the earth.[14]

Ministry in the early Church. Since the identifying of sources in Acts is such a disputed issue, it is not possible to indicate with certainty the Lucan editorial changes of source material. However, it is still possible to highlight some important involvements of Luke which are clearly editorial, at the same time contributing to the development of a theology of ministry.

The early chapters of Acts (1:1 - 4:22) parallel in detail the early sections of the Third Gospel (1:1 - 4:30). Whether Luke is dependent on a Jerusalem source or not, he has edited the material in such a way that the preparation for the period of the ministry of the Church is identical to Jesus'. The gift of sharing in his Spirit, promised by Jesus to his disciples (Lk 24:36-49; Acts 1:8), and reminiscent of Elijah's gift to Elisha for the continuance of his ministry (2 Kings 2:10-13), becomes a community experience. The immediate result of the outpouring of the Spirit and the birth of a new messianic community is the impetus to the ministry of proclamation (Acts 2:14-41), just as it had been for Jesus (Lk 4:16-30).

The main body of Acts shows the history of the Christian missions to the ends of the earth, in fidelity to Jesus' command.[15] It also shows progressive involvement of the baptized in this ministry, whether they be great apostles or unnamed committed Christians (Acts 11:19-26). It demonstrates the evolution of ministry from exclusiveness to universality. This later issue will demand much from Luke's editorial hand whether in the speech of Stephen (Acts 7), the baptism of Cornelius (Acts 10:1 - 11:18), or the conversion of Paul (Acts 9; 22; 26).[16]

We have already seen Luke's editorial paralleling of the ministry of Peter with that of Jesus, and the ministry of Paul with that of Peter. We have also stressed the common compositional material in every area or period of ministry in the Church's evangelical movement to the ends of the earth. Each of these issues stamps the Lucan composition with the interests of ministry. We are shown preparations for the Church's ministry, its origin in the Holy Spirit, and the need for ecclesial commissioning. We see who can be involved in ministry, what ought to be the basic content of the proclamation, and to whom it is directed. Potential obstacles and ideological problems are discussed, and ecclesial responses presented. The common preparation and similar structuring of each ministry gives us a concrete model for pastoral planning. All this is part of the Lucan imprint on the material of Acts.

Luke's Commentators and the Theology of Luke-Acts

We have already seen some of the criteria used by commentators in identitying the main aim of Luke-Acts. Now, in this final section we turn to a selection of the commentators who specifically address Luke's aims in his two-volumed work.[17]

Problem solving. Since the earliest critical studies, it has been suggested that Luke's prime concerns are pastoral theology and the practical desire to solve the immediate problems of his Church. F. C. Baur saw the great problem in the opposing positions of the Judaizers and Peter on the one hand, and Paul, with his cry for freedom from the Law, on the other. Other commentators saw the dehistoricizing of the gospel events by gnostic Christians as the key issue demanding a response. More recently, C. H. Talbert has offered a series of articles portraying the Lucan writings as a defense against Gnosticism. A third problem, which Luke-Acts is seen to correct, is the position of those who viewed the kingdom of God only in terms of Jesus' immediate return. Conzelmann would certainly be the major commentator in this position. A fourth example of a problem current for the Lucan Church is the relationship of Christianity and Judaism. Some writers consider this the pervasive motif of Luke-Acts.[18] We have considered the position of J. Knox, who also sees Luke's motivation as problem solving. For him, Luke-Acts is an early apologetic response to Marcionism.

Luke is indeed interested in facing up to and solving problems that confront his Church, but problem solving is not his principal motive. If it were, letters would have served him better and more directly. Some authors' careful sifting of material to identify a few supportive passages is not persuasive, and still less are positions which force Luke through later philosophical thought. However, these positions have highlighted well Luke's ecclesial concerns and pastoral motivations. They show his understanding of ministry to be both practical and incarnational.

Legal defense. Some commentators, appreciating Luke's tendency to problem solving, have underlined one key issue which they then embrace as the one reason why Luke undertook this task. A. R. C. Leaney states it well: "There can be little doubt that Luke was influenced, among other considerations, by the desirability of showing that Christianity was politically innocent; he probably also wished to show that Paul in particular was wrongly regarded as a political offender."[19] J. Munck shares the same conviction. The desire to present a defense of Christianity and Paul is "the real purpose." C. B. Caird, who comments only on the Third Gospel, says it is the "first great apologia for the Christian faith." E. R. Goodenough, commenting on Acts, decides that it is written to Theophilus to correct the disturbing rumors about Paul.[20]

It is difficult to justify such amassing of material, such meticulous concern for sources and parallels, if only to present an apologetic, or a legal defense. Moreover, there is no early Church evidence that Luke ever played this role. The possibility seems unlikely.

The significance of these positions is the openness to the State found in parts of Luke-Acts. This is certainly an interest of Luke's, though not prime. The dialogic approach he takes, the distinctions he maintains between Church and State are ministerially valuable.

Judeo-Christian dialogue. Some suggest that Acts in particular tries to persuade Jews to become Christians. Others see Christianity as a Jewish sect which becomes a universal religion, the Jews are called, in Luke's writings, to face up to this issue. Rather than the contrasting of Judaism and Christianity, other commentators have identified in Luke-Acts a more dialogic approach. Cadbury had already noted: "I suspect the author's motive is more faithfully represented by such sentences as: God sent the word unto the children of Israel, preaching good tidings of peace by Jesus Christ. God visited the Gentiles, to take out of them a people for his name. Neither against the law of the Jews, nor against the temple, nor against Caesar, have I sinned at all."[21] More recently, F. Danker has taken the position that Luke wants to show that Israel's mission as servant can still find fulfillment through Jesus. He expresses Luke's purpose as follows: "God the Great Benefactor, reaches out to his world at the time appointed through his rejected Servant-Benefactor Jesus and through his Benefactor-Servant- Community, Israel-the Church."[22] This dialogic and integrative approach is also taken by E. Franklin, who sees Luke emphasizing that Jesus can really be accepted as Lord by both Jew and Gentile. "What Luke does is to try to account for Israel's disbelief in a way that does not cause a denial of her history and which leaves open her contact with God's promises."[23]

Connected with the Jewish-Christian relationship is the theme of promise and fulfillment, well developed by such commentators as P. Schubert, P. Minear, N. Dahl, and L. Johnson.[24] In each case, the realization of God's salvific plan is continued in the Church. There is continuity with the old, but realization in the Church.

The Judeo-Christian dialogue present in various forms in Luke deserves highlighting, as does his theme of fulfillment. In each case, the point of arrival is Jesus and his continued presence to all through the Church. Unless the Lucan purpose is a static historical statement, it must be understood as open to expansion through the ministry of the Church. Factually, this is what happens.

Ecclesiological interests. A. Julicher suggested that Luke's purpose was to present an edifying account of the power of God in the apostles. J.B. Lightfoot likewise saw Luke as edifying his readers with the history of the Christian Church. Others see the two volumes more as a systematic reflection on the nature of the Church.[25] Kasemann and followers consider Luke's purpose to be the legitimizing of Church structures current in Luke's day.

J. Dupont has documented well his conviction that Luke is establishing for his time the legitimacy of the Church's mission to the Gentiles. While not agreeing totally with Dupont, Haenchen identifies similar Lucan concerns: "In reality Luke the historian is wrestling, from the first page to the last, with the problem of the mission to the Gentiles without the law. His entire presentation is influenced by this."[26] Others think that Acts simply portrays the Church's fidelity to the commands of the gospel. According to Metzger, it is a record of what led up to the establishing of the Church and its subsequent expansion. In this regard, Talbert considers Luke-Acts to be modeled on the typical biographies of great philosophers and their disciples. Thus, the two volumes portray the Church's relationship to her master.[27]

These considerations are crucial to any evaluation of Lucan writings. The ecclesiological and missionary dimensions of the work are clear and strong. However, the Gentile mission is secured through the power of the Word in the ministries of the Church. The Church of Luke's day needed not just information, but challenge. Christians are called to play a vital role in sharing the mission of the Spirit-guided Church.

Historical aims. W. Ward Gasque, F. F. Bruce, and others strongly emphasize Luke's aims to write the history of the early Church. A similar emphasis has been given by such writers as Drury, who compares Luke's work to biographical forms of his day. These historical and biographical interests of Luke's do not place him among the secular, for in his time all historians and biographers worked from philosophies and/or theologies of history. They were theologians precisely because they were historians or biographers. However, Luke's primary emphasis, say some, is to write the history of the early Church.[28]

Reactions to this aim have been frequent. Commentators see that Luke subordinates history to his theological concerns, and is no longer historically reliable. This is not a criticism of his competence, but is true to the aim which Luke sets himself. According to Conzelmann, Luke's primary purpose is theological and ecclesiological. Faced with the delay of the Second Coming, Luke reinterprets eschatology, integrating the time of waiting into God's plan of salvation history. The writing of history, even of salvation history, was hardly the point.

By giving us an accurate *typical* history, and by stressing the way we should live as Church in this time of waiting, Luke calls on each Christian "to look 'up, back, and ahead' to see that God's salvation has been revealed in certain 'foundational events' of the past which are the basis and clue to his mission."[29] The emphasis is not on history, nor on the time of waiting, but rather on how we should live in mutual ministry during this time.

Evangelical purpose. I. H. Marshall has reacted strongly to Conzelmann's position. "It is our thesis that the idea of salvation supplies the key to the theology of Luke. Not salvation-history but salvation itself is the theme which occupied the mind of Luke in both parts of his work."[30] According to Marshall, Luke presents Jesus as the Savior of the lost. The Christian's response is always, "What must I do to be saved?" The Acts is the spreading of the Word of salvation.

A. George, among others, has supported this position. While common to all gospel tradition, the theology of salvation is a central concern of Luke's. George also highlights Luke's characteristic insistence on the salvation of the People of God.[31]

These evangelical aims are more acceptable than some of the other suggestions. The power of the Spirit and the emphasis on the Word are more appropriate in Luke's concern for the proclamation of salvation. However, and especially in Acts, Luke adds to this common tradition that the proclamation of salvation is now carried out through the ministry of the Church. The power of God's gift is transmitted through intermediaries, to the ends of the earth.

Luke's Vision

Luke's is the only gospel which presents the solemn anointing of Jesus for his ministry of the Good News (Lk 4:18-19), and it alone clarifies Jesus' awareness that his Father had sent him to minister (Lk 4:43). At the calling of the Twelve, given a new context in Luke, Jesus specifically gives the Twelve a name which will describe their future ministry (Lk 6:13-14). Luke alone complements the choice and missioning of the Twelve with the call and ministry of the seventy-two, an episode of cosmic and ecclesial significance (Lk 10:1-16). In the final parable before his entry into Jerusalem, Jesus comments on the prudent use of talents. In Luke's gospel, Jesus adds this valuable warning: "Invest this until I get back" (Lk 19:13). This use of talents for the benefit of others is seen in the dedication of the early Christians. Their commitment to ministry is well expressed by Paul: "I put no value on my life if only I can finish my race and complete the service to which I have been assigned by the Lord Jesus" (Acts 20:24).

Luke gives us Jesus' ministry of the Word and the Church's self-dedication to prolong this ministry. The two periods of preparation stress the initiative of God in calling to ministry. The disciple-ministers are baptized, and filled with the Holy Spirit, their life-work based on the Word. They are warned of continuous temptations regarding the style of their ministry, and reminded of the paschal significance of the opposition they will face.

The ministry itself consists in preaching, teaching, and healing. Ministers must always be aware that they are called by God for this work, and God will give success in spite of all trials. When growth and new situations arise, disciples should call forth others to share in this work of the Lord, so that the ministry is continually extended.

Ministry, though not institutionalized in Luke, is certainly ecclesial. The Christian, baptized into ministry, realizes that it is in the very nature of the Church that together we prolong and extend the ministry of the Lord.

The Third Gospel has a variety of motifs and themes. Luke is clearly interested in the nature and role of the Church. The picture he details, repeated in each period of ministry, is this: empowered with the boldness of the Spirit, the Church's task is to bring Christ's salvation to all. This is done through ministries built upon those of Jesus himself. As Jesus brought salvation through his ministry of calling to faith, so the Church brings Jesus' salvation by continuing that ministry.

Chapter Four
IMAGES OF GOD

Everything has been given over to me by my Father. No one knows the Son except the Father, and no one knows the Father except the Son — and anyone to whom the Son wishes to reveal him. (Lk 10:22)

The ministry of Jesus in the gospel and of the Church in Acts is one of handing on the self-revelation of God. We can only know God when God reveals himself. Otherwise, God remains hidden and unexpressed. Spirituality deals with the evolution of life to fullness, and is always conditioned by our understanding of God. The search for a deeper knowledge of God inheres in all world religions. In the passage at the beginning of this chapter, Luke repeats the conviction of the other synoptics that Jesus has brought the Father's full revelation, ending our laborious search. Later, in Acts 20:27, Paul will state that, for him, the entire content of the Christian proclamation is the revelation of God and his will to humankind.

The revelation of God and our appreciation of it is a slow and difficult evolution. Yet, our image of God is crucial to spiritual life. If the image is unsatisfactory, weak, irrelevant, and without appeal, we move into crises of faith and the "death-of-God." If our image does not evolve, we can easily become fossilized in the worship of an image of God from the past. If not constantly open to the challenges of scripture, we can end up adoring a God of our own creation.

Luke's two-part work is a significant contribution to our understanding of God and of the role of His image in Christian life. His is the only New Testament work that gives us the disciples' relationship to Jesus and his message both before *and* after the resurrection. In doing so, he stresses that the resurrection is the key to unlock our understanding of God. In the other synoptics, it is never clear whether Jesus is presented as he was experienced during his ministry, or as revealed later, after the resurrection. Generally, it is the latter. Luke alone offers the possibility of a distinction.[1] Luke writes for a Gentile audience, and in Acts deals with many audiences of varied social backgrounds, cultures, and religious beliefs. He changes and adapts these images of God, thereby showing how the same God appeals in different ways. By drawing on the traditions of the early Church more extensively than his predecessors, he clarifies in his two works, the image of God in light of the questions of his own day.[2] For Luke, our knowledge of God evolves, and, as it does, so must our spirituality as well. He shows continuity between the Old Testament period of the infancy narratives, the Jesus period, and the post-resurrection period of the Church. Yet, with growing awareness, there is also development in the appreciation of who God is revealed to be in Jesus.

God The Most High - Our Father

Luke's image of God is a combination of accepted source material and contributions specific to the third evangelist. Since in general he shows freedom in the use of his source material, it can be presumed that if he takes over material relevant to the image of God from his sources, it is because it agrees with his own theological convictions. In general, Luke's image of God is taken from the Old Testament tradition. A detailed portrait is presented in the infancy narratives, but the many other references throughout the gospel and Acts are consistent with it. Gradually, through the teachings of Jesus and the growing awareness of the Church, preliminary notions of Trinity develop and distinctions are introduced.

The Father as Sovereign Lord. The title that best describes Luke's image of God the Father is "Sovereign Lord," used by Simeon in his canticle (Lk 2:29) and by the early Church in prayer after Peter and John's release from prison (Acts 4:24). This is complemented by the frequently used title "Most High God" (Lk 1:35, 76; 6:35; 8:28; Acts 16:17). He is mighty, holy, and strong (1:49-51), a God of Glory (Lk 2:9; Acts 7:2). He is a living God (Lk 20:37-38), the Creator of heavens and earth (Acts 4:24; 14:15;

17:24). He is the omnipotent director of world history (Acts 7:32-34; 13:17-30), commanding his angels constantly to do his bidding (Lk 1:11, 19, 26; 2:9; 4:10; 12:8; Acts 5:19; 8:26;10:3, 12:7, 11, 23; 27:23), speaking through the prophets (Lk 1:70; Acts 3:18-21), and guiding his ministers (Acts 16:6). The Father is the inspiration of scripture (Lk 11:49) and of the Law which guides men's lives (Lk 2:23, 24, 39). With the coming of Jesus, himself sent by the Father (Lk 4:18; 7:16), God's kingdom is brought to earth (Lk 4:43; 8:1), his Word is preached (Lk 3:2; 5:1; Acts 6:7; 12:24; 13:5, 46-49; 18:11), and his Spirit poured out (Lk 4:18; 11:13). In each case, the Father is recognized as the source. This image of the omnipotent Lord God is enriched by two further emphases of Luke.[3] The first is the fatherly quality of God: He is Jesus' Father (Lk 1:32; 2:49; 10:21; 22:29; 23:34, 46) and our Father (Lk 6:36; 11:2, 12:30). The second is Luke's strong emphasis that the Father is God, our Savior (Lk 1:47, 68-69, 71, 74; 2:30; 3:6; 4:18; Acts 28:28). In this, Luke differs from other New Testament writers who generally refer exclusively to Jesus in this way.

A major insight of Luke into the image of the Sovereign Lord is that he is merciful (Lk 1:50, 54, 58, 72, 78; 6:36; 18:13). When Matthew speaks of the perfection of God (Mt 5:48), Luke changes the statement to read: "Be compassionate, as your Father is compassionate" (Lk 6:36). This merciful God listens to the prayers of his servants (Lk 2:29-32; Acts 10:31) and helps those who call on him (Lk 1:54, 69). He exalts the lowly, the empty, and helpless (Lk 1:25, 52-58; 4:18). He protects his children and provides for their needs (Lk 12:6-31). His eye constantly on the needs of the Gentile world, Luke stresses that the Father's merciful concerns are universal (Lk 3:6, 23-38; 6:35), extending even to the ungrateful and the wicked (Lk 6:35). Later, with the growing awareness of the Church, we read that God shows no partiality (Acts 10:34), but grants life-giving repentance and salvation to all (Acts 11:17-18; 14:27).

The Father's plan for the world. God's universal sovereignty is seen in his control of world and salvation history. According to Luke, God the Father determined, ordained, and fixed the events of world development and the saving events of Jesus' life (Lk 22:22; Acts 2:23; 10:42; 17:26, 31). The Father has a plan for the world, and Jesus carries out the Father's intent. This saving plan includes Jesus' death for the salvation of us all (Acts 2:23; 4:28; 20:27). Luke's notion of God's plan is also stressed by his constant use of Greek "pro"-compounds. This indicates "God is directing everything in the salvation process according to his plan."[4] Luke also stresses the Father's influence on history by referring to events which take place "as it is written" (Lk 18:31; 22:37). He sees it is necessary that this plan be carried out (Lk 13:33; 17:25; 19:5; 21:9; 22:37; 24:7, 26). "Must (dei) occurs 44 times in Lucan writings out of the 102 times it is found in the New Testament. The Lucan 'must' expresses God's governing providence in the life of Jesus, as well as the necessity of accomplishing his Father's salvific will."[5] As part of this plan, the Father directs the development of Old Testament times (Acts 7:2-53) and sends John the Baptist (Lk 7:27-28). When John begins to preach, the Father precedes him with Spirit and power (Lk 1:16-17). In Jesus' ministry, the crowd recognizes the coming of God (Lk 7:16) and the fulfillment of what God announced through the prophets (Acts 3:18-26). He directs the freeing of Peter and John, and calls for the ongoing preaching of his word (Acts 5:19-20). Later, he delivers Peter miraculously, again for the benefit of the Church (Acts 12:11-17). His power works miracles through the apostles (Acts 13:11; 19:11), directs their ministry (Acts 6:10; 27:23), and opens their minds and hearts to new understandings of his will (Acts 10:15; 14:27; 15:14). Finally, the work of the Church must go on until the Father ends it, and he alone knows when that will be (Acts 1:7).

The Father's plan carried out by Jesus. Jesus, who lives in complete conformity to this plan, executes it faithfully for his Father.[6] Jesus is often not even presented as the acting subject of his ministry. More frequently, he is the means or embodiment of God's plan. Peter states the position well on the day of Pentecost: "Jesus the Nazorean was a man whom God sent to you with miracles, wonders, and signs as his credentials. These God worked through him in your midst, as you well know" (Acts 2:22). From childhood on, Jesus is aware that he must do his Father's will (Lk 2:49). He is sent by the Father, presented by him (Lk 3:22), anointed by him (Lk 4:18-19; Acts 4:27; 10:38), and attested by him (Acts 2:22). When he works miracles, Jesus attributes the power to the Father (Lk 8:39; 11:20), and Luke explicitly recognizes that "the power of the Lord made him heal" (Lk 5:17).[7] From early life until his last breath, Jesus is directed by his Father's will (Lk 2:49; 22:42; 23:46).

The Father's plan, however, includes the exaltation of his Son. The Father glorifies Jesus (Acts 3:13; 5:31), raises him (Acts 2:22-24, 30-32; 3:15, 26; 4:10; 5:30; 10:38-40; 13:30-33; 17:31), makes him Lord and Messiah (Acts 2:34-36), exalts him and ordains him to be Judge of the living and the dead (Acts 10:42; 17:31), and places him at his own right hand (Lk 22:69).

Conzelmann has suggested that "the status of Jesus is something that is bestowed upon him entirely by God."[8] Certainly God's power is clearly seen in the Incarnate Son. God is the Sovereign Lord whose will, plan, and intervention are seen in Jesus.

The Father and the believer. Luke's image of God the Father evokes in the believer awe and wonder before his acts (Lk 5:26; 9:43; Acts 2:11; 3:10), reverential fear (Lk 1:50; 12:5; 23:40), and adoration (Lk 4:8). The most common reaction of the people is one of praise and blessing (Lk 2:14, 20, 28; 5:25-26; 7:16; 17:15; 18:43; 19:37; 24:53; Acts 2:47; 3:8-9; 4:21).

Jesus tells us to be at peace because of the Father's work in the Kingdom (Lk 12:32) and his merciful concerns, which should give us confidence (Lk 11:13). We should serve him in holiness and righteousness (Lk 1:75), never neglecting the justice and love of God (Lk 11:42). He reads our hearts (Acts 1:24), and shows his approval by granting the Holy Spirit (Lk 11:13; Acts 15:8-9). The Father knows what we need and gives us his blessings (Lk 12:30-31), particularly the promise and gift of the Holy Spirit (Lk 24:49; Acts 1:4-5; 2:17-21).

We are his servant-slaves (Lk 1:38; 2:29), though he, as Sovereign Lord, has no need of our service (Acts 17:24-31). Whatever we do, we are empty before him (Lk 18:13); yet he demands absolute and exclusive dedication (Lk 4:8; 10:27; 16:13; Acts 4:19).

Jesus – A Joy to be Shared by the World's People

Scholars, commentators, artists, and preachers. Luke's writings have always been a quarry from which scholars, commentators, artists, and preachers have mined their images of Jesus. His more human Christ has always contrasted favorable with Mark's rather harsh presentation, Matthew's overstylized "new-Moses," and John's exalted, glorified Word. On the day of Pentecost, Peter said to the crowd: "May a season of refreshment be granted you by the Lord when he sends you Jesus, already designated as your Messiah" (Acts 3:20). It seems that the image of the compassionate Lord, presented by our "enthusiast for Christ," has more frequently brought refreshment to searching disciples than have those of the other evangelists. This trend has continued into our times, complemented with some searching studies on the Christology of Luke.

Danker sees the Lucan Jesus after the fashion of Hellenistic public benefactors, who brought peace and salvation to their subjects. He sees Luke stressing Jesus' role as bringer of peace, protector and savior of the world. This benefactor is Son of God from birth, Christ and Lord. Finally, he delegates to his Church his work as benefactor.[9]

For Drury, "Luke's Jesus is the epitome and compendium of the men whom God raised up: he is. . . most strikingly of all a prophet in the mould of Elijah. . . .we have a Jesus who is a link in time's chain, himself the ligature of old and new, the middle of time."[10]

Marshall says Luke's Jesus is the promised Savior whose message is not about the Kingdom, but about himself. Jesus brings in himself the blessings of salvation, and so the early Church can say: "Believe in the Lord Jesus, and you will be saved" (Acts 16:31).

In his studies of Luke's writings, Conzelmann states that "The part played by Jesus in redemptive history and his status have no metaphysical basis, but are entirely the gift of God."[11] According to Conzelmann, Luke's preferred titles for Jesus are "Christ" and "Lord," all others meaning the same as these two. Jesus is the center of history because he is the instrument of the Father's salvation for the world. Conzelmann sees no difference of role between the earthly and exalted Lord; Jesus' actions for the Father are always gifts from the Father, and always manifest subordination to the Father.

Other commentators see the Lucan Jesus as "bringer of Messianic salvation to the Gentiles,"[12] Christ and Lord for Jews and Gentiles,[13] and King.[14]

Moule believes he can identify in the Lucan writings an attempt by the author to explain how people viewed Jesus before and after his resurrection. Moule thinks he has identified in Luke two clearly distinct presentations of Jesus. Only after faith in the resurrection do the disciples acknowledge the exalted one as Lord, Savior, Son, Prophet, bestower of the Spirit, and Son of Man.[15]

The child will be great. The early chapters of Luke's gospel "form a prologue, telling the reader who Jesus is, or rather, perhaps, who he is to be revealed to be later on."[16] We are told that the child will be Great, Son of the Most High (Lk 1:32), a light of revelation for the Gentiles, and the glory of Israel (Lk 2:32). He is mightier than the Baptist, and will himself baptize with the Holy Spirit (Lk 3:16). His kingdom will be everlasting (Lk 1:33), but he himself will always be a sign of contradiction, determining the rise and fall of many (Lk 2:34).

Early witnesses proclaim the child to be the Lord (Lk 1:43), the shepherd of Israel (Lk 2:12), the Anointed of the Lord (Lk 2:26), and the Son of God (Lk 1:35). Angelic witnesses proclaim Luke's major theological conviction in these early narratives, as they announce to the child's mother, and later to the shepherds at Bethlehem, that "This day in David's city a savior has been born to you, the Messiah and Lord" (Lk 2:11; also 1:31-32).[17] These infancy chapters, among the most concentrated theological statements of Luke, form an anticipatory revelation of who, in the resurrection faith of the Church, Jesus is acknowledged to be.

Whatever is said about the Christology of Luke, it seems clear that these early chapters are creedal for him. The child is a descendant of David, the fulfillment of Israel's hopes, and their Messiah. However, he is also a revelation to the Gentiles, their Lord and God. For all the world he is King, Lord, Son of God, and Savior.

The ministry of Jesus. Luke's description of the ministry of Jesus begins with the complex presentation of Jesus' baptism, temptations, and his commissioning in the synagogue in Nazareth. Already, in these early episodes of Jesus' public life, we see those qualities which will be identifiable throughout his ministry, those witnessed to by the early Church. Jesus is loyal to his Father; committed to the mission he has received; sensitive to people, their hopes, and their needs; a prophetic challenge to a sinful world; and constantly growing in awareness of who he is for others.

Already, in the infancy narratives, Luke has highlighted Jesus' total dedication to his Father's will (Lk 2:49). Twice during his Son's ministry the Father's voice will be heard confirming Jesus' role and mission (Lk 3:22; 9:35), and we are reminded often that the Father's Spirit and power are constantly with him (Lk 4:14, 18, 36; 5:17; 6:19; 8:46; 10:21; 11:22). The Lord Jesus dedicates himself to the will of the Father, even to death. He preaches his word, declares his greatness, acknowledges his power (Lk 8:39), and challenges the disciples to pray to the Father (Lk 11:1-4). Nothing better shows Jesus' relationship to the Father than his own life of constant prayer (Lk 3:21; 5:16; 6:12; 9:28; 11:1; 22:32, 41, 44). What was anticipated in Jerusalem (Lk 2:49) reaches its climax in Gethsemane (Lk 22:42) and on Calvary (Lk 23:46), where Jesus' loyalty and filial obedience are seen to perfection.[18]

Jesus shows his loyalty to his Father by his total commitment to his mission. He withstands all temptations to political or spectacular missianism (Lk 4:1-13; 23:35-43). He realizes that he must fulfill scripture (Lk 4:21), and is aware that the Father has sent him to minister (Lk 4:43). Frequently, "by redactional summaries, compositions, and through the use of special traditions," Luke portrays Jesus' Galilean ministry as the fulfillment of the Words of God in scripture.[19] Once this ministry is finished, he recommits himself with the determination to go on to Jerusalem and what awaits him there (Lk 9:51).

Luke, who sees the perfection of God in compassion (Lk 6:36), portrays Jesus as sensitive and compassionate to all. He is moved to pity at the anguish of others (Lk 7:13), and frequently works miracles to cure the sick, exorcise the possessed, and calm the fearful.[20] Most of Jesus' audience were poor. He identifies with their feelings, bringing understanding and relief (Lk 4:18; 7:22; 16:19-31), and condemns others' abuse of riches (Lk 6:24-26; 12:13-21; 14:33; 16:9, 19-31; 18:22). In a society where women are oppressed, he shows concern for their needs (Lk 13:11-17; 15:8-10; 18:1-8), friendship (Lk 10:38-42), appreciation (Lk 23:27-31), and forgiveness (Lk 7:36-50). To all who are burdened with their own sin, he brings mercy and forgiveness (Lk 5:20; 7:36-50; 15; 19:1-10; 23:34, 39-43).

From the earliest times of his public ministry, Jesus prophetically challenges the standards and values of his day. Faced with the temptations of life's alternatives, he abandons the easy and comfortable, insisting on fidelity and responsibility (Lk 4:1-12). Aware that he has been sent by his Father to preach the

Good News, he is willing to confront his own townspeople with the message, albeit anticipating their rejection (Lk 4:16-30). Later, he travels to the larger town of Capernaum to give a major sermon on the new value system he brings to the world (Lk 6:17-49). He challenges the spiritual leaders of the day (Lk 6:3-11) and the nation's spiritual values (Lk 6:5). He tells all that he appreciates real character, not outward appearances (Lk 7:24-28), and has no time for hollow men (Lk 11:42) and their insincerity (Lk 20:45-47). He teaches with authority (Lk 4:32-36), has power over demons (Lk 4:35-41), and gives this power and authority to others for spreading his message (Lk 9:1; 10:19).

Just as Jesus is proclaimed Messiah, Lord, and Son of God in the infancy narratives,[21] he is also recognized as such throughout the Third Gospel by demonic, angelic, and divine voices (Lk 2:11; 3:22; 4:34; 8:28; 9:35). When crowds enthusiastically follow him (Lk 5:15-16), he tells them that the practical conclusion of their recognition is obedience to his word (Lk 6:46-49). When people and cities do not realize what he represents, Jesus condemns their blindness (Lk 10:13-16; 13:34-35; 19:41-44). Some of the crowds later acknowledge him, and when the Pharisees criticize this public acclaim Jesus replies: "If they were to keep silence, I tell you the very stones would cry out" (Lk 19:40). When Peter solemnly proclaims Jesus as the anointed of God (Lk 9:20), thereby affirming the fulfillment of Simeon's prophecy (Lk 2:26) and anticipating the ironic disbelief of the crowds (Lk 23:35), Jesus acknowledges this faith, revealing awareness of his own future. At the beginning of his journey to Jerusalem, Jesus shows clear awareness of what lies ahead (Lk 9:51). He confirms this during the mission (Lk 13:32-33), at his supper (Lk 22:16), and, finally, in the garden (Lk 22:42-43).

The Lucan Jesus is loyal to his Father and committed to his mission. He is one with his people, a challenge to his times, and aware of his life's role.

Luke's Christological synthesis. In reading Luke's work we must identify more than his general portrait of Jesus as described throughout the ministry; we must seek, too, to identify Luke's Christological synthesis. Luke deviates from available models by adding many inspired insights of his own, presenting a distinctive image of Jesus. His work is not an invention, but implies his acceptance of the historical reliability of the episodes he uses. He reflects on the material of tradition, giving a new synthesis. The Lucan Jesus brings in the new era of God's creative action, he is the fulfillment of all promises, the complete instrument of God, our salvation, and the object of the Church's faith.

The first time the world encounters Jesus publicly, we are presented with a creation story. The main lines of development of the baptism of Jesus are the same as in any of the creation stories of the Bible (Lk 3:21-22; Genesis 1:1 - 2:4; 8:6-14; Exodus 14:15-31). The Spirit of God hovers over the water, heralding a new creation, and there follows in each case a new exposition of the teachings of God. Jesus' baptism, too, is the beginning of God's creative interventions in our world and life. His teachings are like new wine (Lk 5:38), his mission a new covenant (Lk 22:20). This approach is identifiable in each of the synoptics, but Luke emphasizes the creational characteristics of the baptism by his later parallel presentation of the baptism of the Church at Pentecost, also presented as a creation story. The baptism of Jesus begins the new era of God's creative activity in our lives. It also begins the process of recognition of who Jesus is, a process that ends in ecclesial recognition and faith at Pentcost.

The coming of Jesus signifies the beginning of the fulfillment of God's promises (Lk 1:68; 2:26, 30). His ministry begins with a solemn acknowledgement of this (Lk 4:21), and the accent on fulfillment is repeated at key moments in the ministry (Lk 13:33). Luke's journey narrative (Lk 9:51 - 19:27) can be viewed as the fulfillment of Old Testament prophecies of the Way of the Lord.[22] At the end of his life, Jesus will look back over all that has happened, seeing it as the fulfillment of the Father's will and promise (Lk 22:37; 24:26, 44-46). Later, the early Church will see the post-resurrectional involvement of Jesus as further proof of his fulfillment of the promise (Acts 2:17-21, 34-35; 47). The Jews expected a Davidic servant of the Lord, and Jesus is he (Lk 1:32; 18:38-39). The scriptures promised a great prophet, and Jesus is recognized as such (Lk 4:24; 7:16, 39; 9:19; 13:33; 24:19). In fact, Luke portrays Jesus as a prophet in the power of Moses and Elijah. "Like Moses, he is a spirit-filled figure (4:14), chooses out seventy (10:1), takes part in an exodus (9:31), and is rejected by those to whom he is sent (7:23)."[23] As Elijah chose Elisha, Jesus chooses his own disciples, and like Elijah leaves the land of his own people (Lk 4:25-27). Elijah raises the son of the widow Zarephath, and Jesus raises the son of the widow of Nain

(Lk 7:11-17); Jesus, like Elijah, has the power to call down fire from heaven (Lk 9:54); both are eventually taken up to heaven, and both send down their spirit on their disciples.[24]

The Jews identified in the Old Testament the promise of a king, and Luke is careful to document his belief in the fulfillment of this hope. Luke alone presents the announcement of the royal messiah (Lk 1:32-33); he introduces the kingdom as the object of Jesus' work in Marcan contexts not containing it (Lk 4:43; 9:2), and states that the gospel's explicit content is the kingdom (Lk 8:1; 16:16). The allegory of the royal pretender is exclusive to Luke (Lk 19:12-27), as is the title "King" given to Jesus during the royal entry (Lk 19:28-44). During the supper the Lucan Jesus promises the kingdom to his disciples (Lk 22:28-30), and is presented as king before the Sanhedrin (Lk 22:67-70), on Calvary (Lk 23:40-43), and at the Ascension enthronement (Acts 1:6-11).[25]

The Lucan Jesus is more than the fulfillment of a selection of prophecies: he is the full and complete instrument of God. A prophet and king, he is also recognized as the Lord's anointed (Lk 2:11, 26; 4:41; 9:20; 24:26, 46). Moreover, this acknowledgement precedes his baptism, indicating that Jesus is not just anointed as such later, but is Messiah from birth (Lk 2:11, 26).

Jesus generally referred to himself as the Son of Man,[26] others referred to him as Lord,[27] and he is proclaimed as Son of God.[28] He is also seen as the Servant (Lk 22:27), the bestower of the Spirit (Lk 3:16; 24:49), and the Savior (Lk 2:11, 30; 19:10). The crowds frequently addressed him as Master (Lk 5:5, 8:24, 45; 9:33; 17:13) and Teacher (Lk 8:49; 9:38; 10:25; 11:45; 12:13; 18:18; 19:39; 20:21, 28, 39; 21:7; 22:11).

Conzelmann has suggested that some titles in Luke, such as Christ, Lord, or Son, mean the same thing, and that in other cases, — Son of Man, or Righteous One — Luke is no longer aware of the titles' original meaning.[29] It seems to me, however, that Luke is presenting us with Jesus who fulfills the expectations of various stands of tradition. More important than the independent use of titles referred to by Conzelmann is the simultaneous listing of several titles (Lk 1:32-35; 2:11; 22:67-70). In each case, they affirm that Jesus fulfills a tradition. On three other occasions, Jesus' divine sonship is identified with his messiahship (Lk 1:32-35; 3:22; 9:35). This does not mean that both titles are reduced to the same concept, but rather emphasizes the absolute originality of Jesus, the total newness of his messiahship. Caird has suggested that it is Luke's contention that Jesus himself is the one who has united some of these titles, referring them thus to himself.[30]

The Lord Jesus, the anointed of God, appears in Luke as a powerful orator and performer of mighty deeds. The title "Lord," more frequently used for God the Father elsewhere in the scriptures, is in the Lucan works used for Jesus, all divine overtones intact. Luke edits Mark to emphasize Jesus' power (Lk 4:31-44; 5:17-26; 8:40-48) and the audience's reverence for him (Lk 5:17-30; 6:1-11; 8:22-25). On the other hand, he omits certain of Mark's sayings which could be construed as showing Jesus mistaken about the end.[31]

The early church will recognize Jesus as the Holy and Righteous One (Acts 2:27; 3:14; 7:52; 13:35; 22:14), the author of life (Acts 3:15), and the source of forgiveness and salvation (Lk 5:21; Acts 13:38, 15:11; 16:31). The instrument of God's designs, he obediently accepts the ministry given him by his Father (Lk 9:31). Having carried it out faithfully, he enters into glory (Lk 24:26) and is received up into heaven (Acts 1:2, 11, 22; 2:34). In heaven he has a place at God's right hand (Lk 20:42; 22:69; Acts 2:34), and is now standing as he watches over his Church (Acts 7:55-56). One day he himself will return as judge (Lk 9:26; 12:36-38; 18:8; 19:23; 21:27; Acts 1:11).[32]

It has been common, recently, to play down the power of Luke's image of Jesus, insisting rather on presumed subordinationism in Luke.[33] Since the Church does not get away from this type of problem for over four hundred years, it seems unrealistic to expect Luke to have a mature exposition. Jesus certainly lives for his Father, accomplishes his will and serves his glory. This seems to be the correct spiritual approach for one who has taken on the helplessness of creatureliness.[34] In general, however, it must be stated that Luke's Jesus is the full and complete instrument of God, fulfilling all expectations: the revelation of God for both Jew and Gentile.

Luke's unified and powerful portrait of Christ as Lord was not presented with the threat of subordinationism in mind, but probably as a response to Gnosticism and docetism.[35] This Servant of the Lord who brings in a new era, fulfills the promises, and is the instrument of the Father's work, Luke also understands to be our very salvation (Lk 2:30). "The Son of Man has come to search out and save what was lost" (Lk 19:10).

Marshall has insisted that Luke's prime concern is to expound on the doctrine of God and his plan for our salvation. This salvation is revealed in Jesus, proclaimed by the early Church, and longed for by the disciple. Jesus is this savior (Lk 2:11, 30), and to everyone the Church can say: "Believe in the Lord Jesus, and you will be saved" (Acts 16:31).

Jesus heals and saves throughout his ministry. He brings redemption from all forms of bondage, pouring out the Lord's messianic blessings on the people. Luke's soteriology is, however, different from other New Testament writers', particularly Paul's. In Luke it is not so much the death of Jesus which saves, but the life and death of Jesus which affect people in so far as, by means of them, Jesus enters his glory (Lk 24:26), becoming the "author of Life" (Acts 3:15) and salvation of all (Acts 5:31).[36]

The final component of Luke's Christology is that Jesus is now the object of our faith. Moule has shown well how, in Acts, the early Church explicitly attributes to Jesus titles and concepts not used by Luke in the Third Gospel. On the other hand, some of the early Church's formulations are really no different from the powerful syntheses of the infancy narratives.[37] He is the Christ,[38] the Lord.[39] Now, however, he is also recognized as the Son of Man (Acts 7:56), the Son of God (Acts 9:20; 13:33), the eschatological prophet (Acts 3:22-23), the Suffering Servant of the Lord (Acts 3:26; 4:27, 30; 8:32-33), the Just One (Acts 22:14), and the Savior (Acts 5:31).

The Church believes that in Jesus has come fulfillment (Acts 3:18) and a season of refreshment (Acts 3:20). They see Jesus as the object of their preaching (Acts 4:18; 5:42; 9:20; 18:5; 28:31), the initiator of true conversion (Acts 3:26), and the source of the common life they share (Acts 9:5). Signs and wonders are worked in his name (Acts 4:30), people are cured (Acts 3:6, 16; 4:10), exorcised (Acts 16:18), baptized (Acts 2:38; 8:16; 10:48; 19:5; 22:16), and saved (Acts 4:12). The early disciples call on the name of the Lord (Acts 9:20) and seek forgiveness in his name (Acts 2:38; 10:43; 22:16). They are willing to suffer and die for that name (Acts 5:41; 21:13).

There is no single, clear, and exclusive Christological position in Luke's work. I have already referred to the different Christologies of the first four chapters of Acts. "This indicates that the author himself knew something of the Christological diversity in the early Church."[40] However, the ministry is found between the theological affirmations of the infancy narratives and the faith formulations of Acts. While a pluralism of appreciation is evident, it is also true that the main lines of Luke's convictions are equally present. On one level we see a Jesus loyal to his Father and committed to his mission; he is sensitive to his people, critical of a sinful world, and grows in awareness of his mission. On a deeper level, the Lucan Jesus brings in a new era of God's creative love. This Jesus is the welcome fulfillment of all promises; more than an adopted instrument of God, he is, indeed, our salvation and the object of our faith.

The Holy Spirit

The expression "Holy Spirit" appears four times in Mark, five times in Matthew, thirteen times in Luke, and forty-one times in Acts. This clearly-identified concern of Luke has led to him being called the evangelist of the Holy Spirit. He certainly mentions the role of the Holy Spirit more than any other gospel writer, and highlights the Spirit's impact on the life of the Church. He stresses the Spirit's guidance of the early community, his involvement in its ministry. However, a theology of the Holy Spirit is not Luke's prime concern or contribution. However, as in other areas of gospel proclamation, Luke's secondary aims remain sources of substantial information.

Signals that the times of waiting are over. Looking back over the time of expectation for the coming of the Lord, Luke sees the Holy Spirit as the source of inspiration in those scriptures foretelling the coming of Christ (Acts 1:16; 4:25; 28:25). This prophetical power of the Spirit of God is particularly seen in the Old Testament representatives who bear witness to Jesus in the infancy narratives: John the Baptist (Lk 1:15), Elizabeth (1:41), Zechariah (1:67), Mary (1:35), and Simeon (2:25-27). The event to which they bear witness is presented by Luke as a Spirit-filled celebration. It culminates in the conception of Jesus, which Luke attributes to the Holy Spirit (Lk 1:35). In the conception of new life in Jesus, we see anticipated the conception of all Christian life. It is achieved exclusively through the initiative of God in the power of his Spirit. As the story develops, the Spirit reveals the coming of the Lord to Simeon (Lk 2:26), inspiring him to go to the temple to proclaim Jesus' messiahship (Lk 2:27). The infancy narratives are so structured that every event and person presented is explicitly stated as filled with the Holy Spirit. Here the fulfillment of the prophecies concerning the outpouring of the Spirit on all messianic people is a sign that the times of waiting are over (Joel 3:1-2; Isaiah 44:3; Ezekiel 11:18-20). The presence of the Spirit here indicates the beginning of a new period of God's creative interventions. This first pentecost anticipates the universal outpouring of Acts.

This synthesis of the Spirit's activity, given in the annunciation and birth scenes, is complemented with the first public presentation of Jesus at his baptism. This event, a creation story with the intervention of the Spirit, portrays Luke's understanding of the relationship between Spirit, Father, and Son. The Spirit is sent down on Jesus by the Father, as Jesus later promises to do for the Church (Acts 2:33). The Spirit is from the Father and is always the Father's promise (Lk 24:48-49). Unlike Mark, who sees the Spirit take possession of Jesus and send him out to the desert (Mk 1:12), Luke states that Jesus is filled with the Spirit (Lk 4:1), acts in the power of the Spirit (Lk 4:14), and is anointed with the Spirit by the Father (Acts 10:38). He thus avoids Mark's placing of Jesus as subordinate to the Spirit. In Luke's theological understanding, Jesus is so full of the Spirit that later he will be the source of the Spirit for everyone (Lk 3:16; 24:49; Acts 2:32-33; 11:16). In fact, in the early Church, the Spirit will be known as Jesus' Spirit (Acts 16:7).

Gives birth to the messianic community. Since the Holy Spirit is the sign that the messianic promises have reached their fulfillment in Jesus' birth and ministry, Jesus shares this Spirit with the messianic community he establishes (Lk 3:16; 24:49; Acts 1:5-8; 2:33). The early Church soon realizes that it is the reception of the Holy Spirit that constitutes membership in this messianic community. Jesus had told them this (Acts 1:4-5), they experienced it (Acts 2:33), and soon became aware of its necessity (Acts 2:38). When the Samaritans receive the word but not the Spirit, it seems to the early Church that something essential is lacking, and Peter and John are sent to bring the Samaritans the gift of the Spirit. This confirms their entrance into the Church (Acts 8:14-16). Later, when Cornelius receives the Spirit, Peter feels obliged to welcome him into the Church (Acts 10:44-48; 15:8). The clearest conviction of the necessary link between belief and the reception of the Holy Spirit is shown in Paul's reaction to the Ephesians (Acts 19:1-7). Membership in the Church is established through the reception of the Spirit, and those dedicated to the Name have the Spirit as their life.

The new life brought by the Spirit is one of power. His powerful interventions are seen at the beginnings of the lives and ministries of both Jesus and the Church. Elsewhere, however, a close connection is recognized between the Holy Spirit and power (Acts 10:38), and the words are often interchangeable (Lk 4:36; 5:17; 24:49; Acts 1:4, 8).[41] Jesus and the apostles exercise power, but that power is the energy of the Holy Spirit.

The new life of the Spirit is powerful not only in its external interventions, but even more so in the inner quality of life of the believers. Navone expressed this well when he said: "Lucan style is characterized by these 'plentitude formulas' in which is described the fullness of the Spirit."[42] The early disciples are filled with the Holy Spirit and boldness (Acts 4:31); the deacons must be men filled with wisdom and the Spirit (Acts 6:3). Stephen is "a man full of faith and the Holy Spirit" (Acts 6:5), as is Barnabas (Acts 11:24). Stephen is "filled with grace and power" (Acts 6:8), the disciples are "filled with joy and the Holy Spirit" (Acts 13:52), and we constantly read that believers are "filled with the Holy Spirit" (Acts 2:4).

Those who receive the Holy Spirit also experience his presence in joy (Lk 10:21; Acts 9:31; 13:52), in ecstatic prayer and tongues (Acts 2:4; 10:46; 19:6), in prophecy (Acts 2:18; 19:6), in peace and consolation (Acts 9:31).

This special gift of God to the community (Lk 11:13) is so identified with it that those who offend the community's life, as do Ananias and Sapphira, are seen to deceive the Spirit himself (Acts 5:3-9).

Inspires, directs, and leads the Church. The Spirit inspires, directs, and leads Jesus in every step of his early ministry (Lk 4:1-14; Acts 10:38). In fact, the Church acknowledges that the Holy Spirit also guided Jesus in his choice of apostles (Acts 1:2). From the earliest days of the Church, the Spirit prompts the leaders to boldly proclaim Jesus (Acts 2:4; 4:8), and they themselves see that their very ability to bear witness is the exclusive result of obedience to the Spirit (Acts 5:32). The Holy Spirit initiates and directs the early mission of Philip (Acts 8:29-39), challenges Peter in a vision (Acts 10:19), and explains in detail what he must do (Acts 11:12). In the Council of Jerusalem the decisions are attributed to a Spirit-guided discernment of the good of the Church (Acts 15:28). Paul and Timothy are guided by the Spirit in choosing the area of mission (Acts 16:6-7), and Paul's final journey is full of the Spirit's guidance (Acts 20:22-23; 21:4).

The guidance of the Holy Spirit is particularly evident in the pastoral planning and direction of the Church's ministries. Before his departure, Jesus assures the apostles that they will be able to continue his work once the Spirit is with them (Acts 1:8). Jesus himself had started thus (Lk 4:1), and his followers will do likewise. We have already noted the balancing of the ministry of Jesus and that of the Church.

The Holy Spirit chooses the ministers and assigns them their mission (Acts 8:29; 10:19; 13:2-4). When Church leaders delegate others for ministry, they seek men filled with the Spirit (Acts 6:3). In Luke's work the Spirit empowers the early leaders for their ministry. H. Marshall has expressed Luke's position clearly: "It therefore seems likely that Luke especially understood the gift of the Holy Spirit as equipping the Church for mission, and consequently that he regarded the essence of being a Christian as the activity of mission."[43] In their ministry of proclamation, the disciples are filled with the Holy Spirit (Acts 2:4; 4:8; 6:5; 7:55; 9:17; 11:24; 13:4), courageously and boldly presenting the message (Acts 4:8, 31; 5:32). When the audience is not receptive, it is seen as opposing the Spirit himself (Acts 7:51). The Spirit's involvement in the ministry of the Church also includes specifying who should be ministered to (Acts 8:29; 10:19), which areas should be evangelized (Acts 13:4), and which avoided (Acts 16:6-7). He strengthens the disciples in their need, supports them in persecution (Acts 13:52), and gradually enlightens the Church to the Gentile mission (Acts 10:17-21; 13:46-52; 15:28; 28:23-28).

The Church's awareness that the Spirit is directing the ministry is well portrayed in the way Luke consistently relates the community's apostolic prayer to the Holy Spirit for the expansion of the Church.[44]

Major components of a Lucan theology of the Holy Spirit. Luke's references to the Holy Spirit are many. In them, his major convictions can be identified, and out of them emerge the major components of a Lucan theology of the Holy Spirit. For Luke, the Spirit, already present in the time of expectancy, heralds the new period and is the herald of the fulfillment of all hopes. In the infancy narratives, and later in the early chapters of Acts, the Spirit is the sign that the times of waiting are over.

The Spirit not only heralds and proclaims the new era, but by his outpouring on the persons of the Messiah and the people of the messianic community, he *is* the new life. His presence and faithful reception constitute the believers as Church. The fellowship of the Lord is the result of the presence of the Spirit in the lives of Christ's disciples. Moreover, the quality of the community's life is maintained by the Spirit, who guarantees faithfulness, joy, prayer, peace, consolation, boldness, and prophetic testimony.

In Acts, Luke parallels Jesus' ascent to receive the Spirit with Moses' ascent of Mount Sinai to receive the law.[45] For Luke, the Spirit is to the Christian what the law was for the Jew: the constant revelation of God's guidance and challenge. He reveals God's will and truth to Church leaders and disciples everywhere.

His guidance and challenge are especially seen in his call to witness and minister. He calls disciples to fearless confession of the Lord Jesus. In every stage of the expansion of the Word, Luke portrays the directional involvement of the Holy Spirit.

Finally, in Luke's synthesis, the Holy Spirit is understood as the promise of the Father and the Spirit of Jesus. He is the Father's gift and pledge. Not a substitute for Jesus, he is the assurance that Jesus is still alive and active in the Church.

Ongoing Presence of God

Based upon actual events. Luke gives us a clear and substantial portrait of God, Father, Son, and Spirit. He is careful to show how his reflections and theological synthesis are based upon actual events in Jesus' life. He takes care to document Jesus' ministry its time (Lk 1:5; 2:1-2; 3:1-22) and place (Lk 2:1-5, 12, 22, 37; 24:25-32). These events, however, were observed by disciples who were Jesus' constant companions (Acts 1:21-26; Lk 24:32), who never failed him.[46] These eyewitnesses testify to the authenticity of the events (Lk 21:12; 24:48; Acts 1:8), and Luke relates this to us (Lk 1:1-4).

Luke shows that many other people — some disinterested, some later Jesus' opponents — still bear witness to Jesus' greatness, to the authenticity of his life and message. These impressed unbelievers, who as a whole hung on his words

(Lk 19:48), are amazed at his teaching (Lk 4:36), acknowledging that they "have seen incredible things" (Lk 5:26). These impartial witnesses contribute significantly to establishing for Luke the historical reliability of the events.[47]

The powerful presence of God in Jesus, witnessed by many and represented in the gospel, is not over and done with. God's presence continues to be actively involved in the lives of the disciples.

Merciful interventions of the Sovereign Lord. The merciful interventions of the Sovereign Lord reach their climax in Jesus' resurrection and continue in the miracles performed for those in need. These miracles, in turn, confirm Jesus' claims. Luke sees the miracles as a prolongation of the power which the Father showed in raising Jesus (Acts 4:29-33). For all of us, this power is acknowledged in the Father's initiative, drawing us to conversion (Acts 5:31; 11:18).[48]

Elsewhere, by use of passive verbs, Luke shows the Father's continuing direction of his plan through the visions given to chosen disciples (Acts 9:3-9; 10:3-8). In this way, Luke shows how his own Church's pastoral initiatives are rooted in the will of God. In so doing, he underlines his own conviction that God still directs the Church.

Jesus remains ever-present. Jesus continues to act as savior (Acts 4:12), leader (Acts 5:31), judge (Acts 10:42), and as the forgiver of sin (Acts 13:38). He is especially powerful through his name (Acts 2:21, 38; 3:6-16; 4:7, 10, 12, 30; 5:28). For Luke the post-resurrection Jesus identifies himself with his Church, continuing to be present in his disciples (Acts 9:4) and their courageous witnessing (Acts 18:9-11). Moreover, as God's plan was carried out through Jesus' obedience, so now is Jesus' ministry continued in the obedience of his faithful disciples (Acts 5:29-32; 20:22-24). In a later chapter we shall see how Luke, in the last chapter of the gospel and the first four chapters of Acts, singles out the various ways in which Jesus is continually present to his Church: in the scriptures, in Christian fellowship, in the eucharist, in the joy and peace of community, in prayer, and in Church leaders.[49]

The era of the Holy Spirit. We now find ourselves in the era of the Holy Spirit. While water is the outward sign of our entrance into the Church, the Spirit within constitutes us as Church.

There is such a close bond between the Spirit and the community of believers that he is identified with their ongoing existence. "It is the Spirit that informs and animates the community, which indeed, apart from the Spirit, would not be a community but an aggregate of individuals."[50] The Spirit is now our life, inspiring, directing, and challenging the disciples. He prays in them, prophesies through them, and is their peace and consolation. For the believer, he is also present in the events of history, constantly calling us to the Way of the Lord (Acts 7:51-53).

Rooted in the revelation of the Old Testament, Luke complements the revelation of God with the teachings of Jesus and the spiritual experiences of the early Church. His portrait is at once powerful and awesome, encouraging and salvational, a challenge and a perennial call to growth and life.

Chapter Five
CHURCH AND LIFE

The Church was at peace. It was being built up and was making steady progress in the fear of the Lord; at the same time it enjoyed the increased consolation of the Holy Spirit. (Acts 9:31)

By the addition of Acts, Luke offers us the most detailed description of the early Church's life, work, and self-understanding available in the New Testament. In the decades immediately following the death of Jesus, the disciples eagerly looked forward to their Master's return. By the time Luke writes, the Church has grown considerably, and is well developed in the larger cities of the empire.[1] Interested in its own future growth and history, it is certainly not a Church awaiting the immediate return of the Lord.

It is not difficult to imagine, however, what a period of crisis this must have been for believers. Why did the time of waiting for the Lord seem endless? Why should there be a Church? If the end of the age was to be the next act in the redemptive drama of God, what meaning could be found for the Church as an ongoing institution?[2] Where is Jesus' guidance now to be found?

It is part of Luke's greatness that he faces up to these problems and tries to provide answers. He interprets the period of waiting as part of the Father's will, rooting the need for the existence of the Church in the directives of the Father who, through visions, theophanies, and the guidance of his Spirit, establishes the Church and the major lines of its early history. He looks back to the origins of the Church and, with historical reliability, presents the typical features of its life, the strengths and weaknesses of its members.

By the time Luke has finished, we have in two parts a basis for the first simple ecclesiological synthesis of Christianity. He addresses the issues of the nature of the Church and why it continues. He makes substantial contributions to an understanding of early structures in the Church, gives ecclesial living a fine ascetical challenge, and opens his own era to an ecclesial strategy for the world. In reality, Luke ushers in the age of the Church.

As in the case of his christology, Luke does not force uniformity on the reader. Rather, he leaves a pluralism in interpretation where he finds it in his sources. His own convictions, preferences, and syntheses are still identifiable and, when material does not accord with his position, he seems to have deliberately omitted it.[3]

In today's oppressed world, we long for the Lord's return to establish peace, justice, and right. We experience a general increase in questions concerning the necessity for the Church, as well as many views challenging ecclesistical structures. Yet, there is an appreciation as never before of the positive aspects of the Church as community, and an increasing longing to share with the needy of the world. These are Lucan interests. They seem to have been vital issues for his time, and he addressed them creatively, with fidelity to the received tradition. Luke is a disciple with an acute sense of Church, and shows forcefully how this ecclesial characteristic is, and must be, an integral part of our spiritual lives.

The Nature Of The Church In Luke

Soon after the presentation of Jesus' ascension, Luke portrays growing community awareness among the early disciples (Acts 1:12-14; 2:41-47; 5:12-14). Traces of this community identity were already noticeable in the later ministry of Jesus (Lk 22:1-23), but after Pentecost, Luke sees the disciples as part of a new reality. As their self-understanding grows, Luke, reflecting on their origins, presents us with his synthesis of their awareness. In Luke-Acts, the early disciples see themselves as the community of Israel's hopes, the community of the end times, of universal vision, the community with an historical mission — the community of God.

The community of Israel's hopes. Throughout the gospel Luke presents many episodes which highlight Judaism's inadequacy as the instrument of God: the parable of the fig tree that is given a last chance (Lk 13:6-9); the conflict between Jesus and the Pharisees on the meaning of sabbath salvation (Lk 13:10-17); the Jewish leaders' complaints about Jesus' treatment of the outcasts who need God's mercy (Lk 15:1-10); the parable of the unjust steward who squanders his master's wealth (Lk 16:1-13); the parable of Lazarus and of the rich man who did not listen to Moses and the prophets (Lk 16:19-31). All these episodes - exclusive to Luke - have the same aim. To them can be added others, common to the synoptics, which Luke integrates into his presentation: the saying of the false leaven of the Pharisees (Lk 12:1), and the parable of the wicked tenants (Lk 20:9-19).

Luke clearly sees the Christian community as the successor to Israel. In some ways, Jesus' final journey to Jerusalem is also a journey to ecclesial consciousness. The teachings of this section give reasons for the failure and rejection of Judaism, and look forward to the Church.[4]

For Luke, the Church is the community of Israel's hopes. He sees the Christian community as the remnant of the last days (Acts 2:21, 47), the heritage of Abraham (Acts 3:25), and the eschatological Zion that witnesses the day of the Lord (Acts 2:22, 39). The Church is the new Qahal, the new assembly of the Lord's people (Acts 2:17-41; 5:11; 8:1, 3; 9:31; 11:22, 26).[5]

Luke, who speaks of Christians as "children of the prophets" and "heirs of the covenant" (Acts 3:25), is also careful to interrupt his account of the early Church with that of the election of Matthias.[6] Thus, before the Spirit's creative baptism, we have the twelve pillars or patriarchs on which the new Israel is founded. The account of Pentecost is portrayed by Luke as a new Sinai event. He skillfully introduces many details which highlight his convictions that this is the beginning of the new Israel.[7] When Peter speaks at Pentecost, he likens Jesus' ascent into heaven and reception of the promised Spirit to Moses' ascent of Mount Sinai to receive the law. Then Acts unfolds the history of this new community as a continuation of salvation history. "The Church represents the continuity of redemptive history, and to this degree is 'Israel.'[8]

In Luke's gospel this identification of the Church with Israel, and the documentation of its growth, had already been anticipated in the parables on the mustard seed (Lk 13:18-19) and the sower (Lk 8:11-15). While referring to the kingdom, they seem to speak of the Church. This was noted by G. W. H. Lampe, who, speaking of the former parable, says: "We have the picture of the growth, like mustard seed or leaven, of the kingdom of God, in this Lucan context virtually identified, it would seem, with the Church."[9] In his general treatment of the kingdom, Luke gives signs of its anticipated arrival (Lk 10:9; 11:20; 17:20-21), but insists — right up to the eve of the passion—that it is not yet here (Lk 19:11; 22:18; 23:42). On the eve of the passion, he speaks of it as very close (Lk 22:18), and assures the apostles of a governing place when it is established (Lk 22:25-30). After his passion (Lk 24:26), Jesus speaks of the kingdom (Acts 1:3) as if it were now here. The kingdom expected by Israel is now the ongoing expectation of the Church.

The hopes of Israel to recognize the Messiah, to be the true children of Abraham and the prophets, to be the beneficiaries of God's interventions, and to witness the kingdom, are portrayed by Luke as attained, not by the Israel of old, but by the new Israel of the Church.

The community of the end times. Peter's first speech at Pentecost explains to the crowds the meaning of the day's events. Luke makes clear in Peter's speech that the Church is here recognized as the community of the end times. He quotes Joel's prophecy of the last days (Acts 2:17), and speaks of the wonders and signs of God which herald the coming of the end (Acts 2:22, 39, 43).

We are twice told that Jesus is the eschatological prophet foretold by Moses (Acts 2:22-23; 7:37). One of the signs of the messianic community of the end times was the general outpouring on it of the Holy Spirit of God. Luke leaves us in no doubt on this issue (Acts 2:17, 33; 4:31; 8:17; 10:44-48; 19:1-7). The foundation of the Church is characterized by this prophesied outpouring of the Spirit.

Jacques Dupont's exegesis of the passages describing the early Church (Acts 2:42-45; 4:32-35) led him to the conviction that Luke here presents the early Church as the faithful community of the end times. Moses had foretold that a sign of the eschatological community would be the assurance that it would contain no needy person (Deuteronomy 15:4). Twice Luke assures us that this is true of the early Church. Dupont adds that since the Old Testament is not quoted here, the link of the

Church with the community of the end times was probably in the consciousness of Christians before Luke's redaction.[10]

Events are described in terms of the end times, and Jesus is presented as the eschatological prophet. That these are the messianic times is confirmed by the visible outpouring of the Spirit on the community and by the community's own qualities of life and sharing. Luke makes his position clear with a few brief references. The dedication and missionary work of the early Christians confirms this conviction that the Church is the community of the end times.

The community with a universal vision. Another component of the early Church is its awareness of its universal mission. That Jesus brings universal salvation is heralded in the infancy narratives, confirmed in his first address at Nazareth, and celebrated in the Supper. The Church then receives the commission from the Lord to proclaim his name to the ends of the earth (Lk 24:47; Acts 1:8). In some ways, Acts is Luke's presentation of the Church's fidelity to this mandate of the Lord, and in Acts we see the gradual development of the Church. As the drama unfolds, considerable symbolic emphasis is given to Athens, the cultural center of the world (Acts 17:16-34), and Rome, the political center (Acts 28:14-30). The structure of Acts shows the Church as the community with a universal vision.

Luke underlines this point more than once. The nature of the Church is symbolically portrayed at Pentecost. All the world witnesses the birth of the Church (Acts 2:8-11), and the first baptism is of three thousand people, representatives of the world.[11] The gift of tongues on Pentecost, and particularly the crowd's ability to understand (Acts 2:8), is to be seen as Luke's conviction that Pentecost is the reversal of Babel (Gn 11:1-9). The Church is the community with the universal mission of unifying the people.

What is symbolized at Pentecost is lived out by the early Church. Soon, the Church recognized that Paul was called to be the apostle to the Gentiles (Acts 9:13-16), and later Peter was obedient to the call of God's universal will when he baptized Cornelius (Acts 10:24-48). The Church sees the persecutions as positively helping in the universal spread of the Word (Acts 8:4-5; 11:19-26). The missionaries journey far, also calling the Gentiles (Acts 13:46-49). The Church confronts and resolves problems which could impede the universality of her call (Acts 15:1-31). Finally, the Church is kept informed of the progress of the Word, rejoicing at the entrance of the Gentiles and the fulfillment of the Lord's command (Acts 11:1-18; 14:27-28; 15:6-11).

The community with an historical mission. Studies of Luke have generally divided into two camps: one considers history and eschatology as opposites; the second sees history and eschatology so intimately linked that history is the workshop of God.[12] Scholars who present the former accuse Luke of historicizing the message and abandoning primitive eschatology. They would, as we have already seen, accuse him of "early Catholicism." This position no longer holds the ground it used to. Instead of reducing it, Luke reinterprets eschatology. In fact, some expectation of the imminent end is still identifiable.[13] However, for such pastoral reasons as the avoidance of false apocalypticism and laxity, Luke emphasizes the way we should live in the time of waiting, and, "Thanks to him, the early Church did not collapse into an hysterical futurist eschatology."[14] It seems quite out of place to ask Luke to choose between eschatology and salvation history when, for him, this division does not exist. He uses history at the service of the proclamation of the eschatological events of Jesus, seeing the Church as a community with a historical mission. However, it is equally clear that this history is nothing more than epilogue, since the saving event came in Jesus. Luke believes the eschatological gift of the Spirit is in the Church to proclaim the message. However, the continuing existence of the Church and its need to be faithful in this time of waiting lead to problems of another kind, and Luke believes that the Church was guided to face them. For Luke, the establishing of the Church is part of the fulfillment of God's will. The historical mission of the Church is to spread the Word: the Eleven are witnesses for it (Lk 21:13), Simon must strengthen the others in it (Lk 22:31-32), the deacons are chosen to facilitate it (Acts 6:1-7), and even persecution is seen as a means for accomplishing it (Lk 21:12-13). The Church which Luke describes is not "early Catholic," but a Church aware of its mission to all in this time of waiting.

The community of God. In the second chapter of Acts, Luke portrays Peter already appreciating that the Church is the community of God, called by the Father in the name of Jesus and endowed with the gift of the Spirit (Acts 2:38-39).

The interventions of God, so powerful in the infancy narratives, continue in the Church. To empower his Church in preaching, the Father sends the promised Spirit (Lk 24:49; Acts 1:5; 2:1-12; 5:32), and to support and confirm his ministers' efforts, he works wonders and signs (Acts 2:43; 5:12-14; 6:8; 15:12; 19:11). He gives directions through visions (Acts 10:1-24; 15:7-11) and through the services of his angels (Acts 8:26; 12:7-11). The early Church preaches God's salvation in Jesus and feels, above all, the need to be obedient to his will (Acts 4:19; 5:19-21, 29). The Church prays to God (Acts 4:23-31), attributes its success to him (Acts 19:20; 21:29), and praises him (Acts 21:20). The early Church certainly sees itself as the community of God.

This community consists of those who are baptized into Jesus Christ (Acts 2:38) and become one body with him (Acts 9:5). This Jesus is the cornerstone of the saved (Acts 4:11), and there is no longer salvation except in him (Acts 4:12). He continues to be present to his Church in many ways, as we shall see, but is encountered especially in scripture and the eucharist (Lk 24:32; Acts 2:42-45; 4:32-35; 20:7).

This community of God, dedicated to Jesus, is also the community formed by the outpouring of the Spirit. The promise of the Father (Lk 24:48-49; Acts 1:5) is poured out on the Church in each of the foundation stories: in Jerusalem (Acts 2:1-4), Samaria (Acts 8:14-17), the Gentile Church (Acts 10:44), and Ephesus (Acts 19:6). We have already seen that the Spirit chooses and designates the ministers, empowers them, and brings them joy and consolation in their ministry. The Church and the Spirit are so intimately united that they testify with one voice (Acts 5:29-32) and must be respected as one reality (Acts 5:3). Leaders of the community of the outpoured Spirit are given their authority from the Spirit (acts 20:28-31) by means of an intensified reception of his gifts (Acts 6:6; 9:17; 13:3). The Spirit who guides his Church also warns it of impending dangers (Acts 11:18; 16:7; 20:23; 21:11).

The Church of Luke is portrayed as the community of Israel's hopes, the community of the end times, the community of universal vision, the community with an historical mission, and the community of God. As an early ecclesiological synthesis, it is superb. It gives us history and roots, present reality and call to commitment, future vision and hopes.

Ecclesial Community

The meaning of Acts is essentially ecclesial. Luke gives us a clear picture of the nature, common bonds, structure, daily living, and mission of the Church. What does Luke consider the common bonds which unite the disciples into a real community? After the departure of Jesus, we are presented with a new corporate life of the Church, in which the believers are so closely united that they are truly brothers and sisters.[15] What is it that unites them so intimately? Later in this chapter we shall see the ascetical practices and forms of sharing which characterize their ecclesial living. Here we examine Luke's emphasis on the nature of their community life. It is a community in salvation, based on shared commitment, constantly challenged by the Word, and open to the Spirit; it is a paschal community growing through opposition.

The community of the saved. In Acts, salvation means belonging to the community of the saved. The group of witnesses formed by Jesus was commisioned to extend his work to all (Lk 24:48). This commission, and the disciples' consciousness of themselves as a specially chosen group, is reinforced in Luke's second ascension story. This story has been referred to as "the ecclesiastical and historical interpretation, with the accent on the work of the Spirit in the Church."[16] The disciples return from the ascension with joy in the realization that the messianic promises are fulfilled in them (Lk 24:52). From the early days after the ascension, they are profoundly aware that they are now a special group (Acts 1:13-14; 2:42-47; 5:12-13, 42) saved in the name of the Lord (Acts 2:21; 4:12).

When others accept the Lord's call, they are "added" to the group (Acts 2:41; 5:14). In fact, we read explicitly: "Day by day the Lord added to their number those who were being saved" (Acts 2:47). When Cornelius has a vision, he is told that Peter will instruct him in how to be saved (Acts 11:14), and, when Peter arrives, he baptizes Cornelius and his household. A similar episode takes place in Paul's missionary work (Acts 16:30-31). In both instances, the story ends with the seekers being united to the Church. Part of the proclamation of the early Church is a call to membership in the community of salvation. S. Brown states it this way: "Luke sees the salvation of the individual as indissolubly connected with the Church, since only through the latter's historical mediation is the Christian enrolled in the present phase of salvation history.''[17] Moreover, Luke's connections of some of the episodes are significant. The direct result of the Pentecost experience, at least in its literary presentation, is the healthy community life of the early disciples (Acts 2:42-45). This leads to the group's being held in high esteem and praise (Acts 2:47), and the Lord's addition of others to their group (Acts 2:47). The community is of sign value to others, drawing them to the community of salvation.

The community's conditions for membership. The conditions for membership in this comunity are laid down by Peter: repentance, belief in Jesus, baptism, and reception of the Spirit (Acts 2:38). Repentance and change of life are necessary for the belief to be authentic. Repentance has, in places, practically the same meaning as discipleship. Belief in Jesus is the condition for baptism "in the name of Jesus." This commitment of the disciple to the name of Jesus would mean, for the Hellenistic readers of Luke, a transfer of ownership of themselves to Jesus. For any of Luke's audience with Jewish background, it meant their dedication to Jesus, their endowment with his saving blessing.[18] The gift of the Spirit is the climax of entrance into the group of the believers, for the Spirit seals the faith.

The above four stages of initiation are sometimes understood as included in the fullness of any one of them. God gives the Gentiles "life-giving repentance" (Acts 11:18), and Philip baptizes the eunuch (Acts 8:38). In both cases, the issue is their admission into the Church.

After initiation must follow a life of conformity with what the community considers to be the will of God.[19] Ananias and Sapphira fail in this, their initiation of no value (Acts 5:1-11).

Belonging to the Christian community is not something achieved once and for all. The Christian must "remain in the faith." We have already seen that the Church's task was to preserve and pass on the Word of Jesus. Everyone who has been baptized shares in his task. Perseverance in faith "is something active and dynamic: it means 'holding fast to the word' (Lk 8:15), 'keeping the word' (Lk 11:28), 'doing the word' (Lk 8:21).''[20]

The community of ongoing fidelity to Word and Spirit. Ongoing fidelity to Word and Spirit is crucial to Luke's vision of ecclesial commitment. Already in the gospel he has modified the parable of the sower (Lk 8:4-15), making it a parable on the dynamism of the seed which is the Word of Jesus.[21] The disciple is threatened with exclusion from the community if he or she does not listen. The ecclesial community is formed by the Word, which is their very life. In fact, in places Luke seems to identify the Word of God with the community itself (Acts 12:24; 19:20).[22] The early Church prays that they will always proclaim it with boldness (Acts 4:29-31), and when the apostles see this responsibility threatened, they anoint the seven deacons (Acts 6:2-7). Although this latter group is commissioned to look after the charitable needs of the community, they actually spend their time in proclaiming the Word. When the Gentiles receive the Word (Acts 11:1), and Paul proclaims it (Acts 13:5; 17:13), we are basically dealing with a proclamation about Jesus. This Word, to which the community must be faithful, has an internal dynamic growth of its own in the community; it increases, grows, and multitplies (Acts 6:7; 12:24). The disciples, seeing its power, glorify the Word (Acts 13:48-49).

The ecclesial community, called to salvation in Jesus, is entrusted with his Word as guide and challenge. When Paul leaves the elders of Miletus for the last time, he says: "I commend you now to the Lord, and to that gracious word of his which can enlarge you, and give you a share among all who are consecrated to him" (Acts 20:32).

In addition to being open to the constant challenge of the Word, the early Church is also a community sensitive to the continual and varied guidance of the Holy Spirit. His guidance is seen in his inspiration of scripture (Acts 4:25) and in the common deliberations of Church leaders (Acts 15:28). All feel the need to obey his calls, whether to action (Acts 5:32) or inaction (Acts 16:6). Obedience to the Spirit is required of individual Church leaders like Peter (Acts 10:44-48), and of communities (Acts 13:1-3). The Church sees the Spirit present in everyone, so that Ananias' hypocrisy and the Jewish leaders' lack of faith are explicitly attributed to their resitance of the Holy Spirit (Acts 5:3; 7:51). The same Spirit who guides Church leaders (Acts 20:28) also speaks out through local prophetic figures (Acts 11:28-30; 21:11), and even entire communities (Acts 21:4-6).

The paschal community growing through trials. Finally, we see the Church in Luke as the paschal community which grows through trials. In the Third Gospel, Jesus "must" suffer. His passion is part of the divine plan leading to resurrection and growth. This same passover is part of the life of the early Church. There is some kind of problem, opposition, or persecution in every period of the Church's ministry in Acts. This is deliberately structured by Luke to highlight this young community's essential role of suffering. In the early days after Pentecost, Peter heals the lame man at the gate of the temple, preaching there as well. Both he and John are arrested, imprisoned overnight, then brought before the high priest to be challenged in their work. When released, they identify with Jesus' suffering, and, together with their community, rejoice and ask for more boldness in their ministry (Acts 4:23-31).

Soon they are arrested again and, when released by an angel, are recaptured and tried. Their words move Gamaliel to support them, but the Council still has them flogged, releasing them with further warnings (Acts 5:30-42).

Stephen becomes the first disciple to imitate his master in death (Acts 7:54-60). Luke so structures this section as to model Stephen's death on the Lord's, thereby presenting Jesus as the protomartyr and exemplar.

Stephen's death by stoning leads to a general persecution of the Church (Acts 8:1; 9:1-2), but this results beneficially for the spreading of the Word (Acts 8:4; 11:19). Persecution continues: Paul's life is threatened (Acts 9:29), and Herod treats many others violently, killing James, the brother of John (Acts 12:1-2). In order to ingratiate himself with the Jews, Herod imprisons Peter (Acts 12:3-5), but Peter escapes, leaving Jerusalem to spread the Word afar (Acts 12:17).

This element of persecution and physical suffering is a constant throughout the journeys, but always the ministry goes on, stimulated even by the persecutions: Paul and Barnabas are reviled by the Jews, but this moves them to the Gentiles (Acts 13:46); Paul and Silas are flogged and imprisoned at the instigation of the economically powerful, but this leads to conversion and new life (Acts 16:19-34); jealous Jews later attack the same two missionaries, but when they escape and are pursued, this results in Paul's challenge to Athens, the heart of the cultural world (Acts 17:5-15). When Paul is reviled in Macedonia, he goes to the Gentile (Acts 18:5-8); finally he returns to Jerusalem, where he is rejected by all, but as a result brings the Word to

Rome (Acts 21 - 28).

As far as Luke is concerned, the blood of the missionaries is the seed of the Church, and the paschal element is essential to Christian growth: "We must undergo many trials if we are to enter into the reign of God" (Acts 14:22).

Ecclesial Structuring

In the infancy narratives and throughout his ministry, Jesus is recognized as a person of authority (Lk 1:32-33; 4:32-36; 5:17; 9:1; 10:19). However, he consistently rejects certain styles of authority (Lk 2:16; 4:6-8; 19:24-27). Luke often speaks of authority in his stories, but it is clear that this is not Jesus' way (Lk 7:8; 12:11; 19:17; 20:20; 23:7). His exercise of authority is different, but authority he certainly has! When Jesus was asked, "By what authority do you do these things?" (Lk 20:2), Luke precedes the question with Jesus' teaching, instead of the cleansing of the temple as in his source, Mark. Jesus' public ministry is one of authoritative teaching. Eventually the gospel ends with Jesus portrayed as the high priest solemnly blessing his people (Lk 24:50).

Matthew's gospel ends with Jesus saying "Full authority has been given to me. . . I am with you always" (Mt 28:18-20), but in Luke this becomes "Recall those words I spoke to you when I was still with you" (Lk 24:44). In Acts, Jesus is not present to exercise power, but uses mediators to recall those words (Acts 1:2; 8:35; 9:6, 10).[23] He has specially chosen the principal mediators (Acts 1:2), twice warning them about the use of authority and privilege (Lk 9:46-48; 22:24-27). Jesus came as a servant (Acts 4:27), and they, too, must be servants (Acts 4:29-30).[24]

In Acts it is presumed that the Pharisees and Sadducees are finished as leaders; that Jesus' authority is now exercised in the Church. In Acts we witness a "process of ecclesialization" in which Jesus' authority in the Spirit is now focused in the Church.[25] His authority is to be used for the spread of the Word. In Luke, authority at the service of mission and ministry is certainly more important than any form of authority in a structured organizational role. It is unwise to speak simply of institutionalization and Luke's "catholicizing tendencies."

We read principally in Luke of God's "people". This is the prime reality.[26] Any structuring is to facilitate the people's growth in the Spirit. "The institutional does not by itself guarantee the presence of the Spirit. The facts are, as Luke sees them, that the Spirit mobilizes those who are receptive to its power, and the institutional is the earthly matrix in which those endowed by the Spirit act."[27]

There seem to be in Acts varied forms of Church structure. There are collegial forms of ecclesial structuring as well as monarchical forms; spontaneous Spirit-guided interventions and conciliar interventions; city structures and provincial structures.

The Twelve. The Twelve is the most important structure of the Church in Acts. Already, in the Third Gospel, Jesus chose the Twelve and specifically named them apostles (Lk 6:12-16). They accompany Jesus in his ministry (Lk 8:1-3), are empowered and sent to preach and heal (Lk 9:1-11), are close participants in the miracle of the multiplication of loaves (Lk 9:12-17), and are told in confidence about the coming passion events in Jerusalem (Lk 18:31-34). After Jesus' death, when the women find the empty tomb, they report this to the Eleven (Lk 24:9), as do the disciples who journeyed to Emmaus (Lk 24:33).

If we are to presume that the Twelve were the ones at the Last Supper — although it is not stated explicitly, and a larger group could be implied — it is then significant in the Lucan redaction that anything negative stated about the apostles is completely omitted (Mk 14:27, 50), and Luke's editing shows them in a more responsible light (Lk 22:49-54).

After Pentecost we find the Twelve together for the first public presentation of the early Church (Acts 2:14), and later they collegially recommend the appointing of the seven deacons (Acts 6:1-6). After this, we hear no more of the Twelve. There are about twenty references to "the apostles," but it is not clear whether is meant the Twelve, or a larger group. There are certainly examples where some authority is exercised by a larger group (Acts 1:23; 11:1-18; 15:2).

What is the role of the Twelve in the community? When Judas betrays the Lord, he is replaced by Matthias (Acts 1:15-26), but when James dies, he is not replaced (Acts 12:2). "The real problem in Acts . . . [is] . . .why the Twelve disappear as an authoritative and an administrative group within a relatively short time after the need was felt to reconstitute it by the election of Matthias."[28] What role did they occupy historically, and what purpose do they have in Luke's presentation? We have little historical information other than the preceding references. It seems unlikely that they did significantly more than this; the synoptics do not even agree on their names. Their purpose lies in two directions. The first is precisely that they are the Twelve and, as such, declare "the nature of the new community as that of eschatological Israel."[29] Earlier in the gospel, Jesus descended with the Twelve to meet the people (Lk 6:17), as Moses descended in Exodus (Ex 32:15; 34:29). The Twelve embody the theological conviction of the early Church that they are the new Israel.

The second purpose of the Twelve is to be historical links of witness between the early Church and the earthly Jesus. The candidate chosen to take Judas' place must have known Jesus from his baptism until the ascension (Acts 1:21-26). The Twelve always accompany Jesus, observing, and reporting on him reliably. This is their purpose, namely they are authoritative and credible links. Marshall draws a significant conclusion: "If there is no salvation *extra ecclesiam*, it is not because the Church possesses the gospel but because salvation is through Christ and his Word is committed to the apostles."[30]

The seven deacons. This fidelity to the Word leads the Twelve to recommend that seven deacons be chosen for the table service (Acts 6:1-3). This episode is redactionally presented in two significant steps: the community chooses the candidates as they did in Matthias' case (Acts 1:23), and, the authoritative body of the apostles imposes hands and commissions the deacons.[31] Although designated for charitable activites, even these seven factually preach, debate, and work wonders in support of the Word (Acts 6:8; 7:1-53; 8:26-40). The deacons seem to exercise remarkable freedom in their ministry. Stephen's sermon, with its Samaritan overtones, could hardly have been considered orthodox and acceptable by those early disciples in Jerusalem; those willing to confront even Peter for what they considered unorthodox behavior (Acts 11:3).

Peter. In the early Palestinian-based Church, Peter stands out as an accepted leader. In the Third Gospel, his call is given significant attention (Lk 5:1-11). It is to Peter that Jesus says: "From now on you will be catching men" (Lk 5:10). Jesus goes to Peter's home and cures his mother-in-law (Lk 4:38-39), and Peter is later listed first among the apostles, his name changed by Jesus (Lk 6:14). He solemnly professes faith in Jesus (Lk 9:20), witnesses the transfiguration (Lk 9:28), and with John prepares the last supper (Lk 22:8). Luke acknowledges Peter's denial, but stresses that Jesus assured Peter he would repent and strengthen the others (Lk 22:31-32).

In the Acts, Peter is again named first in the list of the Eleven (Acts 1:13). He leads in the suggestion to elect Matthias (Acts 1:15-26), is the great preacher of the early Church (Acts 2:14-36; 3:12-26; 10:34-43) and the spokesman before Jewish authorities (Acts 4:8-12; 5:29-32), and a man of authority (Acts 5:1-11; 15:7-11). Peter is portrayed as a great miracle worker (Acts 3:1-10; 5:1-11, 15), and some of his miracles parallel Jesus' miracles in the Third Gospel (Acts 9:32-42). He is also the object of special divine protection (Acts 5:17-21; 10:9-48; 12:6-11).[32]

According to Luke, Peter authoritatively inaugurates the Church's mission to the Gentiles by his acceptance of Cornelius into the community (Acts 10:1 - 11:18). Considering later actions of Peter and other claims of Paul (Ga 2:11-14), it is not clear whether this episode is totally historical or whether Luke, firmly convinced of God's will in the entrance of the Gentiles, roots and legitimizes it in the authority of Peter. In either case, it is clear that Luke considers Peter the prime leader of the early Church.

Although Peter is the recognized leader of the early Church, he seemingly departs Jerusalem after his miraculous release from prison (Acts 12:17), leaving James in authority (Acts 12:17; 21:18). Later, Peter returns for the council of Jerusalem and plays a leading role (Acts 15:7-12).

When a practical pastoral problem with important doctrinal implications confronts Paul and Barnabas (Acts 15:1-2), they decide to refer it to the Jerusalem Church. It seems this Mother Church has authority over early missionary enterprises. The authority group, which seems to be a collegial form of government, is "the apostles and presbyters" (Acts 15:2, 6, 22, 23). During the Council, Peter speaks from an obviously key position, but it is James whose last word and recommendation is accepted (Acts 15:1-29).[33]

The portrait of Peter in Acts is complex. He is very different from the Peter we meet in the other synoptics. At times it seems that Luke describes the Peter who must have been, at others the

Peter whom Luke decided *needed* to have been for the Church in those times.

Paul. The other great figure of Acts is Paul. His vision and conversion, which Luke repeats three times (Acts 9:1-19; 22:3-21; 26:9-18), are intended to show the divine origin of his call and mission to the Gentiles. His journeys take him throughout Asia Minor and Europe, where he preaches to both Jew and Gentile. He is a miracle worker (Acts 16:16-18; 19:11-19), some of his miracles paralleling those of Jesus and Peter (Acts 14:8-13; 20:7-12). Like Peter, he is the object of special divine protection (Acts 9:3-19; 16:10, 25-31; 18:9; 20:23; 21:10-11; 26:19: 27:23-24). When eventually arrested and put on trial, the whole episode reflects Jesus' trials (Acts ch 22-26).

Paul begins his missionary work with Barnabas (Acts 13:1-3). Before they leave, the prophets and teachers impose hands on them in some form of ordination or commissioning ceremony (Acts 13:3). Already during this first journey Paul and Barnabas have installed presbyters in every Church (Acts 14:23). Paul travels in his second missionary journey with Silas (Acts 15:40), and while he visits many "congregations" and meets the "brothers," there is no reference to any structuring of the Church. However, it seems reasonable to conclude that Paul and his companions continued the pastoral practice of the first mission (Acts 14:23). In the third journey, Paul summons the presbyters of Ephesus to hear his sermon (Acts 20:17), urging them to watch over the flock (Acts 20:28).

Paul seems to be the main authority in his ministry. Wherever he travels in Acts, he sets up Church structures that do not conform to those of the Jerusalem Church; this is confirmed by the major Pauline letters. He respects the authority of the Jerusalem Church (Acts 15:2; 21:18), but does not imitate it in governmental form.

Pluralism. The ecclesial structuring of the early Church as portrayed by Luke is pluralistic. The powerful leaders Peter, Paul, and James have their own style of government while showing respect for the body of a Church greater than they are. Jerusalem seems to have its form of government, Miletus and Antioch theirs. At one time we see the Spirit in the judgment of wise leaders at the Council, later in the charismatic leaders of Antioch, and occasionally in the prophetic challenge of individuals such as Agabus. Besides missionaries explicitly delegated by the Church, we also meet Apollos (Acts 18:24 - 19:1), Aquila, Priscilla (Acts 18:1-4, 18-21), and unamed committed Christians (Acts 11:19), each preaching the Word of God. At one time we are presented with structured and regulated leadership, at another with charismatic leadership. We see again the ecclesialization of the Spirit who manifests his guiding authority as he chooses.

Acts shows us a new way of exercising Church power. Problems are faced up to and usually solved (Acts 6:1-7; 9:26-30; 11:1-18; 15:1-6). There is always respect for the Church, and a willingness to explain why one acts differently (Acts 11:4; 21:18-21). This is part of the community asceticism of Acts.

I think it is also challenging that Luke portrays the Church leaders as the embodiment of his theology, as he does with the Twelve. They are presented as the new Israel, and Paul is described as the apostle of Gentile entry into the Church. Luke is stating strongly that Church leaders should embody the ecclesiology of the day.

He is also convinced that present beliefs are and must be rooted in the past, and much of his redactional work supports this. However, not willing to force uniformity on disparate sources, he honestly gives us a pluralistic approach.

When he speaks of the leaders of the day, there is always some delegation and commissioning by the Church. The Twelve, themselves called and commissioned by Jesus, mandate the deacons; the local Antiochean Church mandates Paul and Barnabas; and Paul and Barnabas commission the elders. However, these mission confirmations often come after the community as a whole has already chosen the people they want.

Ecclesial Living

In Luke's approach, the Church is neither a place of refuge nor an institution offering ready-made salvation. Church is a way of living, the expression of our faith and commitment to Christ. Conversion "is not a once-for-all total change, but a process to be worked out in *medio ecclesiae*. The communitarian nature of Christian faith is expressed literally and radically in the lifestyle of the primitive church."[34] It is this communitarian lifestyle we now consider. The following chapter on discipleship includes teachings of an individual and personal nature, but here we concentrate on four major manifestations of the early Church's community asceticism. The early Church is a worshipping, a sharing, a poor, and a joyful Church.

A prayerful Church. The atmosphere created by Luke for the infancy narratives is permeated by personal prayer (Lk 2:37, 51), community prayer (Lk 1:46-55, 68-79; 2:20, 24-32, 41), and ritual prayer (Lk 2:13-14, 22, 41). This emphasis on prayer is highlighted in Jesus' life. Jesus stated that prayer was one of humanity's prime commitments (Lk 4:8). Jesus often goes away to pray during his ministry (Lk 6:12; 9:18, 28; 10:21-22; 11:1; 22:41-44; 23:46). Jesus' ministry and interventions in people's lives often stimulate them to awe and prayers of praise to God (Lk 5:26; 7:16; 13:13; 18:43; 19:36-38). Jesus' final meal is the ritual prayer of Passover (Lk 22:15-20).

This emphasis on prayer is continued by the early Christians, who see themselves as a worshipping Church. The apostles prize prayer so highly that they reorganize the early Church to include time for worship and prayer (Acts 6:4). The leaders are models of community prayer: Peter (Acts 3:1; 10:9), John (Acts 3:1), and Paul (Acts 16:25; 20:7, 36; 21:26; 22:17; 24:18; 27:35).

Luke presents the early communities as examples of a worshipping Church. The Church in the upper room "devoted themselves to constant prayer" (Acts 1:14), including the communal request for guidance in the election of Judas' successor (Acts 1:24-25). After Pentecost, the Jerusalem Church was noted for its prayer (Acts 2:42-45; 4:32-35). . They went to the temple daily for prayer (Lk 24:52-53; Acts 2:46), prayed together in their homes (Acts 4:24-30; 12:12), and, in the face of God's merciful designs, easily moved to community prayer (Acts 11:18). Not only Jerusalem, but Antioch (Acts 13:2-3) and Tyre (Acts 21:5) are prayerful communities.

The special moment of community prayer in the early Church is the breaking of bread; this is both the messianic banquet and the recelebration of the Lord's supper. Meals shared with Jesus were something special (Lk 9:16-17; 22:14-20; 24:30-35, 41-43): a participation in the messianic banquet. Navone has claimed that Luke strategically places a banquet at every major moment in gospel and Acts and, understood messianically, the banquet theme is a type of "primitive ecclesiology."[35] Fellowship is a part of being Church, and table conversation shared in reflection and faith is generally revelatory of the invitation to enter into radical transformation with Christ.[36]

The breaking of bread is not only a messianic banquet, but also the major ritual celebration of the early Church. The early Jerusalem Church celebrated in their homes (Acts 2:46), and we know that Paul celebrated this liturgy in Troas (Acts 20:7-11). For Luke, the community recognizes the presence of Jesus in their midst in the breaking of bread (Lk 24:30-31). It is a moment of special prayer and worship.

A sharing Church. The early Church is sustained by prayer and worship in their common commitment to the Lord. The disciples, however, also live as a truly sharing Church. Two major descriptions of the early Church, provided for us by Luke in two of his summaries, highlight the major areas of sharing: the instruction of the apostles, common life, the breaking of bread, and prayer (Acts 2:42-47; 4:32-35). In almost every city referred to in Acts, we see the group gathering for instruction. We have also seen sharing in prayer and worship. These three are more formal kinds of sharing, but what else was involved in their common life?

The community of believers, we are told, are of one heart and one mind (Acts 4:32). They seem to delight in taking their meals together (Acts 2:46-47), and sharing with others what they have seen and heard of Jesus (Acts 4:20; Lk 24:13-35). They share their faith with enthusiasm and joy. This union extends to all the Church. Wherever Paul travels he calls on the local communities, whose sharing in faith and love is always evident (Acts 15:30-33; 18:22; 21:7-14). In fact, it is this real bond of union that leads Paul and Barnabas to "go back and see how the brothers are getting on in each of the towns" (Acts 15:36). This common bond of faith and love is also seen in the practical sharing of hospitality. It is already present in the early journeys of Paul (Acts 16:14-15, 34), and is particularly noticeable in the generous welcome given him by the Church of Rome (Acts 28:15).

Another concrete form of sharing is their mutual encouragement in faith (Acts 16:40; 18:27), and on other occasions we see the community interested in the apostolic involvement of the missionaries, eagerly listening to their sharing of what the Lord had done through them (Acts 14:27-28; 15:4).

The depth of their sharing is seen in the disciples' willingness to share their material goods. When Paul returns to Jerusalem, it is "to bring alms to my own people" (Acts 24:17). In Jerusalem, Barnabas sells land and brings the money to the apostles (Acts 4:37). In fact, we are twice told that the Jerusalem community "shared all things in common, they would sell their property and goods, dividing everything on the basis of each one's need" (Acts 2:44-45). Later we are told: "None of them ever claimed anything as his own; rather, everything was held in common" (Acts 4:32). Although these are general descriptions of Luke, they seem more than an ideal. After all, the Church appointed seven deacons to help in the daily distribution (Acts 6:1-6). This implies a lot of distribution, itself dependent on extensive giving. Their deep union in faith leads the Jerusalem Church to union in material goods.[37]

When we look at this sharing Church, we see many forms of faith sharing: instruction, prayer, worship, common property, meals, shared faith responses to Jesus, hospitality, mutual encouragement and support in faith. These will be complemented later with shared poverty, joy, vision, and mission.

A poor Church. Luke-Acts is unquestionably the major call to poverty in the New Testament. The infancy narratives are peopled with the poor, who recognize and welcome the messianic event. The gospel is brought to the poor (Lk 4:18; 7:22), and throughout we hear warnings against the rich (Lk 6:24-26; 12:13-21; 14:33; 16:9, 19-31; 18:22). The disciples must be ready to leave all things (Lk 5:11 instead of Mt 4:18-22; also 14:33), renounce all goods (Lk 14:33), sell all, and give away the proceeds in alms (Lk 11:41; 12:33 instead of Mt 6:20). For any who still question the relative importance of poverty and riches, Luke alone has the parable of Lazarus and the rich man (Lk 16:19-31). Luke's two volumes are a message of hope for the poor (Lk 6:20-23) and a major confrontation to the rich who are not part of the poor Church.[38] In Luke alone we read of the rich fool whose wealth became his security (Lk 12:13-21), of Simon to whom Peter cries "May you and your money rot" (Acts 8:20), of Judas, and of Ananias and Sapphira, whose deaths "foreshadow the fate that awaits the Christian who remains attached to 'unrighteous mammon.'"[39]

The gospel challenges us to absolute detachment, incarnated in the Church by the willingness to make sure that there is no needy person in the community (Acts 4:34). Attachment is condemned, good use accepted—for the wealthy are also part of the community (Lk 19:1-10; Acts 10:1-4; 16:14)—but the removal of need is the principal way of living as a member of a poor Church. S. Brown synthesizes the call well: "In the Age of the Church it means the abandonment of the proprietary spirit, with the practical consequence that the Christian puts his property at the disposal of the community, being willing even to part with it altogether, if the common good requires this."[40]

Luke's own community, for whom these volumes are written, is made up of both rich and poor.[41] The former are a little too attached to their wealth, and it is to these that Luke says: "No servant can serve two masters. . .You cannot give yourself to God and money" (Lk 16:13). "Sell what you have and give alms" (Lk 12:33); "When you have a reception, invite beggars. . .you will be repaid in the resurrection of the just" (Lk 14:13-14). On the lips of John the Baptist, preparing for the entrance of the Lord, comes the answer to the questions: "What ought we to do?" In reply he said, "Let the man with two coats give to him who has none. The man who has food should do the same" (Lk 3:10-11).

Luke gives the challenge of poverty to all from Jesus, models of poverty in Church leaders, examples of poor Churches, and the call to choose prudently and well.

A joyful Church. Luke creates an atmosphere suggesting appropriate attitudes for the events described. An atmosphere of joy permeates his work. Joy, praise, glory, blessing, peace are words especially used by Luke.[42] The annunciation and birth of the Savior is an event of great messianic joy (Lk 1:14, 41, 58; 2:10). The crowds rejoice at Jesus' words during his ministry (Lk 4:15; 13:17), and are overwhelmed with joy and praise at his miracles (Lk 5:26; 7:16; 13:13; 17:15-16; 18:43; 19:37). Luke shows God rejoicing at a sinner's repentance (Lk ch 15), Jesus rejoicing with his disciples (Lk 10:21), the seventy-two rejoicing in their ministry (Lk 10:17), and individuals rejoicing in their conversion (Lk 19:6). We are reminded that the greatest reason for joy is having our names written in heaven (Lk 10:20). Finally, at the foot of the cross, symbolically in the name of humanity, the centurion gives joyful praise to God (Lk 23:47).

This messianic joy which permeates Luke's gospel — its teachings, miracles, banquets, and people—comes to a climax in the last chapter. The appearances of the Risen Lord on the first day of the week symbolize a new creation. This new life to which the Lord gives birth is filled with joy (Lk 24:41, 52), blessing (Lk 24:30, 50, 51, 53), praise (Lk 24:53), and peace (Lk 24:36).

Born in the Easter mystery, the Church is a joyful Church. This is seen in the continuing messianic and eschatological joy developed in the gospel. Joy is communal and ecclesial, found in true conversion and the development of the missionary work of the Church.

The new Jerusalem Church finds joy in its shared life and faith (Acts 2:46), receiving even the experience of suffering with ecclesial joy (Acts 5:41; 12:14). Conversions and baptisms are joyful moments for Church and recipients, the freedom and new-found life shared in joy (Acts 8:39; 16:34).

It is particularly in the success of the Church's ministry to the Word that we witness the joy of the faithful. After Philip's ministry in Samaria, we are told that "The rejoicing in that town rose to fever pitch" (Acts 8:8). When Barnabas arrives in Antioch, "he rejoiced to see the evidence of God's favor" (Acts 11:23). The news of the Gentile entry into the Church is always welcomed with joy by the new communities (Acts 11:18; 13:48; 15:3, 31; 21:20). Ministers of the Word are blessed in their work as they see the Church expand and develop. Barnabas rejoiced (Acts 11:23), and later "The disciples could not but be filled with joy and the Holy Spirit" (Acts 13:52).

It should also be stressed that Luke presents the theme of joy in significant structural form. Refrains, a typical stylistic characteristic of Luke, bring out important theological motifs as he progresses through the developing ministry, and one of the constant refrains is joy (Acts 8:8, 39; 13:48, 52; 16:34).

Ecclesial living in Luke is both fulfilling and satisfying. He calls the disciples to be a prayerful, sharing, poor, and joyful Church. These are complemented with Church's role of universal missionary concern.

Ecclesial Spirituality

Luke-Acts gives a fine synthesis of the life, work, and self-understanding of the early Church. Luke's presentation balances fidelity to tradition with inspired interpretation. Much of what he says reveals how the Church of apostolic times really lived. Other parts speak more clearly of Luke's own Church; of what they thought Church life ought to be, based on what was known of those earlier times. This balance between fidelity to the past and creative interpretation is perhaps Luke's most important teaching for our own times. We as Church must be faithful to the past, but we must make that past alive, meaningful, and prophetically challenging today.

Luke answers for his Church the question of how disciples should live in this time of waiting for the Lord's return. His insights, profoundly centered on ecclesial life, are equally valuable for us as we, too, await the Lord's return.

We must continue to reflect on the nature of the Church and make it newly visible to each generation. The Church is a community which fulfills hopes; a community for our times, a community with a universal vision and an historically important mission; above all, the Church is a community of God.

In the Church, according to Luke, we are baptized into a new corporate life. We must constantly intensify our awareness of this, and live as parts of this ecclesial reality. For us, as for the early Christians, salvation is found in a community based on faith. We are in process of becoming Church and must live out our call each day in fidelity to Word and Spirit. Church is more an asceticism in which we live than a place to be entered.

The Church is structured for the enabling of the Spirit, but leaders are valuable when and if they embody the ecclesiology of the day. Within the Church we all have varied responsibilities and lifestyles, but, like the seven deacons, no matter the task assigned, our prime responsibility is to the Word. Moreover, Luke's pluralistic presentation has important spiritual challenges in the area of ecumenism.

Our life today in the Church requires deep sharing and ongoing conversion. This happens in the heart of the Church, for conversion means to be Church. Life now, as in Luke's time, means prayer, sharing poverty, and joy. These are not extra qualities, but essential. They recreate us as the Church Luke speaks of; they make us credible.

Chapter Six
THE CALL TO DISCIPLESHIP

Jesus said to all: "Whoever wishes to be my follower must deny his very self, take up his cross each day, and follow in my steps." (Lk 9:23)

Matthew restricts the use of the word "disciple" to the Twelve close associates of Jesus. Luke, however, uses the word for a much larger audience. While "disciple" is still distinct from "the crowd," Luke applies it broadly to all believers.[1] Even during the time of Jesus' ministry, however, the disciples live within a hierarchical arrangement dominated by the actual Twelve.

In the Third Gospel, this large group of disciples follows Jesus wherever he goes. He is their Lord, they his servants. They travel with Jesus throughout his ministry, and standing by him in his time of suffering (Lk 22:49). No disciple ever leaves Jesus' presence except at his command.[2] Later, Jesus must leave this group in Gethsemane. They have journeyed with him, stood by, and stayed with him, and Luke now describes Jesus' withdrawal with a word which portrays Jesus as tearing himself away from his close friends.[3]

Luke is the only New Testament writer to apply the term "disciple" in the period following the resurrection. Other New Testament writings use it only to describe followers of the earthly Jesus. In Luke, however, even after Easter, we still have "disciples" who now follow the Way in the Church (Acts 9:2). They remain in the local Church, living the life they understand Jesus to want from them. They only leave the Church to go on mission when expressly commissioned to do so.

Teachings on discipleship are extensive in Luke's Gospel. In Acts, discipleship is centered on living the community life of the Church (as we saw in the last chapter); the special call of the disciple is always a call to ministry. The major teachings on discipleship in Acts are contained in the many solemn commissioning accounts.

This chapter considers first the call of the disciples to commit themselves to Jesus. Secondly, it examines Luke's special notion of discipleship as a following of the Lord along the way of life. Thirdly, it focuses on Luke's presentation of Jesus' teaching on discipleship in the Third Gospel. Fourthly, it deals with discipleship in the Church as seen in Acts. Finally, since "today" is a characteristic emphasis of Luke, we shall reflect on his concerns for discipleship today

The Call Of The Disciple

Call accounts. There are four major call scenes in the gospel of Luke. The first is the call of Mary to cooperate with God's plan (Lk 1:26-38). The remaining three are explicit calls to discipleship: the call of the first disciples (Lk 5:1-11), the call and mission of the Twelve (Lk 6:12-16; and 9:1-6), and the call and mission of the seventy-two (Lk 10:1-20). In each of these four calls we find five common themes; these can be understood as Luke's theological requirements for discipleship. In each call, the initiative is the Lord's; no one asks to be his disciple (Lk 1:26-28; 5:1-4; 9:1; 10:1-3). Secondly, discipleship requires a reform and new direction to life (Lk 1:38; 5:8; the reform for the accounts of the Twelve and the seventy-two is implicit in Lk 5:1-11). Part of this required reform is detachment (Lk 1:34; 5:11; 9:3; 10:4). The fourth common component of discipleship is mission or ministry, and in each call disciples are committed mission (Lk 1:31; 5:10; 9:2; 10:9). Finally, each disciple is called to show faith in the Lord who calls and to be baptized in his name (Lk 1:37-38, 45; 5:5; for the Twelve it is implicit in 5:5; 10:20).

Four other scenes complement the above. These are partial accounts stressing the initiative of the Lord and the need for detachment: the call of Levi (Lk 5:27-32), the general call to discipleship (Lk 14:25-35), the challenge to the rich young man (Lk 18:18-30), and the call to Zacchaeus (Lk 19:1-10).

Calls to discipleship continue in the post-resurrection period and are frequently found in the sermons in Acts. In a selection of the more developed accounts, we find still present the five characteristics of Luke's theology of discipleship. These are:

Peter's first discourse and call to the crowds (Acts 2:14-39); his second sermon, interrupted by the temple guards (Acts 3:11-26); the call of Paul (Acts 9:1-22); Peter's call to Cornelius (Acts 10:1-48); and, finally, Paul's sermon in Pisidian Antioch (Acts 13:16-41). The initiative, previously shown by Jesus, is now identified in either the miracles and wonders of God, which arouse the participants to awe and fear (Acts 2:1-13; 3:1-10; 9:3-9; 10:1-8), or in the dedicated initiative of ministers of the early Church (Acts 2:14; 3:11-12; 9:10-16; 10:9-23; 13:16). The challenge to reform of life is always present (Acts 2:38; 3:19; in Paul's case it is evident in the contrast given by Luke). The theme of detachment is implied in their call to the baptism, to the symbolic stripping of oneself and commitment to the Church (Acts 2:38; 10:47-48). The fourth component of discipleship, mission, is seen in the reception of the Holy Spirit, which in Acts is the guide and inspirer of the Church's ministry (Acts 2:38; 9:17; 10:44-46; the other two call accounts are interrupted by temple guards or the crowd). Faith, the final component, is presented in each account. In Acts, faith means acceptance of the *kerygma* and belief in the centrality of Jesus Christ to history, life, and salvation (Acts 2:22-36; 3:12-26; 9:20; 10:34-43; 13:16-41). The many other partial calls of Acts contain one or more of these, but no other requirements are introduced.

Divine initiative. In Luke-Acts no one earns discipleship. In fact, the two best candidates (by human standards), the faithful and observant religious leader (Lk 18:9-14) and the devout and morally upright young man (Lk 18:18-30), are given as examples of people not ready for the Lord's call. Significantly, Luke places these episodes on each side of Jesus' meeting with the little children, reminding us that "The reign of God belongs to such as these" (Lk 18:17).

In the gospel, Jesus chooses whom he wants. The initiative of God is also the predominant element in any calls through the Church in Acts. The calls of the Ethiopian, of Paul, and of Cornelius are preceded by divine interventions. On other occasions, when the ministers of the Church are working hard to win over people to Christ, we are told that the initiative of God went before them to prepare the hearts of the recipients (Acts 13:48; 16:14). The missionaries themselves are aware that, as they work, the Lord "confirmed the message with his grace" (Acts 14:3).

Paul sees his whole ministry as "bearing witness to the gospel of God's grace" (Acts 20:24, 32), and Peter, speaking of the Gentiles' entry into the Church, stressed divine grace and initiative in all calls: "Our belief is. . . that we are saved by the favor of the Lord Jesus and so are they" (Acts 15:11). Although on occasions it seems that people invite Jesus into their lives (Lk 24:28-29), they see eventually that Jesus is the host, they the guests at his invitation (Lk 24:30).

Conversion. The preparatory ministry of John the Baptist leads to conversion (Lk 1:16-17). Jesus himself said: "I have not come to invite the self-righteous to a change of heart, but sinners" (Lk 5:32). When a woman spoke in praise of Jesus' mother, he took occasion to emphasize the greater relationship based on true and obedient conversion to his word (Lk 11:27-28). Jesus then reminded the crowd that when Jonah challenged Nineveh, "they reformed, but you have a greater than Jonah here" (Lk 11:32). Earlier, Jesus had condemned Chorazin, Bethsaida, and Capernaum because they had shown no conversion (Lk 10:13-15) On another occasion, when the crowd lamented Pilate's killing of some Galileans, Jesus replied: "I tell you, you will all come to the same end unless you reform" (Lk 13:3-5). His entire ministry was a challenge to conversion, and his last words to his disciples were "penance for the remission of sins is to be preached to all the nations" (Lk 24:47).[4]

The concepts of repentance and conversion are of particular interest to Luke.[5] Our commitment to God in Jesus involves two phases: a turning away from sin and towards God. For the former, negative part, Luke generally uses "repentance;" for the latter, complete change of life-direction, he uses "conversion."

True conversion is the result of faith in Jesus. It implies turning one's back on previous lifestyles and journeying towards the Lord. This return to the Lord is a life commitment, never partial or suspended (Lk 11:24-26). True conversion is, in some ways, indistinguishable from discipleship.

The essence of true conversion in Luke is best seen in his systematic expositions in Acts.[6] There, the Church's missionary preaching consistently presents four elements of true conversion. First, conversion is always to the person of Jesus, not to abstract truths (Acts 9:35, 42; 11:21, 24). It therefore calls for the development of a relationship uniting the individual to God and implying a practical change of lifestyle. Conversion means becoming a follower of the Way (Acts 9:2; 18:25-26; 19:9, 23). Secondly, the point of departure for conversion is the awareness of sin in life. No matter the audience, the early ministers always arouse a sense of sin and guilt, a need for the healing forgiveness heralded by the Good News (Acts 2:37; 3:13-14; 4:10-11; 8:20-22; 10:43). Thirdly, all conversion is stimulated by the realization that the all-powerful God is actively involved in our lives, in Christ's resurrection, in miracles, or deep within the hearts of all (Acts 2:24-32; 4:29-30, 33; 11:18). This becomes a determining motive for conversion. The fourth element of conversion is the realization that the Lord to whom we are called will return as our judge (Acts 17:30-31). However, he will be the universal judge, evaluating the conduct of his people, the Church.

The call to discipleship in Luke starts with repentance and grows through conversion. Motivated by a sense of sin in our lives, by the realization that the Lord is our judge, and by belief that God is actively interested in our lives, we, as disciples, turn our backs on evil and journey with the Lord to God.

Detachment and ministry. A third component of the call accounts is detachment, ritually celebrated in baptismal immersion. Because we have dealt with poverty and detachment already, however, the reader is referred to that section. Note, the importance of Luke's connection of mission and ministry with all discipleship: in Luke, every disciple is a disciple/minister, not in the sense of a hierarchical minister but in that of ministry of one kind or another being a vital and essential part of any committed disciple's life. However, since these topics are dealt with elsewhere in the book, we shall not repeat them here.

Faith. The fifth component of the call to discipleship is faith in the Lord Jesus. Jesus values faith highly, and when he finds it, attributes to it salvation, spiritual or material. "Your faith has been your salvation" (Lk 17:19; also 5:20; 8:48-50; 18:42). When the disciples are afraid because of the storm, Jesus challenges them with "Where is your faith?" (Lk 8:25), a criticism he will repeat to the two disciples on the way to Emmaus (Lk 24:25). During Jesus' ministry the disciples ask, "Lord, increase our faith" (Lk 17:5), and before the passion, Jesus says to Peter, "I have prayed for you that your faith may never fail" (Lk 22:32). In sadness, Jesus says, "When the Son of Man comes, will he find any faith?"

(Lk 18:8). Even in these references, Luke modifies his sources. Luke's understanding is specific and clear. Belief is a once-and-for-all event, and believing is identical with becoming a Christian.[7] In Luke the believer is the disciple (Acts 6:7; 14:22; 18:27), the object of faith is Jesus (Acts 9:42; 11:17; 14:23; 16:31; 20:21; 22:19; 24:24). Faith is the total personal redirection of life to Jesus and his new values. It is a commitment that touches the depth of one's being and personality and, once made, the believer's faith is permanent, though always capable of increase (Lk 17:5; Acts 16:5) or threat from sin (Lk 22:32). In its origins, faith is linked to grace as a free and unearned gift (Lk 1:30, 45; Acts 15:11), but a person fails when the gift is not accepted (Lk 1:13, 20). Faith purifies our hearts (Acts 15:9), bringing forgiveness (Lk 5:20; 7:50; Acts 26:18) and salvation (Lk 17:19).

Faith, once received, must be fostered lest the believer "fall away in time of temptation" (Lk 8:13). The believer must constantly "hear the word in a spirit of openness, retain it, and bear fruit through perseverance" (Lk 8:15). He must also "hear the word of God and act upon it" (Lk 8:21).

Persons who respond to the gracious initiative of God, repenting and reforming their lives, show the genuineness of their repentance by detachment and total conversion to the Lord. This conversion begins in life-directed faith, is sealed in baptism, and manifested in discipleship.

The Following of Christ

Followers of the Way. In Luke, the word "follow" is reserved for the disciple's necessary attitude to Jesus. The disciple follows Jesus wherever he goes, never leaving him, except at his command, and then only to return when the mission is accomplished. In Luke, neither John the Baptist nor the apostles have any followers; Jesus alone is to be followed.[8]

In Luke-Acts, the teachings on following Jesus take place during a series of journeys in which the disciples take part, and the reader/disciple is invited to join. Following Jesus in the journey of life becomes so crucial for the understanding of discipleship that Luke eventually refers to the disciples as followers of the Way (Acts 9:2; 18:25-26; 19:9, 23; 22:4; 24:14, 22).

The concept of the "Way of the Lord" is already present in the Old Testament. Together with the Hellenistic interest in the journeys of great heros, this no doubt influenced Luke. In Luke-Acts we find a series of journeys, each with its own teachings for the disciples and followers of the Way: the journey of Mary to visit Elizabeth (Lk 1:39-56), the visit of Joseph and Mary to Bethlehem (Lk 2:1-20), and their journeys to Jerusalem for the purification (Lk 2:22-40) and Passover (Lk 2:41-52).

The whole of Jesus' public ministry is understood by Luke as the Way of the Lord. John heralds the beginnings of the journey (Acts 13:24), and Jesus speaks of the ending exodus (Lk 9:31). After the Transfiguration, the great journey to Jerusalem begins (we shall look at it in more detail later) (Lk 9:51), and following the resurrection, there is the journey to Emmaus (Lk 24:13-35). In the Acts we have the four journeys of Paul, the journeys of Philip, and the fact that the disciples see themselves as followers of the Way. Moreover, when Judas' successor is chosen, he must be a person who shared the company of those who journeyed with Jesus (Acts 1:21). In the first Pentecost sermon, Peter, wanting to tell the crowd who Jesus is, quotes the psalm: "David says of him...you have shown me the paths of life" (Acts 2:25-28).

Journey to Jerusalem. In these Lucan journeys the believer accompanies the Lord, learning what discipleship means. Since this is best seen in the journey to Jerusalem (Lk 9:51 - 19:27), which shows Luke's particular concerns, method, vision, and spirituality, we shall now consider it in a little more detail.

We have seen that the central section of the Third Gospel is presented as a comprehensive ministry, paralleling the earlier ministry of Jesus in Galilee. This section (Lk 9:51 - 19:27; some commentators would extend it to 19:44), presented in the form of a journey to Jerusalem, begins solemnly, stating that Jesus "firmly resolved to proceed toward Jerusalem, and sent messengers on ahead of him" (Lk 9:51). A series of Lucan editorial inserts follows, reinforcing the fact that Jesus and his disciples are "making their way along" (Lk 9:57). We read that Jesus sends seventy-two "in pairs before him to every town and place he intended to visit" (Lk 10:1). "On their journey Jesus entered a village" (Lk 10:38), and later "He went through cities and towns teaching - all the while making his way toward Jerusalem" (Lk 13:22). To a well-intentioned Pharisee who tried to prevent harm to Jesus, he replied, "I must proceed on course today" (Lk 13:33).[9]

At the beginning of this section is a fine example of "echo-diction": the constant repetition of a word to stress the author's aim. The word "follow" is repeated (Lk 9:57, 59, 61), emphasizing to disciple and reader the following of the Lord. Luke even pictorially presents Jesus journeying and walking ahead of his following disciples (Lk 9:57; 14:25).

Mark has traces of a significant journey of Jesus to Jerusalem (Mk 10:17, 32), but in Luke this theme is developed into a comprehensive ministry, with very little source material and only a few skillfully inserted editorial modifications. "This most characteristic journey motif is a piece of deliberate editorial work."[10]

Interpretations of the journey narrative. Different interpretations of the journey narrative have been offered. There have always been supporters of literal historical interpretations. If not original, it is suggested that the present form is a combination of several journeys of Jesus. Others emphasize the literary interests of Luke, paralleling this with the journeys of Hellenistic heros. The present form is thus seen as Luke's literary means of presenting much of his non-Marcan material. The third possibility is that Luke's interests are primarily theological and spiritual. He may be able to root the material of this section, as elsewhere, in historical events and undoubtedly wants to present his material in a format appealing to his Gentile audience, but his prime interests are theological and spiritual.

In this section, Jesus returns to places he has been to before, but now travels in a different way. He travels to Jerusalem (Lk 9:51; 13:22, 33; 17:11; 19:28) and to what awaits him there (Lk 9:22, 43-44; 13:33; 18:31-33), with determination and awareness (Lk 9:51; 13:33). H. Conzelmann has suggested that the journey presents "a stage of Christological development."[11] Jesus' awareness of his need to suffer is portrayed in this journey to suffering. Thus, the journey, in which the disciples are called to follow the Lord, is progressive to the passion. The whole purpose of the journey is presented again very briefly in the incident of Simon following Jesus and carrying the cross (Lk 23:26, 55). The journey is to salvation, and the teaching is the means. Jesus journeys to Jerusalem to achieve our salvation through the cross and resurrection, and the disciple is challenged to realize and integrate this into life (Lk 9:23-25, 46-48; 18:26-29; each challenge is associated with a passion prediction).

In many ways this journey of the disciples with Jesus is a training for them in pastoral and spiritual theology. No sooner has the journey begun (Lk 9:51) than James and John want to bring down fire on a non-accepting Samaritan town (Lk 9:54-55). But Jesus "turned towards them only to reprimand them," a warning to missionaries not to condemn those who do not accept the message. Throughout this journey, discipleship and ministry are frequently connected. The entire section begins with an introduction, a list of requirements for the apostle, and the mission of the seventy-two (Lk 9:51 - 10:20). These three closely-related parts are possibly deliberately integrated by Luke for theological reasons. Jesus sends disciples ahead to prepare the way (Lk 9:51-52), and sends the seventy-two with a similar commission (Lk 10:1-20). Luke, by his personal editing, focuses the disciples' attention on the eventual mission to the Gentiles (Lk 13:22-30; 17:11-19; 19:11-27).[12] This is the future Way of the Lord. Throughout this section the Lucan theme of joy is also especially evident. "In the travel narrative. . . there are 20 references to joy and 10 pericopes in which this theme is basic."[13] Joy must permeate even the paschal dedication required of the disciple/minister who must remain with Jesus at all times. This journey, formative for the disciple, is in some way symbolic of the mission of the whole Church. To be part of the Church is to be called to a dangerous and adventurous journey.[14]

Journeys of the Church. Luke's theme of journey or Way is continued in Acts' description of the life of the Church. In the Third Gospel, people were called to accept Jesus as he journeyed into their lives. In the time of the Church, people are called to accept the Word of the Lord when brought through the journeys of the Church. The proclaiming of the Way of the Lord is now the Church's mission to the ends of the earth.[15] This is best seen in the great missionary journeys of Paul, whose second and third journeys, modeled on the format of Jesus' gospel journey, show in yet another way that the Church journeys as Jesus did.[16] In these journeys of the Church, the Holy Spirit guides the way (Acts 8:29; 10:19; 11:12; 13:4; 16:6-10; 20:22).

Besides Paul's great journeys with their call to the Word, there are other smaller, significant journeys for the disciple/ministers of the Church. Jesus joins two disciples in their journey to Emmaus, and, as they share the crucial questions of the day, they recognize Jesus in scripture, fellowship, and the breaking of bread (Lk 24:13-35). This journey gives us "a complete catechesis, a tiny summary of the whole gospel."[17] The message comes alive as the disciples journey with Jesus. Later, the Ethiopian will encounter Jesus' word in Philip, minister of the Church (Acts 8:26-40). Elsewhere, Peter's journey to Cornelius will be the disciple/minister's journey to the realization of God's plan for universal salvation (Acts 10).

Paul eventually utters the words which challenge any disciple/minister of the Way: "I put no value on my life if only I can finish my race and complete the service to which I have been assigned by the Lord Jesus" (Acts 20:24). Luke presents the Church's task as contining the Lord's journey. The disciple, called through conversion to follow the Lord, journeys with him in life and continues to journey with Jesus in the Church.

Discipleship in Luke

In Luke's gospel no teaching is specifically addressed to the disciples by the earthly Lord anywhere, except during the travel narrative of the journey to Jerusalem. Needless to say, the disciples are presumed to be present during all of Jesus' public preaching, but during the journey to Jerusalem — also an apprenticeship for the disciple/minister — there is a series of teachings addressed exclusively to the disciples. Four themes run through this section: prayer, warnings for the minister, the need for totality of self-gift, and practical pastoral needs for disciples in ministry.

Prayer (Lk 11:1-13; 18:1-8). The theme of prayer is of particular interest to Luke and is dealt with more frequently by him than by any other New Testament writer. The Lucan Jesus is a person of prayer (Lk 5:16; 10:21-22; 22:32, 41-45), and his ministry arouses prayer in others (Lk 5:25-26; 7:16; 13:13). Luke portrays Jesus at prayer before every important step of his ministry (Lk 3:21; 6:12; 9:18, 28; 11:1; 22:41). Moreover, all these passages except the last, Gethsemane, are specific to the third evangelist. Luke's Jesus also teaches prayer, telling his audience to "pray for those who maltreat you" (Lk 6:28), to "ask the harvest-master to send workers to his harvest" (Lk 10:2), and to "pray constantly for the strength to escape whatever is in prospect" (Lk 21:36). Jesus' principle teachings on prayer are, however, reserved for the disciples. Jesus makes two presentations on prayer in the journey section.

The first of these is a small treatise on prayer in three parts: how to pray, the need for persistence in prayer, and confidence in prayer. The disciples have seen how important prayer is for Jesus and, seeing him at prayer (Lk 11:1), approach him and ask him to teach them. The result is the "Our Father." Both the context and the shorter version of Luke are probably more historically accurate. This disciple's prayer stresses the glory and Fatherhood of God, hope for the messianic kingdom and its benefits, and sorrow and forgiveness. Jesus tells the disciples that in their prayer they ought to call God "Father," up to this point a title original and exclusive to Jesus. They, too, may now share this special and intimate relationship. The disciple looking to God as his Father addresses two petitions to him. The passive form suggests that the disciple/minister is asked to acknowledge that the Father sanctifies his own name and spreads his own kingdom. Jesus' words thus become both prayer and warning to the disciple that his or her contributions amount to nothing (Lk 17:10). The whole prayer, in the plural throughout, reminds that prayer must always be communitarian and ecclesial. The disciple prays for three needs of the Church: a share in the bread of tomorrow's eschatological banquet, forgiveness of sins, and protection from the final trial of evil. All three requests are eschatological and refer to the life and requirements necessary for participation in the eschatological community.[18] The disciple's only action in the prayer is forgiveness. It is suggested that universal forgiveness and reconciliation are the necessary attitudes in this time of compassion and salvation.

The short parable which follows (Lk 11:5-8), addressed to the disciples, encourages them to make their simple and confident requests to the Lord with insistence. This parable is found only in Luke. The second short parable, found in the Sermon on the Mount in Matthew, here applies to the disciples (Lk 11:9-13). It is introduced with a solemn claim to authority by Jesus, who urges the disciples to ask and seek continually for what they need.[19] The major teaching is that the disciples should be confident that God will answer their prayer. God's answer to ecclesial prayer is to bestow his Spirit, in Luke the director and guide of the Church's ministry.

The second teaching on prayer for the disciples comes later in the journey (Lk 18:1-8). This parable, again special to Luke, is similar to the previous Lucan parable (Lk 11:5-8), as is the teaching for the disciples: pray at all times with perseverance and insistence. It is a parable which, while addressed to the disciples, probably has Luke's own persecuted Church in mind. They, like the disciples, are urged always to hope and pray with confidence for the coming redemption, realizing that God in his own time will avenge injustice. This teaching of Jesus is followed with the parable on humility in prayer, at which the disciples could well have been present (Lk 18:9-14).

The disciple's prayer is above all for the glorification of the Father and must prepare us for the end. It should be approached frequently, with insistence and confidence that the Father's Spirit will always be given.

Warnings for the disciple/minister (Lk 12:1-53). This section begins with an interesting Lucan touch. Although thousands crowd around Jesus, he still has an aside for his close disciples. Their training continues "in the field" of missionary work. The material in this section agrees in general with the other synoptics. Luke, however, has combined it, placed it here, and directed it to the disciples. More particularly, he is interested in presenting Jesus' warnings for the disciple/minister to Church leaders of his time, especially those of his own Church.

His first warning is again hypocrisy (Lk 12:1-3). The true disposition of the disciple cannot remain hidden, for eventually everything comes to light. It seems that Jesus here challenges partial and superficial commitments. The disciple must accept Jesus totally.

In the second small incident (Lk 12:4-7) — the only one in the synoptics in which Jesus addresses the disciples as his "friends" — he warns them against fear of physical suffering and persecution, possibly in the contexts of their discipleship and ministry. We must be fearless in our witness to the Lord. In all of life's problems we should avoid weakening in faith, for God is our judge; and we should be confident and encouraged if persecuted, for God is a provident and compassionate Father.

Jesus' third admonition for his disciples is against blasphemy (Lk 12:8-12). The disciple who courageously acknowledges Jesus will later be recognized by him and, in times of trial, aided by God and his Holy Spirit. This reassurance is for the disciple who can respond to the inspiration and presence of the Spirit. Those, however, who in times of persecution refuse this influence, must face the rejection of his Holy Spirit. It has been suggested that Luke is here concerned about apostasy in his own community.[20]

After receiving from the crowd a question motivated by greed (Lk 12:13-15) and responding with the exclusively Lucan parable on the rich fool (Lk 12:16-21), Jesus turns to his disciples to warn them about attachment. He has spoken strongly against greed, avarice, and the irreligious attitudes of the rich fool. Now he highlights for the disciples the real issues involved in attachment. In the last analysis they are a denial of God's providential care of us. Jesus wants disciples who are not constantly anxious, but who trust in Providence and prefer quality of life rather than quantities of possessions. The dedicated disciple must be single-minded in his or her search for the Kingdom and its extension.

There follows a collection of teachings on readiness for the Lord's return (Lk 12:35-53). No new audience has been named, and we can presume that he still speaks to the disciples. Although directed to the disciples in general, there do seem to be diferences between the first part (Lk 12:35-40) and the second (Lk 12:41-53). The former urgently emphasizes a disciple's vigilant readiness for the Lord's return. Since some of Luke's own Church may have lost interest in the Second Coming, this could have been tailored for them. The second part emphasizes not vigilance, but the faith needed in Church leaders awaiting the Lord. They will be judged according to their faithfulness to the Church and its needs during Jesus' absence. "More will be asked of a man to whom more has been entrusted" (Lk 12:48).

Discipleship and total commitment (Lk 14:25-30; 17:22-37; 18:28-33). Jesus' expectations when calling the first disciples (Lk 5:1-11) and Levi (Lk 5:27-28) indicate his desire for total response. Before he begins the journey to Jerusalem, Jesus says to all: "Whoever wishes to be my follower must deny his very self, take up his cross each day, and follow in my steps" (Lk 9:23). Later he gives practical examples of this (Lk 9:57-62). He shows the rich young man that his expectations of a disciple are rigorous (Lk 18:22), and, for all, he describes what to expect (Lk 21:10-19).

Twice during the journey Jesus states the demands of discipleship. Having just spoken of the messianic meal, Jesus tells those disciples who hope to be there that there must be no half-heartedness in their commitment (Lk 14:25-30): discipleship and commitment have priority over family, possessions, and life itself. This is a difficult challenge, not to be undertaken without full awareness of what it implies. Here Luke gives us two parables exclusive to him which warn against rash and hasty commitments. Luke ends by pointing out that: "A fully sacrificing disciple is like salt and is useful for society to preserve and purify and add flavor to it. But a half committed one is like tasteless salt which is useless for any purpose and is thrown out like rubbish."[21] This demanding teaching is repeated (Lk 18:28-30) when Jesus assures Peter that his fidelity to this call will be generously rewarded.

The disciple dedicated to the Lord must live as if the Lord were returning any moment. Just before this account (Lk 17:22-37), Jesus tells a Pharisee who had been asking for signs, that there will be none. There will be no time to prepare for the Lord's return. Rather, the disciple must live in preparedness, so that when the Lord chooses to come, the disciple will neither hesitate nor turn back. His decision during life must always be for the Lord. The single-minded dedication of a lifetime is the disciple's true preparation. Even in this description of the end, Luke skillfully inserts the notion that the Son, returning as judge, must first suffer and be rejected (Lk 17:25). This combination of two Christological components, Jesus as Son of Man and Jesus as the Suffering Servant, must then be reflected in the life of the disciple (Lk 17:33). Jesus later repeats this thought (Lk 18:31-33), showing again the total commitment he expects. This will be required of the disciples, but, unfortunately, they again fail to understand.

Pastoral needs for the disciple/minister (Lk 16:1-8; 17:1-10; 18:15-17). Of the many teachings of this section, Luke thought one series particularly suitable for the disciples. The first is the unusual story of the crafty manager who, having been fired by the owner, reduces the accounts of his master's debtors (Lk 16:1-8). In context, this story is part of a collection on the correct use of money. However, when applied to the disciples by Jesus, it highlights the manager's initiative and foresight. The enterprising manager is also, in his dedication, an example of one who achieves and secures his own goals. In using this story, Jesus "must surely also wish that his disciples would show as much resourcefulness in God's business as men of the world do in their own affairs."[22] The fact that this story is exclusive to Luke might tell us something about the disciples of his day, who needed challenging in initiative and dedication to their own real self-interests in Christ.

After completing the section on the correct use of money, Luke directs to the disciples four teachings found scattered in the other synoptics (Lk 17:1-10). The first piece of pastoral advice for the disciple is to avoid giving scandal. Those who give scandal to the little ones of the Church could well be Church leaders of Luke's day. They are told to beware of themselves in this, to avoid all scandal, even the unintended.

There follows a warning to disciples of all generations to challenge the wrongdoer in the Church. In doing so, however, the disciple must never be arrogant or self-righteous, but always show a spirit of forgiveness and reconciliation to those who repent.

A factor which further limits the effectiveness of the disciple as an instrument of the Lord is weak faith; here, again, Jesus challenges the disciples.

The final saying of Jesus recorded in this section is the reminder that disciples must take no self-satisfaction in their work. All servants of the Lord are poor and empty, since he is the master, the source of all effectiveness in the work of the Church. This theme is developed later when Luke returns to the Marcan outline (Lk 18:15-17). Here, Jesus again stresses that no one earns life in the kingdom. Before this short story is the parable of the Pharisee and the publican (Lk 18:9-15), and after it the story of the rich young man (Lk 18:18-30). Both are examples of self-righteousness in which the protagonist thinks he is earning salvation. Jesus points out the children in this scene, saying, "The reign of God belongs to such as these" (Lk 18:16). It is interesting that where Matthew has Jesus rebuke the disciples for scolding the children, Luke omits it, thus preserving a constant, positive relationship between the disciples and their Lord.

Jesus' ongoing teaching on discipleship in Acts. We have already seen that, for Luke, disciples are the believers of all Christian communities who have rooted their lives in Jesus (Acts 6:7; 14:22; 18:27). In Acts, discipleship is living as Jesus taught in this time of waiting. The disciples' lives are given to the Lord and are under his direction. Baptism, seen in Acts as the sealing of this commitment, has a two-fold form and emphasis. We are told that disciples are baptised "in the name of the Lord Jesus" (Acts 2:38; 10:48), and sometimes that baptism is "for the purpose of the Lord Jesus" (Acts 8:16; 19:5; Greek preposition "eis").

Since ministry is a prime concern of Luke's, the disciple is also involved in ministry. For Luke, ministry follows on baptism and is an intimate part of discipleship. Later, the community of ministers is structured to facilitate response to the Spirit. However, hierarchical ministries are secondary, developed to facilitate the more fundamental ecclesial ministry resulting from the initial commitment to Jesus. Discipleship in Acts means continuing to live as Jesus taught and being open to Jesus' further calls and direction.

The early Christians lived out the teachings of Jesus in their local communities. They responded by living as the eschatological community, a Church of God with hope, relevance, vision, and mission; as a Church of salvation, based on the Word and the Spirit and growing paschally; and as a prayerful, sharing, poor, and joyful Church. Their commitment as disciples is to live ecclesially, since this is seen as the embodiment of Jesus' teachings. We have already seen how important the life of the Church is in Acts. Much of the disciple's ministry and commitment are shown in service to the Church itself.

Discipleship has a second thrust in Acts. Jesus' teaching on discipleship does not end after his death. Directly or indirectly, the Risen Lord visits the disciples of the Churches to give them specific directions in discipleship and ministry. In Acts alone are nineteen accounts of divine interventions, the purpose of which is to commission disciples for specific tasks. These, together with two such episodes in the last chapter of the Third Gospel, give us a total of twenty-one commission accounts in the post-Easter period.[23]

Commissions are given to the women at the tomb, the Eleven, the apostles, Philip, Paul, Ananias, Cornelius, Peter, and prophet leaders of the Antiochean Church. We read of three interventions in Peter's life, nine in Paul's. The women at the tomb are left to take their own initiative; the Eleven are given the Church's program of action to the ends of the earth; the apostles are told to preach with courage; Philip is given directions that lead the

Church towards the Gentile world; Ananias is told what to do with Paul; Cornelius is directed to send for Peter; the prophets of Antioch are inspired to designate Paul and Barnabas for ministry; Peter is told to begin admitting Gentiles into the Church, and later given directions on escaping from prison; Paul is sent to Ananias, urged to go to Macedonia, encouraged to preach fearlessly, and told on other occasions to leave Jerusalem for Rome to appeal to the Emperor. Sometimes the directions are specific and personal; on other occasions they are major directives for the development of the Church's mission. The disciples and the whole Church continue to learn from the Lord. Their obedient response to his call and commission is their continuing discipleship in the period of the Church.

In this section we have seen some of the teachings which Luke considered particularly appropriate for Jesus' disciples. The teachings are given while the disciples follow the Lord to Jerusalem and what awaits him there. Called to develop a life of prayer with perseverance and confidence, the disciples are warned against hypocrisy, fear, blasphemy, attachment, and lack of vigilance. The disciples' commitment must be total, having priority over family, possessions, and life itself. The disciples must live each day as if the Lord's return is imminent. In pastoral service the disciples must show initiative and single-minded dedication, avoid scandal, challenge the wrongdoer, and grow in faith and forgiveness. Finally, the disciples must realize at all times that life and salvation are gift and grace, and cannot be personally earned or ministerially achieved. The Lord's teachings are lived out ecclesially, complemented by openness to the ongoing inspiration and commissions of the Lord.

In this chapter on discipleship we have seen the common characteristics of Lucan call accounts: the call is from God and demands conversion, detachment, ministry, and faith. The disciple is, above all, called to follow Jesus to Jerusalem. During the journey the Lord teaches his disciples, giving them guidance in prayer, warning them what to avoid, challenging them to total commitment, and dealing with practical pastoral needs. In Acts, discipleship is seen in living-as-Church and being open to personal commissions from the Lord. This teaching on discipleship is not a historical presentation alone. Rooted in history, it is also a proclamation to today's disciples.

Discipleship Today

We have noted that Luke seems to direct his teaching on discipleship to the needs of his own Church. Luke's work is not history alone, but history at the service of *kerygma*. The main issue is to proclaim the Word to concrete circumstances. He is rooted in the past, but brings the challenge of that past fresh to each situation. In Luke-Acts we are presented with a series of new beginnings in which the disciple/reader is eventually caught up. More than any other New Testament writer, Luke stresses the words "now" and "today": now is the time, today is special. The disciple is called again in these new beginnings, reminded that no matter the date in history, today and now is the time for response.

New beginnings. Luke-Acts creates an atmosphere of newness, stating over and over again that a new era now begins, and we are a part of it. A series of new beginnings punctuates the presentation: the birth of Jesus and the infancy narratives end one age (Lk 2:29-32), joyfully announcing a new age beginning for all (Lk 1:43-44, 50, 55, 67-79; 2:38). The creative Spirit intervenes (Lk 1:35) and the hoped-for Savior is born (Lk 2:11). It is to Luke's credit that this brings a new beginning to every Christmas.

For readers steeped in the Old Testament (and some of Luke's readers would be), the account of Jesus' baptism is a creation story heralding the new era beginning for us (Lk 3:21-22). The supper, too, ends one era and brings in a new beginning (Lk 22:16, 20). The passion and death are the new beginning of the kingdom, heralded on the eve (Lk 22:16) and established in the resurrection (Acts 1:3).

The resurrection is the great new beginning, and each of the appearances of the Risen Lord is on the first day of the week, the day of new creation. This event is the center of history (Lk 24:27), and all the future will take this as its starting point (Lk 24:46-49). In Acts many miracles are understood as manifestations of God's resurrectional power alive in that moment (Acts 4:29-33). These are small resurrections for the churches to see.

Pentecost, too, parallels a creation account (Acts 2:1-4). It is also the reversal of Babel (Acts 2:5-12), the renewal of Sinai, and the beginning of the Jewish nation (Acts 2:32-33). Besides the great Pentecost, several smaller pentecosts herald new beginnings of messianic times for local churches (Acts 8:14-19; 10:44-48; 19:1-7).

Certainly, the birth of this new period in history is recapitulated in the soul of the true disciple of any time.

Now. The call of the disciple to begin anew with Jesus is also stressed by Luke's frequent use of the words "now" and "today." The messianic period begins with Mary's acknowledgement that from now on she is to be called blessed (Lk 1:48). Simeon, a representative of the Old Testament, publically acclaims, "Now, Master, you can dismiss your servant" (Lk 2:29), since the time of salvation is here. Peter is told, "From now on you will be catching men" (Lk 5:10). The great sermon condemns three times those whose consolation is now, those who are full and laugh now, but blesses those who now weep (Lk 6:21, 24-25). Jesus recognizes the conflicts that can arise from the challenge of his message: "From now on a household of five will be divided" (Lk 12:52). Later, Jesus laments over Jerusalem: "If only you would have known the path to peace this day [now]" (Lk 19:42). At the supper, Jesus says he will [now] not drink until the kingdom is set up (Lk 22:18), and adds: "Now, however, the man who has a purse must carry it" (Lk 22:36). Before the Sanhedrin he says: "From now on, the Son of Man will have his seat at the right hand of the Power of God" (Lk 22:69).[24]

The events which luke describes happen again for his audience. "The 'now' of Jesus. . . is the present of Luke's contemporaries," and Luke considers each sacred event of the past "as a message event, that is, as an event that simply cannot be noted objectively and made a fact of history; it is an event one must confront as a listener."[25]

Today. In Luke, the decision for or against the Lord and discipleship is made now, today; the events of our salvation come to each disciple today.[26] We are not merely reading history — we are listening to the proclamation of our salvation. The disciples, listening to Luke, hear that today in David's city a Savior is born (Lk 2:11), that today scripture is fulfilled, the Lord is coming to bring glad tidings, liberty, sight, and release (Lk 4:14-21). Zaccheus becomes each of us listening to the Lord: "I mean to stay at your house today." We know that if we accept discipleship, the Lord will say, "Today salvation has come to this house" (Lk 19:5, 9). Disciples everywhere can identify with the crowd's joyful acclaim: "We have seen incredible things today" (Lk 5:26). It is for all disciples that Jesus journeys today to Jerusalem (Lk 13:32-33; 24:21), and, sadly, the disciples acknowledge that the Lord's words are sometimes even for them: "The cock will not crow today until you have three times denied that you know me" (Lk 22:34). However, the Lord's mercy is ever present, and the disciples trust that other words, too, are meant just for them: "This day you will be with me in paradise" (Lk 23:43).

Luke writes about Jesus' past to challenge men and women to decide now. Today Christ calls us (Lk 19:5, 9), saying "Come along, everything is ready now" (Lk 14:17). He warns, however, that "Whoever wishes to be my follower must deny his very self, take up his cross each day, and follow in my steps" (Lk 9:23).

Chapter Seven
UNIVERSAL CONCERNS

Give, and it shall be given to you. Good measure pressed down, shaken together, running over, will they pour into the fold of your garment. For the measure you measure with will be measured back to you. (Lk 6:38)

We have seen Luke's theological positions relevant to the image of God, the Church, and discipleship. We have also seen that a strong sense of mission is generated by each explanation. The Father, as Sovereign Lord, has a plan for salvation history. This plan, brought to fullness in Jesus, is continued in the mission of the Church. Jesus, ever obedient to his Father's will, is continually present to us in the mission of the Church; and the Spirit, now the power of God, guides and directs the ministry of the Church. The Church is a faith community with an historical mission, and discipleship in Luke is the following of Jesus, being open to the ongoing commissions of the Lord. In Luke we do not see an emphasis on higher righteousness or moral reform, but rather on missionary enterprise and ecclesial ministry. The disciple, called to a participation in the Church's mission (Acts 1:8), in no way achieves salvation through ministry (Lk 17:10). Luke has been accused of holding positions which support salvation by works, but this is not true. He is well aware that salvation comes through faith and is sealed with the gift of the Holy Spirit. The Spirit himself continues the mission of the Church (Acts 1:8; 20:22). The Church's involvement in ministry manifests faithfulness in response to the inspiration and guidance of the Holy Spirit

The mission of the Church is one of universal salvation: salvation of the whole person, of every person. The word "to save," used so frequently by Luke, can mean to heal (Lk 17:19; 18:42), to exorcize (Lk 8:36), to avoid death (Lk 6:9), or to raise from the dead (Lk 8:50). It can also refer to total healing as a result of faith (Lk 7:50; 8:48; 17:19; 18:42). In some cases, physical salvation is a call to belief in the spiritual salvation God offers. Even physical salvation is a call to faith in God, to openness to his saving power. The Church calls all: "Believe in the Lord Jesus and you will be saved" (Acts 16:31). This salvation is total: from the corruption of the times we live in (Acts 2:40), from all forms of illness (Acts 3:4-10), from condemnation (Acts 8:22-24), and from selfish individualism (Acts 2:47). In fact, it is total salvation in Jesus (Acts 2:21; 4:12).

Luke has special concern for the salvation of all and the quality of their lives, including all the underprivileged of his time. He is interested in social justice and the theology of charity to all. His Church, reaching out in peace to the world, is dedicated to the universality of salvation.

The Charter Sermon

After Jesus' baptism and temptations (Lk 3:21 - 4:13), Luke presents his inaugural sermon in the synagogue in Nazareth (Lk 4:14-30). There follow some early manifestations of Jesus' messianic power, both in his teachings (Lk 4:31-32; 4:42-44) and his miracles (Lk 4:33-41; 5:12-26). Luke then documents for us the calls of the first disciples (Lk 5:1-11, 27-32). All this precedes the solemn presentation of the great discourse on the plain. This sermon is the charter sermon for the new religion and is characterized throughout with the universal concerns which Luke sees as essential to Christianity. Like most charters, written after the organization has been in existence for some time, this sermon presupposes knowledge and lived acceptance of the gospel message. The sermon does not itself present a way of salvation, but is rather a synthesis of the new levels of awareness required by the committed disciple. The sermon clarifies that Christianity has a new audience and a new set of values. It demands new attitudes and sets a new goal. It establishes new criteria for religious authenticity and fidelity. This sermon, permeated with concern for the underprivileged and outcast, is a statement of commitment to social justice and reform, fostering outreach to all in peace. It reminds Christianity of its mission of universal salvation.

A new audience for Christianity. Matthew's Sermon on the Mount (Mt chs. 5, 6, 7) is over three times the length of Luke's Sermon on the Plain. The basic teachings in both are the same, but Matthew has expanded his with material from other sermons of Jesus. The final form has been edited into a major confrontation with Judaism. Luke omits material of exclusively Jewish importance, hence of little interest to his Gentile audience (Mt 5:17 - 6:18), and places other teachings elsewhere in his gospel. The result of the two evangelists' differing editorial contributions is to make Matthew's sermon the major collection of Jesus' teachings, a sort of new Sinai experience, while Luke's is more of a charter, highlighting the essential characteristics of the new religion. Luke takes the teaching out of its Jewish milieu, interpreting it for universal application.

In Luke's version, Jesus has spent the night in prayer (Lk 6:12), as he generally does before major events. He then chooses the Twelve, to whom he gives the name and mission of apostles (Lk 6:13). With these Twelve as the foundation of the new Israel, he descends the mountain, and, like Moses surrounded by the twelve tribes, solemnly presents himself to the waiting crowds (Lk 6:17; Ex 19:24; 32:15; 34:29). In Matthew, the audience is the disciples (Mt 5:1-2), whereas in Luke Jesus speaks to the disciples (Lk 6:20) in the hearing of crowds from Judea, Jerusalem, Tyre, and Sidon (Lk 7:1), from throughout Palestine and the neighboring Gentile countries. Among the crowds are the sick and possessed, for whom society could not or would not provide. The new audience of Luke's sermon represents the new audience of Christianity: people in need, the helpless and abandoned, Jews and Gentiles alike, anyone who truly longs to be healed, people who long even now to touch Jesus, convinced of his power to cure and to save (Lk 6:19).

New values. Jesus speaks to his disciples in the hearing of the crowd, outlining the new values of the kingdom (Lk 6:20-26). The four beatitudes in Luke are probably Jesus' original four, to which Matthew added. Jesus reverses the accepted values of society, showing what he considers necessary for life in the kingdom. Luke's presentation, more direct, is in the second person and speaks of conditions "now." He contrasts the accepted values of a materially-minded world with the value system of

God. He calls "blessed" those who are materially poor, who lack the necessities of life, whose oppressed lives are joyless, and who are outcasts of society. He does not say that these qualities are necessary to enter the kingdom, but that those in these conditions more readily open to God. The sick and troubled long for the saving power of Jesus (Lk 6:18-19). Jesus does not proclaim the blessedness of misfortune, but the desirability of attitudes which can result from the awareness of helplessness and need in such situations. To the oppressed of society, the have-nots, those who constantly weep at their distress, and those whose faith is mocked by society, Jesus brings glad tidings of liberty, healing, and release (Lk 4:18).

Luke adds four woes to the beatitudes, this contrast parallelism underlining the forcefulness of his challenge. His statements are not condemnations or curses; he says instead that people who are now rich, full, satisfied with life, and objects of popularity are religiously unfortunate. Their satisfaction can easily stunt their aspirations for God. If filled with what they have, they are unlikely to recognize the poverty, hunger, sorrow, and loneliness which only God can fill.

Luke gives to the beatitudes and woes a strong social perspective. He avoids the spiritual interpretations of Matthew, stressing instead the Church's mission to the underprivileged, the needy of all kinds, the outcasts of society, and all people open to God. The basic outline of the teaching, traceable certainly to Jesus, encourages those in need to capitalize on the positive potential of their conditions. It is not an acceptance of social injustice, nor merely a restatement of Old Testament belief in the eternal reversal of roles. It is rather a highlighting of the potential values in deprivation and the potential obstacles in possessions, relevant to true appreciation of God's reign in our lives.

A new goal. The new goal of Christianity is universal love. This section, solemnly introduced by Jesus and directed to the crowd, is presented as the Lord's command. Luke uses inclusion here to emphasize the issue, twice stating the need of love of enemies (Lk 6:27-35). Since the audience would be accustomed to the challenge of loving one's neighbor, this call to love also one's enemy is in practice a call to universal Christian love. Luke stresses this vision by adding "everyone" to his sources (Lk 6:30). The love to be shown is *agape,* or genuine Christian love. This is the first time Luke uses this word. Those who curse, abuse, or rob us, those who act aggressively towards us, depriving us of the necessities of life, are also our neighbors. The Christian is called to benevolence, unconditional love, and universal concern. We read in Matthew of the need to show love to the outcasts of Jewish society, namely the tax collectors and Gentiles (Mt 5:46-47), but Luke, ever sensitive to these groups, replaces them with a general statement on sinners with which the audience can more readily identify.

Since Luke is concerned about the growing divisions between rich and poor in his own community, he addresses this in the beatitudes and woes, adding to his sources a further recommendation: "Lend without expecting repayment" (Lk 6:35). This, too, is a sign of Christian love.

The motivation for this call to universal love is the love and concern with which God our Father treats all. Here Luke changes Matthew's "Be perfect...", and rounds off the section with the call: "Be compassionate as your Father is compassionate" (Lk 6:36).

New attitudes. Jesus also demands new attitudes in our daily dealings with others, particularly within the community life of the Church (Lk 6:37-42). There should be no judging or condemning of others, no finding fault or destroying good names with petty criticisms. Instead, the disciples should treat others positively, showing compassion, forgiveness, and understanding. No one should present him or herself as a guide until he or she has a good grasp of Christian life (Lk 6:41-42). This will make disciples more compassionate, forgiving, understanding toward others, and more likely to treat others as they themselves would like to be treated (Lk 6:38). These simple attitudes, permeated with benevolence and universal concern, would have a revolutionary impact on community life were they faithfully lived.

New criteria for judging fidelity. Finally, the charter sermon clarifies the new criteria for judging authenticity and fidelity in one's commitment (Lk 6:43-49). In the previous section Luke addressed the warnings of the Lord against hypocritical criticism of others. Now the question is how one can distinguish the true and authentic believer from the hypocrite. Luke uses as part of his response a saying of Jesus' used by Matthew as a warning against false prophets (Mt 7:16). Luke directs the same saying to disciples: "Each tree is known by its yield" (Lk 6:44). The fruit produced tells us what is in the disciple's heart. The test of inner goodness is the evaluation of the disciple's words and deeds (Lk 6:45). Time reveals the nature of each one's commitment.

Moreover, the commitment of each disciple must be not only in word, but in obedience to the teachings of Jesus (Lk 6:46). On this foundation is discipleship built (Lk 6:47). Dedication to Jesus must be total, or disaster will result (Lk 6:49). This is a powerful ending to the charter sermon. Jesus' words to his disciples and the crowds are also addressed to disciples in Luke's community, and to us today: "Any man who desires to come to me will hear my words and put them into practice" (Lk 6:47).

This Sermon on the Plain synthesizes Christianity's need to reach out in iniversal concern to all. The audience of the proclamation is the world, and the message implies a reversal of this world's values. The basic goal is universal love, and the new attitudes which facilitate this include self-criticism, forgiveness, concern, and understanding for all others. Disciples must be doers of the word, for by their fruits will they be judged.

This sermon calls for and fosters peace in the community, and in outreach to others. It directs the Church in its mission to the poor and socially underprivileged. It calls for social betterment and more concrete sharing. It is a charter of the Church; an ecclesial strategy for missions of outreach to all in need.

The Church And The Underprivileged

Luke strongly believes the Church should be open to all minority groups, and should integrate them into the life of the Church. He consistently shows concern for the poor and the oppressed, specifically addresses which attitudes the Church should show to the outcasts of society and religion, and has much to say about women in Church and society. He also seems aware of divergent theological schools within the early Church, representing them fairly as intimate parts of the new community. Towards minority groups, whether based on economic, social, religious, or theological differences, Luke goes out of his way to illustrate the qualities outlined in the charter sermon. He modifies his sources, omits unacceptable statements, adds new stories from his own sources, and structures his work differently. He characterizes in this way the Church's attitude to these various fringe groups. The concern for the underprivileged in Luke-Acts is not the personal creative work of Luke, but further questioning addressed to the Church's oral tradition of Jesus. Luke asks of the oral sources questions his predecessors had not, and in so doing brings to us Jesus-based insights applied to the new developments of his Church.

The poor and the oppressed. The Third Gospel is good news for the poor and the oppressed. They are the ones who celebrate the birth of Jesus as their hope and salvation. Zechariah and Elizabeth are looked down on by their society because they are childless and old, but God values them, raising them up to be his instruments. Mary and Joseph are unknown, of such little concern to society that no suitable accommodation is offered them, even for Mary's delivery. Those who rejoice at Jesus' birth are the shepherds, poor, and ritually unclean. When Jesus is presented in the temple, the old man, Simeon, and Anna, the poor widow, become his heralds to the people.

Luke's Jesus ministers to the poor and oppressed. In his inaugural address in Nazareth, Jesus claims to bring glad tidings to the poor and liberty, recovery, and release to the needy (Lk 4:18). After the great charter sermon, he restates this same mission in reply to the question of John the Baptist: "The blind recover their sight, cripples walk, lepers are cured, the deaf hear, dead men are raised to life, and the poor have the good news preached to them" (Lk 7:22).

Jesus' miraculous power especially benefits the poor and oppressed: the possessed, whom society shuns and fears (Lk 4:33-37; 8:26-39; 9:37-43); the leper, who must publically proclaim himself unclean (Lk 5:12-16; 17:11-19); the paralyzed and helpless (Lk 5:17-26; 6:6-11); the woman with the hemorrhage that makes her ritually unclean (Lk 8:40-48); the widow of Nain, who, having lost her only son, is without relatives in a society that considers that state a curse (Lk 7:11-17); the sinful woman who prostitutes herself (Lk 7:36-50), and Jairus' daughter, dead at twelve, the age her society recognized as the beginning of womanhood (Lk 8:49-56).

In his miracles, in his healing ministry and teachings, Jesus shows the importance of the poor and oppressed for his Church. All his disciples had to be detached from possessions (Lk 18:24-30), his special apostles chosen from the poor

(Lk 5:1-11; 6:12-16) and outcast (Lk 5:27-32). He sends them on mission with advice on detachment and simplicity of life (Lk 9:1-6; 10:1-12). To a man who invites him to a meal, Jesus says, "When you have a reception, invite beggars and the crippled, the lame and the blind" (Lk 14:13). He goes on to explain that the rich, by their attachment to possessions, will not be present at the eschatological banquet; but the poor, the oppressed, and the outcast of society will (Lk 14:16-24). In his great sermon, Jesus stresses the importance of the materially poor and socially underprivileged (Lk 6:17-26). Elsewhere, he calls all to trust in providence, not in possessions (Lk 12:13-31). Jesus welcomes into salvation the wealthy who are already detached (Lk 19:1-10), but the attachment of others, such as that of the rich young man, saddens him (Lk 18:18-23). He points out that possessiveness closes the people to God's call (Lk 16:19-31).

We have already seen how the early Church appreciates and lives out this pastoral preference of Jesus for the poor and oppressed. Wealthy men and women enter the Church, too, but share their wealth, committing themselves, with the Church, to remove need from their midst.

Outcasts of society. Jesus' attitude to the social and religious outcasts of his day is a perennial lesson for the Church. The poor, the diseased, and the possessed are shunned by the community, but welcomed by Jesus. In his ministry he deliberately chooses direct involvement with outcasts in the Palestine of his day.

Tax collectors are representatives of a hated foreign power, constant reminders of Roman occupation. When John the Baptist calls to repentance, tax collectors are among the first to be baptized (Lk 3:12), and they rejoice and praise God for this opportunity (Lk 7:29). Later, Jesus actually chooses one of them to be an apostle (Lk 5:27-32), accepting his invitation to a reception at which many tax collectors are present. When criticized for this by the Pharisees, Jesus replies, "I have not come to invite the self-righteous to a change of heart" (Lk 5:32). Jesus had a real appeal for tax collectors, and they responded enthusiastically to him (Lk 15:1), a fact that the Pharisees disliked intensely (Lk 15:2). Later, "Jesus violates the Jewish laws of ceremonial purity by not merely having contact with a tax-collector, but actually inviting himself to his house for a meal."[1] Zacchaeus responds to Jesus and reforms his life (Lk 19:1-10). It is also worth noting that when Luke reports these incidents, he edits them in such a way as to remove negative judgments. Where Matthew and Mark group tax collectors with sinners, Luke speaks of "tax collectors and others" (Lk 5:29); where Matthew has "tax collectors and prostitutes," Luke generalizes it to "sinners" (Lk 7:34; Mt 21:30-32).

Another group of outcasts in Jesus' day are the Samaritans. In two stories exclusive to him, Luke uses Samaritans as exemplary people, in contrast to the Jews and their leaders: the good Samaritan (Lk 10:33) and the only grateful leper (Lk 17:16). The former story in particular challenges the values of Jewish society by uniting two apparently contradictory words for the same person: Samaritan and neighbor (Lk 10:36).[2]

In a society governed by religious values, public sinners are outcasts: even when they repent, people are slow to associate with them. This is the way the early Church treats Paul (Acts 9:26). Jesus courageously reaches out to these outcasts — the sinful woman (Lk 7:36-50), Zacchaeus (Lk 19:1-10) and the thief (Lk 23:39-43) — drawing each to repentance. This group of religiously unacceptable people, includes the Gentiles. Jesus associates with them, too, commending the quality of their faith (Lk 7:1-10). He manifests his intention to go to the Gentiles (Lk 4:16-30), and his conviction that they will enter the kingdom instead of the chosen people (Lk 13:28-30).[3]

Jesus' practice of calling outcasts is appreciated by the early Church. Peter states the position well: "I begin to see how true it is that God shows no partiality. Rather, the man of any nation who fears God and acts uprightly is acceptable to him" (Acts 10:34-35).

Women and Christianity. Women are certainly underprivileged in Jesus' time. Although presented as equal in the creation story, they are actually treated as men's possessions, second to men in all aspects of social and religious life. In Luke's gospel Jesus shows special concern for women. Luke's editorial skill is at its best here in the positioning of the stories, their balance, parallelism, contrast, and climax, and his choice of episodes from the traditions. He frequently parallels a story about a man with one about a woman, thereby showing their equality before God.[4] Thus, we have Zechariah and Elizabeth, Mary and Joseph, Simeon and Anna, the man who loses a sheep and the woman who loses a coin, the raising of the servant of the centurion and the raising of the son of the widow of Nain, the Twelve and the women who accompanied Jesus (Lk 8:1-3). In each case we are shown that Jesus does for women what he does for men, for they are equal before him. Moreover, Luke contrasts men and women in such a way that women are presented as better examples of discipleship: Zachariah doubts, but Mary believes (Lk 1:18-20; 1:34-35). The Lucan Jesus also uses women in his sermons as examples of the qualities he teaches: Peter's mother-in-law and service (Lk 4:38-39), the penitent women and love (Lk 7:36-50), Magdalene and repentance (Lk 8:2), the hemorrhage victim and faith (Lk 8:40-56), and Mary and prayerful listening to Jesus (Lk 10:38-42). Jesus speaks of his mother's faith (Lk 11:27-28), the perseverance of the widow (Lk 18:1-8), and the consolation of the women on the way to Calvary (Lk 23:27-31). Women in the infancy narratives of Luke are examples of the faith of the great figures of the Old Testament. Anna is the first herald of the messiahship of Jesus (Lk 2:36-38), and later the women at the tomb are the first heralds of the Risen Lord (Lk 24:22-24).

Mary, the mother of Jesus, is presented as the model believer. She is faithful to her religious duties (Lk 2:22-27), obediently responds to the call of God (Lk 1:38), and trusts in his word (Lk 1:45). Her prayers and praise are a synthesis of the best values of the Old Testament, and open us to the call of the New (Lk 1:46-55).

Jesus willingly associates with women and knows their concerns and hopes (Lk 4:38-39; 7:11-17, 36-50; 15:8-10). He has a close friendship with Martha and Mary (Lk 10:38-40) and involves other women in his ministry (Lk 8:1-3). Instead of speaking about "men" as the rest of the Bible, Luke begins to speak of "men and women."[5] Women play important roles in the early Church: the mother of John Mark hosts the gatherings of the local Church in her home (Acts 12:12); Dorcas is an example of charity (Acts 9:36); Priscilla works with her husband in the ministry of the Word (Acts 18:2-3, 18-21); and the conversion of some leading women is noted as a major development for the early Church (Acts 17:4, 12, 34).

Jesus' attitude to women and the early Church's faithful response is a major development in the life of early Church communities, and contrasts with the society of the time. It signals

Jesus' reversal of society's oppression, and the positive integration of another minority into his Church.

Several schools of theology. Jesus' universal concerns, concretely seen in his welcoming of various groups into his Church, is also part of Luke's picture of Christianity. We have already seen his pluralism in Christologies and Church structures. There are also several schools of theology represented in Acts. Luke's own positions are identifiable. It is also possible to identify the positions of James and the elders of Jerusalem (Acts 11:1-18; 15:1-2, 13-29; 21:15-25). Gentile Christianity, the position of which is generally Luke's as well, is particularly stressed in some of the later speeches of Paul. These have an individualism about them, differing from the typical Lucan speeches of Paul. Elsewhere we can identify the theology of Samaritan Christianity, particularly in the speech of Stephen (Acts 7:2-53), which "contains a viewpoint which is not in line with Luke's own theology, though he has incorporated it into Acts with some editing."[6] Luke presents these theological positions fairly, neither diluting them nor merging them. Their differences, clearly identifiable, are still presented as part of the whole. This willingness to present minority theological positions seems yet another instance of the Lucan Church's openness to groups usually treated as outcasts.

The Third Gospel and Acts are forceful in their teachings on the poor and oppressed, the need to welcome all outcasts, to integrate women fully into the life of the Church, and to appreciate the values in all minority positions. Luke's synthesis is as challenging as ever.

Outreach in Justice and Peace

Social sin and injustice. Luke condemns personal sin (Lk 1:20; 3:19; 7:30, 37; 8:4-15; 12:20; 22:22; Acts 8:20; 13:10-11), but his forceful condemnations are more frequently against injustice and social sin. With an acute sense of social injustice, Luke portrays Jesus and the early Church as intensely aware of social sin. In the narrative, in Jesus' teaching and parables, injustice is condemned: ambition (Lk 9:46-48; 14:7-11), violence and revenge (Lk 9:54-55), greed (Lk 12:13-15), possessiveness (Lk 12:16-21), dishonesty (Lk 16:8), and any attitude which ignores the poor (Lk 16:19-31). He confronts the injustice of some aspects of sexual im morality (Lk 16:18), the avoidance of taxes (Lk 20:21-25), entrapment (Lk 20:20), false accusations (Acts 6:13), and bribery (Lk 22:5; Acts 24:26). He is aware that sometimes social sin is the normal order of the day in a corrupt society (Acts 2:40), where public scandal is rampant (Lk 17:1-2), greed leads to inheritance litigation (Lk 12:13-15), and some resort to robbery and mugging (Lk 10:30-37). There is much abuse of power and authority (Lk 22:25-26), and lawyers, called to uphold justice, do nothing to improve legal procedures (Lk 11:46).

He sees evil in its materialistic guise (Acts 8:20; Lk 21:34): keeping up with the Joneses, social acceptance (Lk 14:12), security at any cost (Lk 12:16-21), squandering of wealth (Lk 15:11-24; 16:1), and misuse of other people's property (Lk 16:1-7).

Luke is aware of the injustice perpetrated by political institutions, particularly when supported by corrupt judges (Lk 18:1-8). There is misuse of the pressures of crowds (Acts 13:50; 17:5, 13), false accusation (Acts 17:6; 21:28), and punishment for the condemnation of immoral public figures (Lk 3:20). He speaks of imprisonment without trial (Acts 4:1-3; 16:37), and excessive punishment for what is not even criminal (Lk 23:13-25; Acts 5:40-41). He knows, too, that religious persecutions are instigated for political or social benefits (Lk 13:1-5; 21:12-19; Acts 5:40-41; 8:1-3; 9:1-2; 12:1-3; 13:50; 14:19). The sinful world described by Luke includes slavery (Acts 7:9), conspiracy to murder (Acts 9:23-24; 23:12-14), political rivalries (Lk 9:53), and war (Lk 21:10-11).

Even in the area of religion, injustice is rampant. Outward religious observance often goes with inner sin (Lk 11:39-40; 20:46-47) and injustice (Lk 11:42). Religious hypocrisy (Lk 5:30; 18:9-14) leads to socially accepted — and necessary — generosity but nothing more (Acts 5:1-11). The corrupt and wealthy eventually become impervious to religious values (Lk 16:19-31), but there is no true religion without aid to the poor (Lk 18:18-25). Without a sense of justice, there is danger of commercializing religion itself (Lk 19:45-46; Acts 8:18-21; 16:16; 19:23-40). Injustice within religion is seen in abuse of religious leadership (Lk 20:9-16), false interpretations of scripture which create intolerable religious burdens for the people (Lk 11:52), insistence on the primacy of positive religious law over basic human needs (Lk 6:6-11; 13:10-17), refusal of freedom of conscience (Acts 5:28-32), and indifference of religious leaders to injustice (Lk 10:30-37).

A platform of justice and reform. Jesus comes to bring his Father' word. He frequently condemns unjust social conditions. His first great sermon, the inaugural address in Nazareth, is a platform of justice and reform (Lk 4:18-19), the great charter sermon a challenge to society's values and a reaffirmation of the importance of the poor and oppressed (Lk 6:20-26). These clear positions had already been expected by the poor ones of the Old Testament (Lk 1:46-55), and anticipated in the preaching of John the Baptist. When the latter, preparing for the Lord's coming, is asked by the crowds how they might reform their lives, his answers, without exception, are challenges to social justice (Lk 3:10-14).

Jesus expected renunciation from his followers (Lk 14:33), warning all that: "No servant can serve two masters. . .You cannot give yourself to God and money" (Lk 16:13). Judas (Lk 22:5), the rich man (Lk 16:19-31), the rich young man (Lk 18:18-25), and the rich fool (Lk 12:16-21) are condemned for their possessiveness and lack of concern for the needy. In Acts, Ananias, Sapphira, and Simon are criticized for greed (Acts 5:1-11; 8:9-24). On the other hand, Zacchaeus (Lk 19:1-10), and later Cornelius (Acts 10:2-4), are praised for their social concerns and personal reform.

Jesus' concern for the poor and his warnings against riches are clear and frequent (Lk 2:24-26; 12:13-21; 14:33; 16:9; 18:22-25). His advice to the rich and powerful is, "Make friends for yourselves through your use of this world's goods" (Lk 16:9), and share with those who are in need and cannot repay you (Lk 6:35-38; 14:13-14). After all, "What profit does he show who gains the whole world and destroys himself in the process" (Lk 9:25).

For Jesus there is a close link between discipleship and commitment to social reform. The absence of concrete aid in justice jeopardizes repentance and response to the Lord's call (Lk 16:19-31; 20:47). Conversion and social justice are part of self-dedication to God (Lk 11:41; 12:32-34; 19:8).

Luke presents no developed theology of social involvement, but a solid basis on which to build. The condemnation of social and religious injustices is powerful, the preferences of Jesus clear, and his linking of social justice and discipleship identifiable. The Church responds by establishing a simple religious community of sharing and poverty (Acts 2:44-45; 4:32-35), constantly offering aid to the needy (Acts 6:1; 20:35; 24:17).

The frightening reminder of the disciples' need to examine themselves on social justice is the realization that even Jesus was tempted to possessiveness in goods, reputation, and power (Lk 4:1-13). Yet he chose poverty, service, and a ministry of integral human betterment for all.

A religion of peace. Commitment to the Lord Jesus in faith overflows to others in justice and love. This dedication brings peace to the disciples, calling them to live in peace with all men and women. The coming of Jesus was anticipated as a visitation from God "to guide our feet into the way of peace" (Lk 1:78-79). His birth as the king of peace also brings "peace on earth to those on whom his favor rests" (Lk 2:14). Later, in the temple, Simon witnesses to the peace which is now his at the recognition of the child (Lk 2:29).

Peace is the gift of Jesus' ministry, but it is intimately connected with faith (Lk 7:50; 8:48; 10:5-6). For Luke, faith is the once-and-for-all redirection of life to Jesus, which saves the disciple, resulting in peace. Those who come to Jesus and believe in him leave in peace (Lk 7:50; 8:48), but those who reject Jesus and do not believe lose what peace they had (Lk 19:42). In all these episodes, peace is more than a greeting, it is Jesus' gift of messianic blessing to those who believe. Anyone open to the Lord in faith will be at peace, but when faith is absent, desires for peace are futile. In fact, it can even be said that Jesus, "destined to be the downfall and the rise of many" (Lk 2:34), brings peace to the faithful but absence of peace to those who reject him (Lk 12:51; 14:32). Jesus reminds his ministers, "On entering any house, first say, 'Peace to this house.' If there is a peaceable man there, your peace will rest on him; if not, it will come back to you" (Lk 10:5-6). Towards the end of Jesus' ministry, when he enters Jerusalem in messianic triumph, Luke alone adds that the disciples acclaim Jesus as the bringer of peace (Lk 19:38), a gift which Jesus bestows on his Church after the resurrection (Lk 24:36). Faith in Jesus brings peace to the disciple. This is so strong a belief in the early Church that the object of faith, the very proclamation of the Church, is referred to as "the good news of peace" (Acts 10:36).

This gift of peace is essentially an inner quality and can coexist with persecution. The disciple at peace is also sent out like a lamb among wolves (Lk 10:3). Others' hatred and abuse of the disciples remain (Lk 6:27-34; 10:3-9), and the constancy of this persecution is referred to in the saying on the swords (Lk 22:36-38).[7] It is doubtful that the disciples merely misunderstood this, as Jesus had forcefully warned them against violent reactions (Lk 9:52-56).

Basically an inner gift, peace rooted in faith leads to a style of living fraught with social and political implications. The disciple does not react against oppression but, in peace, sees it as part of the conflict and passover of faith (Lk 6:27-34). Moreover, there is in Luke no trace of open conflict with the State. Rather, as we have seen elsewhere, Luke is concerned to show that Christianity can live peacefully with the State.

Faith in Jesus brings peace; peace even in persecution. However, this peace is not just passive, but socially and politically effective. The attitudes of Christian disciples help to share with the world Jesus' gift of peace.

Luke has a clear picture of the injustice of Jesus' time and that of his own. He is also well aware of situations which are part of our world. Strong in his condemnations, clear in his formulation of Jesus' position in his Church in regard to the disciples' need for commitment to social involvement, he also gives us a profound picture of Jesus' call and challenge to peace. On the one hand interior and personal, this peace also contributes to world peace both socially and politically.

Universal Salvation

Theology of salvation. Luke's many concerns are drawn together in the one great thrust of his writings: "The Son of Man has come to search out and save what was lost" (Lk 19:10). Luke is the only synoptic writer to use the title "Savior" for Jesus (Lk 2:11). He alone stresses that the name "Jesus" was given to the child, a name in New Testament times being indicative of mission and reality (Lk 2:21). The early Church in Acts refers to Jesus as their savior (Acts 5:31; 13:23). Other words referring to salvation are also specifically emphasized by Luke.[8] This emphasis on salvation is not based only on word usage; the atmosphere of the entire work is one of interest in the theology of salvation. Luke sees the Sovereign Lord as the savior with a plan for the world. This saving plan, carried out by the obedient Son, is proclaimed to the world by the missionary endeavors of the early Church.

The time of Jesus is welcomed as a period of merciful salvation by the witnesses of the infancy narratives (Lk 1:47, 68-79; 2:11, 21, 30, 38). Moreover, this early synthesis of Luke's message is then unfolded in gospel and Acts. In other words, Luke's two volumes can be arranged around this central motif of salvation.[9]

As presented in Luke-Acts, salvation is integral. The welcoming of the underprivileged and the outreach to the oppressed are part of the whole process. The whole person and each person is the object of the Lord's saving grace. The Lord saves from physical handicaps (Lk 6:9-10; Acts 4:9-12), demon possession (Lk 8:36), illness (Lk 8:48; 17:19), and death (Lk 8:49-50; 17:33).[10] These cases of healing imply an appreciation in faith of genuine deliverance by the Lord, well expressed by Marshall: "There is some link between the healings wrought by Jesus and the spiritual salvation which He brought to men, a link which is not merely linguistically easy but has its deeper roots in the fact that common to both sets of activity is the power of God revealed in Jesus in response to faith. The power to heal and the authority to save both reside in God."[11] The saving grace of God, experienced in the healings and grounded in faith, culminates in salvation from sin (Lk 5:20; 7:48-50) and total deliverance (Lk 17:19; 18:42; 19:9).

Salvation is only in Jesus (Acts 2:21; 4:12; 15:11; 16:31). In his inaugural sermon, he claims that his ministry brings salvation to all (Lk 3:6) and during his ministry, salvation is found by those who believe in him (Lk 7:48-50; 17:19; 18:42). While Jesus hangs on the cross, the crowd ironically acknowledges both his power and the mystery of the means of our salvation. "He saved others; let him save himself...save yourself and us" (Lk 23:35-39). Jesus saves by being willing to lose his own life (Lk 9:24; 17:33).

To anyone who asks, "What must I do to be saved?" (Acts 16:30), the Church's answer is always: "Believe in the Lord Jesus and you will be saved" (Acts 16:31; also 2:21; 4:12; 15:11). Salvation is not earned, but given by the grace of God because of the obedience of Jesus, who was exalted as the "Author of life" (Acts 3:15) and our "savior" (Acts 5:31).[12]

This salvation is not dispensed by the Church, but its reception is certainly in Luke an ecclesial experience, for it constitutes the believing disciple as a member of the Church, the community of the saved. Salvation comes with faith in Jesus, but this faith is concretely shown in the Word, which is committed to the

Church. It is the disciple/ministers of the Church who, in their proclamation of Jesus, "will make known to you a way of salvation" (Acts 16:17). In fact, Paul and Barnabas can say of themselves, "For thus were we instructed by the Lord: 'I have made you a light to the nations, a means of salvation to the ends of the earth'" (Acts 13:47). Moreover, when Cornelius is instructed to send for Peter, he is told, "In the light of what he will tell you, you shall be saved" (Acts 11:14).

The proclamation of the missionaries consists in the news that we are all "saved by the favor of the Lord Jesus" (Acts 15:11; also 2:47). All that is necessary for the disciple is faith (Acts 13:38-39; 16:30-31). Practices of the law are no longer sufficient (Acts 13:38-39; 15:1-2). The disciple must hear the Word, receive it with joy, live in detachment, retain the Word, and bear fruit through perseverance (Lk 8:11-15).

Salvation of the Gentiles. The theology of salvation in Luke-Acts is given specific emphasis — another confirmation of Luke's universal concerns. The Third Gospel and Acts stress the salvation of the Gentiles. From the infancy narratives onwards, the universal implications of the Good News are stressed. Jesus' birth brings peace to all (Lk 2:14), for he is not only the glory of Israel, but a revealing light to the Gentiles (Lk 2:32). Luke traces Jesus' genealogy not to Abraham, but to Adam, the father of all. Gentiles are present for the great Sermon on the Plain (Lk 6:17-18), and when the Twelve are sent on mission, Luke omits Matthew's charge not to go to the Gentiles (Mt 10:5). Rather, Luke is insistent that the gospel is for all (Lk 24:47).

Dom Jacques Dupont concludes that Luke deliberately highlights the salvation of the Gentiles at all major structural points in Luke-Acts.[13] Luke modifies Mark's presentation of the beginning of Jesus' public ministry, adding that, as a result, "All mankind shall see the salvation of God" (Lk 3:6). This introduction is complemented with the conclusion to both volumes and Paul's last recorded words: "Now you must realize that this salvation of God has been transmitted to the Gentiles — who will heed it" (Acts 28:28). The conclusion of the gospel and the introduction to Acts stress salvation to the ends of the earth, a phrase often used as a euphemism for the Gentile countries (Lk 24:47; Acts 1:8). Dupont insists that in a work which deals with great heroes, their speeches, especially their inaugural speeches, are moments when the author can stress the positions he himself holds dear. In each case in the Third Gospel and Acts, a factual emphasis on the salvation of the Gentiles is effected by deliberate modification of sources (Lk 4:16-30; Acts 2:14-40). A third way to emphasize your own concerns, says Dupont, is to repeat stories containing important teachings. Luke repeats, three times each, the Cornelius episode (Acts 10:9-23, 24-48; 11:1-18) and the conversion of Paul (Acts 9:1-9; 22:5-16; 26:12-18). In the former we have the conversion of the first Gentile, in the latter the conversion of the apostle of the Gentiles.

Luke alone adds a sequel to the gospel; his second work documents for us the ministries of the Church in bringing the Word to the Gentiles.[14] The Church's early ministry is to the Jews (Acts ch 1-6). The speech of Stephen (Acts 7:1-53) signals the first major theological break with Judaism and the first consideration of Samaritan positions. The persecution which follows Stephen's death leads to the spread of the Word, eventually opening contact with the Greeks (Acts 8:4; 11:20). Stephen's death is also followed by the ministry in Samaria and the conversion of those who have historical and religious links with Judaism. The historical and theological move away from Jerusalem has begun. Philip baptizes the Ethiopian who is presented as a proselyte preparing for Judaism (Acts 8:26-40). Then comes the great moment of Paul's conversion (Acts 9:1-19). But the instrument chosen to bring Jesus' name to the Gentiles (Acts 9:15) is left aside until Peter, the recognized leader, has established the acceptability of Gentile entry into the Church (Acts 10:1 -11:18). Paul's work, thus legitimized in Peter, is later sanctioned by the apostolic council (Acts 15:1-29). Once Paul begins his mission to the Gentiles, the Lord guides (Acts 13:47; 16:9) and encourages him (Acts 18:9-10). Paul in particular carries out the universal mandate of the Lord (Acts 1:8; 26:20).

This Lucan description is not only intended to show the historical development of the Church's mission to the Gentiles, but, more importantly, it roots this practice in the early authority of the Church. Luke goes a step further, pointing out that the Church's universal concerns are inspired by God: Peter and Paul have visions, Philip is directed by the Spirit, and every subsequent step to the Gentiles will be directed by the Lord.

Universal salvation. Luke-Acts is placed in the context of world history (Lk 1:5; 2:1-2). Luke sees Jesus as the center of history, prophesied by the Old Testament and proclaimed by the Church. In Jesus, God's "mercy is from age to age on those who fear him" (Lk 1:50). The Church is instructed to go to both Gentiles and Jews, not to one or the other. Peter's words are clear: "I begin to see how true it is that God shows no partiality. Rather, the man of any nation who fears God and acts uprightly is acceptable to him" (Acts 10:34-35). In other words, Luke's insistence on the salvation of the Gentiles is an insistence on universal salvation.

In examining the charter sermon, we have seen that the audience who must hear the Word includes everyone. This universality is shown again at Pentecost and the baptism of the Church (Acts 2:5-12). However, being part of the Church demands a reform of attitudes, for the disciple must know the blessedness of poverty, hunger, sorrow, and rejection. Whatever one's condition, love for all must grow in concrete ways, rooted in the foundation of Christ.

This universal salvation must include the poor and oppressed. It must draw in, through love, the outcast of every culture. This salvation is not truly religious and Christian unless it is total, open to the betterment of every aspect of life, for the Lord's words also imply a challenge to social justice.

Salvation in Jesus is integral and total. It is always a gift, and never earned, but its reception is authenticated in daily living. This daily living consists in a spirituality of universal salvation, a spirituality that calls us to live out the universal concerns of the Good News, welcoming all to the salvation which is Jesus' gift.

Conclusion
LUKE-ACTS AND SPIRITUALITY TODAY

Luke is a model of Christian life, and one of the greatest spiritual leaders of the early Church. His message, rooted in the unique call of Christ, assures us that he has carefully checked the traditions he has received. His sense of responsibility for the message is matched by his readiness to adapt it to a new culture, a new age and new needs. He brings the message of Jesus to life for peoples Jesus never knew.

Luke knows of the great missionaries and evangelists who preceded him. Ecclesially devoted to them, he clearly believes that the spirituality of his own Church should not be enslaved to former patterns and perspectives. Rather, Jesus' message must be delivered in all its freshness to Luke's own Church. The author skillfully fosters in his readers a sense of mystery, awe, wonder, and prayer, so that the proclamation is made as if for the first time.

Luke is not only a model for us today in his vision, commitment, world view, and life, but is unquestionably so in the way he deals with the sources and traditions of our faith. He is respectful of the origins of Christian spirituality, constantly seeking to verify and legitimize his teachings in Jesus. However, Luke also sees that for Christian spirituality to be perennially relevant and authentic, he must also show the need for interpretation (the hermeneutical dimension of spirituality) and the constant exploration of new modes of living out the message (the heuristic dimension of spirituality). Thus he redactionally stresses four characteristics of the call to discipleship: it is ecclesially centered, and prophetically challenges world situations, and it must be pastorally adapted, challenged to grow to fullness.

The spirituality which Luke calls for is neither individualistic nor a passive dependence on God. The spiritual vision he portrays includes a constant call to share Jesus' ministry in the Church. This commitment includes the proclamation of who God is for us. In our daily life he is the Sovereign Lord, mighty and strong, but he is also the compassionate Father, who plans salvation through Jesus. Recognizing the Father's love, the believer is called to confidence, peace, and service.

Luke's spiritual challenge is centered on Jesus, whose life and death are presented as models for the believer. Like Jesus, the believer is called to total commitment to the Father's will and to the mission with which he or she has been entrusted. While sensitive and compassionate, the believer must also prophetically challenge the false values of the world. In his or her ministry the disciple has the aid of Jesus, who brings God's power into our lives Jesus is the embodiment of God's promises, the instrument of salvation.

Christian existence is modeled on Jesus' obedience to the Father. It is an ecclesial life, for the times of waiting are over, and the Spirit inspires, directs, and leads the Church. Spirituality must now include constant openness to the Spirit, who reveals God's guidance and challenge to each generation.

Luke's spirituality is ecclesially centered, building strong community awareness in his audience. They, the community of Israel's hopes, have universal responsibilities and mission. Each believer's salvation is intimately connected with the Church, where his or her repentance, belief, baptism, anointing, and paschal living are celebrated. The believer's commitment to the Lord is not something over and done with in a single moment of confession. Conversion is an ongoing process in the heart of the Church. Each individual is called to live as part of a worshipping, sharing, poor, and joyful Church.

The call of the disciple begins with the initiative of God and implies conversion, detachment, ministry, and continued faith in the Lord Jesus. Christian discipleship is a lifelong journey with Jesus. On this journey, the disciple is called to a life of prayer and absolute dedication to Jesus. The journey includes many obstacles, temptations, and blocks that must be faced and overcome. Moreover, discipleship is not a relationship with only the pre-resurrection Jesus, but is also alive and challenging in the "today" of every generation's Church.

The spiritual challenges of Luke mean total redirection of life for the believer, who now has new values, new goals, new attitudes, and new criteria for authentic fulfillment in life. The Christian redirection of life, well synthesized in Jesus' charter sermon, moves outward to others and their needs in the self-sacrifice of the believer. The poor, oppressed, and outcast must feel the impact of the Lord's love and call. Social sin and injustice must be challenged, and the community of believers known for social reform, peace, and universal sharing of salvation.

I have insisted throughout this work that Luke challenges not only in word, but also by his personal attitudes. For him, all spirituality is based on the foundational revelation of Jesus. However, it must also be interpreted for new situations, and he challenges us to explore new possibilities of lifestyle that can better reflect Jesus' message. This calls for a strong awareness of mission through Jesus, and community growth in the Church. Spirituality implies the redirection of life and fidelity to the ongoing character of call. Finally, the Christian life Luke describes necessitates outreach in service and love to all.

I see Luke's inspired synthesis as fulfilling and enriching. I hear his call as profoundly challenging. I am convinced that his insights are perennially valid.

Appendix
STUDIES OF LUKE-ACTS

As an aid to the spiritual theology presented in the body of this book, we now review briefly the historical development of Lucan studies. We do this for three reasons: first, to give the reader a context in which to insert the present decade of Lucan studies; second, to show the development of historical critical methods and techniques currently in use in biblical studies and presumed throughout this book; and third, to stress that the dynamics at work in the development of a critical approach have themselves clarified the role that Luke can play in our spiritual lives today.

In the last quarter-century, scholars have made us particularly aware of the vision, call, and challenge to ecclesial growth that Luke brings us from Jesus. The journey to this awareness, however, has been slow, and Luke has always evoked a love/hate response. Moreover, there is perhaps no other New Testament writing for which the research is so influenced by philosophical, theological, and denominational prejudice. Some critics are indignant at what they consider to be Luke's compromising of the primitive *kerygma*. Others ridicule his presumed misunderstanding of Paul. Some exalt his literary ability, while others marvel at his historical accuracy. Some commentators interpret Luke with the help of the Hegelian dialectic of history, while others filter his thought through the philosophy of Heidegger. Episcopal-type churches canonize him as the first faithful and accurate chronicler of the beginnings of Christianity, but reformed churches despise his "early Catholicism." He has been viewed as a passive secretary, a faithful transmitter, a compiler with style, an author in his own right, and a great theologian.

In studying the research on Luke, it is difficult to distinguish critical evaluation from the accepted interpretations of the schools or churches: the Tübingen school, British scholarship, the "new look" in German Lucan studies, and the identifiable position of the post-Bultmannians. Scholars do seem to group together under definite theological banners before beginning their Lucan enterprises.

Yet it remains true that, despite frustration, disagreement, and prejudice, great developments have taken place in our understanding of Luke, scholarly research bringing us a period of great appreciation of his work.

In some ways, a study of the history of Lucan research is a study of the critical issues which have faced theology over the years. Moreover, our appreciation of Luke and his work has changed, gradually leading us to the present, when he stands out in prophetical challenge to all.

Luke - The Secretary Companion of Paul (The pre-critical period)

It is not until the eighteenth century that the scientific method is born in the writings of R. Simon (1638-1712), the first to apply critical biblical methods to the New Testament. Prior to the attempt, the general approach was to assume the New Testament to be straight historical records, written by eyewitnesses. The writer of the Third Gospel was presumed to be Luke, the physician from Antioch, who traveled with Paul (as the latter tells us in Col 4:14; Phm 24, and as Luke himself assures us in the "we" sections of Acts). An eyewitness for much of the development of the early Church, Luke unfortunately had not seen Jesus. However, the apostolic origin of the message, seen at the time to be a criterion for canonicity, was guaranteed by Luke's role as Paul's secretary.[1] In fact, "by the latter half of the second century Luke's gospel was widely associated with Paul's apostolic authority. This tendency reached full flower two centuries later when Paul's phrase, 'my gospel,' was widely believed to refer to Luke (Eus. 3,4,7; Rom 16:25; 2 Tim 2:8; cf. 2 C 8:18)."[2] This gospel, basically Paul's, was said to have been written down by his faithful companion, Luke, thought to be a native of Antioch and hence to have had contact with Matthew's gospel of that foundational Church. Moreover, in his travels with Paul, particularly during the latter's house arrest in Rome (Col 4:14; Phm 24), Luke was thought to have had opportunity to meet with Mark, who wrote his gospel there. Hence it was thought that the Lucan text draws on knowledge gained from Matthew and Mark in the major sections of the gospel, and on the message, life, and experience of Paul elsewhere in the Third Gospel and Acts. Where Luke's presentation differs from Matthew's or Mark's, the discrepancies were explained to be variations of the oral traditions. This remained the orthodox position until 1863, when H. J. Holtzmann offered, in *The Synoptic Gospels*, a painstaking study in support of the two-source theory (Mk-Q) of the synoptic gospels.

The early Church's conviction that Luke was to Paul what Mark had been to Peter — that is a faithful transmitter of his gospel — continued to be proclaimed and was generally accepted until the seventeenth and eighteenth centuries. This conviction was particularly strong at the time of the formation of the canon of the New Testament, ca. 150 - 200. Clement of Rome (II, Clem IV), and Justin Martyr (Apol 1:67) are the first to treat the gospels as scripture, but it is the early heretic Marcion who first groups together some New Testament writings as a norm or canon of faith. Marcion rejected the god of the Old Testament and all the teachings of Judaism. In the latter, he includes the preaching of all the Twelve, who, in Marcion's judgment, had corrupted the message of Jesus. Paul was the only true teacher. Consequently, Marcion's canon consists of ten of Paul's letters, together with Paul's gospel written by Luke. This position challenged the early Church to respond, and thus the canon began to be formed. This canon includes four gospels, the letters of Paul, and, among other writings, Acts. The latter, said to be written by a certain Luke who journeyed with Paul, is itself a legitimization of the role now given the Twelve by the early Church. Marcion's position is thus undermined by a "pauline writing."

Whether in the writings of early Church leaders, theologians, and scripture commentators or in convictions surfacing at the time of the canon's emergence, Luke is consistently seen as Paul's disciple, a faithful transmitter of his gospel and the history of his missionary work. Both works are considered to be historically reliable. This is the traditional view until the eighteenth century.

Luke - The Diplomatic Compromiser (Tendency criticism)

This general understanding of Luke was accepted in spite of inconsistencies. For example, there seemed to be discrepancies between Paul's life and teachings in his own letters, and his life and teachings in Acts. Chronological indications in the Lucan gospel differed from those in the other gospels. Sections taken from Mark had been changed. Although Luke writes Acts of Apostles, he really does not deal with any apostles other than Peter. The traditionally accepted position just did not seem tenable. How could these two volumes be the work of a faithful companion of Paul? How could they be historically reliable? They were incomplete, at variance with other parts of revelation.

Peaceful acceptance of tradition gave way to discomfort. Following on the rationalism and enlightenment of the 18th century came scientific methods in the study of history. These were then applied to the Bible, resulting in the science of historical criticism of the Bible. These methods were first used in *The Critical History of the New Testament*, by R. Simon (1689-92). This French Oratorian priest provided us with a method, but it was H. S. Reimarus (1694-1768) who, in the next century, became the catalyst for a deeper understanding of the synoptic gospels. Reimarus was a deist who rejected all orthodox Christianity, and, according to him, the scriptures were not historically reliable. The Jesus of history was very different from the Christ of the gospels. The gospels are creative writings, not historical accounts, and we must, Reimarus insisted, accept the creative element in the Christian tradition.

The 19th Century saw two reactions to these ideas. The first was the development of "the creative element" in the traditions. This is seen in tendency criticism, and has been given new birth in the redaction criticism of recent decades. The other reaction came from source criticism, eventually giving us a new understanding of the synoptic problem. Proponents of tendency criticism directed their attention principally to Acts, while source critics at first directed their research to the gospel of Luke.

The inconsistencies already mentioned were, in the judgment of tendency critics, the result of Luke's selection of material. It was not that he was unable to present the same picture as the other writers, but that he was unwilling to do so because he had in mind definite purposes best achieved by slanting his work in certain ways. In selecting his material, he was led by a tendency, or bias, which colored his presentation.

Tendency criticism is the scholarly attempt to identify the bias or tendency (Tendenz) which motivates a given author in the selection, arrangement, and presentation of his material. The bias is the "creative element" (Reimarus) which the author contributes.

Scholars differed widely in identifying precisely what Luke's bias was.[3] However, they all agreed that, whatever their suggestions, the bias compromised Luke's historical reliability. F. C. Baur merits special attention, standing out as a giant among the tendency critics and the acknowledged founder of the influential Tübingen school. He applies the Hegelian dialectic of history to early Christian developments. In these early years, he sees tension building between a movement calling for freedom from the law, and a reactionary movement insisting on legalistic obedience. The former is among the Gentiles, its major proponent Paul, the latter among the Judaizers, their leader apparently Peter. Luke parallels the work of Jesus with the work of Peter, and that of Paul, putting Peter and Paul on equal footing. He reconciles the two with notable diplomatic ability, legitimizing the Gentile aproach.[4] According to Baur, Luke's identifiable tendency or bias is to write his works in such a way as to legitimize the mission to the Gentiles. Baur's disciples and others suggest different biases, such as apologetic interests (Schrader, 1836), reconciliation in the form of history but not itself historical (Schwegler, 1846), a conciliatory tendency (Zeller, 1854), and so on.

According to the critics, the fundamental motivating force in Luke's selection and arrangement of sources is the reconciliation of two opposing trends in early Christianity. He gives to future generations a picture of Paul gentler in his attitudes toward the Jews. Paul helps the Jewish Church, obediently circulates the recommendations of the Council of Jerusalem (Acts 15:22), circumcizes Timothy (Acts 16:3), and is eventually put on trial, not for his attitudes to the law, but for his belief in the resurrection (Acts 23:6). On the other hand, Peter is now seen as the founder of the Gentile mission (Acts 10), speaking out against overburdening the Gentiles (Acts 15:10), laying aside the prescriptions of law

(Acts 11:3), and upholding Paul and his work (Acts 15:7-12). In all this compromising, Luke, according to the tendency critics, sacrifices historical reliability. In fact, he is not interested in history, but in the furtherance of his biased purpose.

The paradox of this early phase of tendency criticism is that, while its task is to identify the bias of the scripture author, the one feature which stands out is the bias, tendency, or prejudice which influenced the tendency critics themselves. Why force Hegelian dialectic on the early Chruch, making a radical division between Paul and the Judaisers and insisting on tension-filled reactions? Could there not have been a peaceful evolution, as Lechler suggested (1851), or a more open relationship between the two groups (Ritchl, 1857)?

Certainly the basic insight of tendency criticism is valuable and will be furthered by redaction criticism. Unfortunately, this initial insight did not have, at this early stage, the tools for documentation. The tendency critics needed the tools of source and form criticism before they could achieve the full potential of their insight. But this would have to wait.

Luke - The Historian (Source criticism)

The tendency critics responded to the inconsistencies in Luke's work by pointing out that his bias prevented him from introducing material which weakened his purpose. A different explanation was given by the literary and source critics, generally dedicated believers unwilling to accept a Reimarus-type explanation. They were fine scholars who acknowledged that, after Baur, only thorough and critical study and explanation would suffice, and that a return to precritical, fundamentalist, and blind acceptance was no longer possible.

Reactions to the Tübingen school came both from England and Germany from scholars who were masters in the use of the tools of literary criticism. In England, the three great Cambridge scholars, J. B. Lightfoot (1828-1889), B. F. Westcott (1825-1901), and F. J. A. Hort (1828-1892), approached the New Testament with the solid textual critical methods of the day and gave future scholars additional tools for source criticism. In his work on Ignatius of Antioch and Clement of Rome, Lightfoot showed Baur's descriptions of a tension-filled Christianity to be inaccurate. Westcott and Hort provided future scholars with a critical edition of the Greek New

Testament. All three wrote outstanding commentaries. In Germany, A. von Harnack (1851-1930), the renowned nineteenth century protestant scholar, also rejected the ideas of Tübingen. He directed his critical research to the kernel of the problem in his trilogy on Lucan writings, in which he rejected Baur's position and restated Luke's role in the early Church, his relationship to Paul, and the reliability of his presentation.[5]

Another scholar, the British archeologist William Ramsay, faced the crucial issues of New Testament scholarship at this time by zeroing in on Lucan studies. Initially skeptical of the historical reliability of Acts, he was eventually led by his travels and archeological studies to enthusiastically support the historical accuracy of Luke's description of the early Church.[6] His historical studies were a fine complement to theological issues.

Literary criticism has at times been more narrowly defined as source criticism, and the age of New Testament source criticism began in earnest with the insights of K. Lachmann (1835) and C. H. Weisse (1838). The former no longer accepted the position of the precritical period that Matthew and John were the earliest writings, but instead proposed the priority of Mark. Weisse, on the other hand, suggested a second source of traditional material, shared by Matthew and Luke, called Q.

The insights of these two writers were first documented and critically examined toward the end of the nineteenth century in the work of H. J. Holtzmann, and in the early part of the present century in B. H. Streeter's outstanding exposition.[7]

According to source criticism, Mark was the first gospel to be written. It was much earlier than the others, very simple, and reliable as an historical source. Luke used Mark in writing his own gospel, and in general was faithful to Mark's presentation. However, the source critics also identified large sections of Luke's gospel not found in Mark, but present in Matthew. These traditions, shared by Matthew and Luke but not found anywhere else, make up Q. Finally, they concluded that Luke has a source of his own not found anywhere else. Streeter suggested that Mark was written in Rome, ca. 65-70, and Q was from Antioch ca. 50. Luke's private source, L, was from Caesarea ca. 60, and Luke's gospel, as we have it now combined, dates from around 80.

Variations in content between Luke and the other writers, they suggested, stemmed not from bias, but from inavailability of sources. Furthermore, identifiable differences in the same episode are due to slight variations in the oral tradition.

It is not as easy to identify the sources of Acts because we do not have other versions, as we do with the gospels. However, it was suggested that painstaking study can identify sources based on travel notes, people (Timothy, Peter, Barnabas), communities, or places (Antioch, Caesarea). We can see parallel sources (two stories of Stephen, three conversion accounts, two Pentecost descriptions), and read and appreciate the significance of the "We" source.[8] The various hypotheses of Acts' sources inevitably end by concentrating on the skill of the editor who combines such a variety of sources. In other words, later studies on the sources of Acts become early form-critical studies.

Whether we examine Luke's use of Mark or Q, or his duplication of parallel sources, one thing is clear to many source critics: Luke strives to be faithful to his sources, to be as careful and accurate as possible. He attempts to give us an ordered historical account, as he claims. However, an historian's reliability depends on the accuracy of his sources. For some authors these are questionable, and, as a result, Luke's historical reliability is diminished.

Studies in the language and background of the New Testament and research into sources behind the New Testament texts converge in this period on the conviction that Luke's description is accurate, his writings reasonably early; certainly not as late as Baur suggested. Luke was seen as Paul's companion, as showing respect for his sources, and as an historian at least as reliable as other historians of his age.

Luke - The Story-Teller (Form criticism)

Source criticism limited itself to a study of the documents at hand. It had concluded in the theory of the two sources. Luke used Mark and Q. Mark was the earliest gospel; simple, primitive, and historically reliable. But now scholars' attention was directed more to the reliability of these two sources, to what lies behind them, and how Luke uses them?

As early as 1901 W. Wrede, in *The Messianic Secret in the Gospels*, had already stated that Mark's gospel is not primitive, but is itself profound theological reflection. It is not totally historical, but the messianic secret, for example, is a literary device of Mark. J. Wellhausen in his work on the synoptics, and K. L. Schmidt in his work on the historical Jesus, began to sow the seeds of a further stage in critical analysis.[9]

The question at this time is that if the sources behind Luke are themselves theological compositions, can we get behind these sources to the period when the events took place? Can we find out how the stories took shape? This new stage in biblical criticism dissects the writings in such a way as to identify the individual units of tradition shared by them. Often, these individual units (forms) of tradition have different settings in each gospel. The connecting framework, the work of each editor-evangelist, is then set aside as secondary. Once identified, this context of the editor can be removed, and thus, hopefully, the critic moves closer to the primitive message about Jesus. This identification and analyis of the various units of tradition is known as form criticism.

The two great exponents of the form-critical method were Martin Dibelius (1883-1947) and Rudolf Bultmann (1884-1976). Both were interested in the developments which took place in the traditions before the first written records. Dibelius studied the process from early Church traditions forward to the gospels. Bultmann studied the process from the written gospels back to the early traditions behind the written expressions.[10] Of the two, Dibelius had greater immediate impact, but Bultmann has had greater lasting effect. Dibelius was more willing to accept the historical value of identified units of tradition, whereas the more radical Bultmann saw less of historical value and more of the creativity of the writers.

The five fundamental principles on which the theories of Dibelius and Bultmann rest can be stated as follows:[11] (1) the synoptic gospels are popular, sub-literary compositions; (2) they depict the faith of the primitive Christians who created them, not the historical Jesus; (3) they are artificial collections of isolated units of tradition; (4) these units originally had a definite literary form, which can still be detected; and (5) this form was created by a definite social situation. Both Dibelius and Bultmann gave special attention to Luke's writings. They stressed his artistic and literary skills, as the following quotations from their works indicate. Dibelius says:

> The literary understanding of the synoptics begins with the recognition that they are collections of material. The composers

> are only to the smallest extent authors. They are principally collectors, vehicles of tradition, editors. Before all else their labour consists in handing down, grouping, and working over the material which has come to them. Therein also their religious presentation of the material comes to essential expression. Thus they make their influence felt with much less independence than, say, the composer of the Fourth Gospel and much less also than the author of the Book of Acts. The latter is indeed himself an evangelist, but he is much more bound by his material in the Gospel of St. Luke than in the Acts of the Apostles. Here he acts as an author, but in the Gospel rather as a collector and editor. For this reason, St. Luke more than the other synoptics shows the strongest literary character.[12]

From Bultmann we read:

> Luke's chief interest is literary. His ambition was to write his story in a way that would impress even his cultured Greek readers, and he had a special concern to reproduce the right *taksis*, i.e. an evidently historical sequence (1:1-4).
>
> For our purposes it is essential to recognize that the Gospel of Luke is the climax of the history of the Synoptic Tradition is so far as the development which the tradition had undergone from the beginning has attained its greatest success in Luke: the editing and connecting of isolated sections into a coherent continuity.[13]

Relevant to the gospels, then, the evangelist's work is said to be principally the collection, final selection, and arrangement of the material, as are the literary context and framework for the presentation of the units of tradition. Each evangelist writes for the benefit of the local Church, with its needs in mind. Luke stands out as the literary genius in this editorial work, climaxing the development of the synoptic presentation in his gospel and showing himself as a true creative author in Acts. He writes as a proclaimer of faith in a way that attracts his audience. He appeals to them at a level important at that time, the level of artistic and literary development. According to these critics, this means that Acts can no longer be viewed as a chronicle of early Christianity. Rather, it is a literary masterpiece at the service of faith.

Luke - The Theologian (Redaction criticism)

Reimarus' major insight was to highlight the creative element in the Christian tradition. Tendency critics had underscored the impact of the author's tendency on the final documents. Source critics acknowledged the variations in the author's treatment of the sources, and form critics isolated the units of tradition from their connecting framework, laying the latter aside as secondary.

After 1950, biblical scholars and theologians began to give more attention to the evangelist-editor's contribution. At first, this critical study was referred to as tradition criticism and concerned itself precisely with the question of why a tradition was shaped in a given way. In form criticism, editorial work was left aside as secondary and unimportant. Now it is seen as critical to an understanding of the situations in which the New Testament texts were written, and as helpful in reconstructing theological developments in the early Church.

What the critics were actually doing was analyzing the history of the editorial process and the contribution of the evangelist in the composition of his work. E. Haenchen, an outstanding Lucan scholar, refers to this step in biblical criticism as composition criticism, but today it is generally called redaction criticism. It shows the process of reflection in the development of a text and throws light on the issues, circumstances, and dynamics that influenced it. Redaction criticism is described in the following ways: E. Krentz says, "It is in essence a form of *Tendenzkritic* that uses the editorial techniques of the final writer to determine the special interests and concerns that motivated his work."[14] N. Perrin notes, "It is concerned with studying the theological motivation of an author as this is revealed in the collection, arrangement, editing, and modification of traditional material, and in the composition of new material or the creation of new forms within the traditions of early Christianity."[15]

Redaction criticism sees the writers of the New Testament as theologians who imprint their style, interests, and pastoral concerns on their compositions. In Lucan studies, it stresses Luke's role as a theologian, leaving aside the issue of the historical value of the episodes. Studying the editorial process and composition throws light on the concerns of the evangelist himself and increases our knowledge of the communities for which he wrote.

The methods of redaction criticism had in some way been appreciated by the tendency critics, but at the time, they did not have the tools for further documentation. Other scholars had made tentative steps in this direction. Perhaps it is R. H. Lightfoot (1883-1953), in his Bampton lectures (1934), who deserves the title of the first redaction critic. It is, however, R. Bultmann who is really the father of redaction criticism.[16]

Luke and early Catholicism (R. Bultmann, E. Käsemann, and J.C. O'Neill)

In his writings on Luke, Bultmann had played down the historical value of the episodes used by Luke and stressed Luke's creativity in the stories. He claimed that editorial involvement climaxes in Luke, who is so influenced by community needs that his final work, while a brilliant composition, loses the original message of Jesus and deviates from the early *kerygma*. According to Bultmann, the primitive proclamation of the Good News was eschatological, consisting of a call to immediate repentance and decision, and underlining the need to find salvation only in he who called: Jesus the Lord. Bultmann claimed that, in Luke, this original eschatological call was unfortunately lost, and we are now presented with a Church which, with its ecclesiastical offices, authority, and sacraments, has become the indirect source, channel, and guarantor of the tradition. To describe this vision of mediated salvation, E. Käsemann uses the term "early Catholicism".

Since Bultmann and Käsemann, it has been common practice among protestant scholars to rebuke Luke with betrayal of the real message, and to consider him the initiator of the early catholicizing tendencies, which, it is thought, later bloom in the Pastoral Letters and in the writings of the early bishops, Ignatius and Polycarp. The notion of "early catholicism" includes the rejection of the immediacy of the end and the resulting institutionalizing of the Church in the time of waiting. The Church is established with ecclesiastical offices and an authority passed on through legitimate succession. The institutional Church offers guarantees for the rightness and necessity of Christian faith, monopolizes official interpretation. Through tradition, teaching, and sacraments, the institutional Church becomes the channel of grace.

Critics who hold this position are convinced that Luke, in the selection of his material and its arrangement, in his substantial changes and personal interpretations, creates a theological position different from the primitive *kerygma*. He gives us the nascent Catholic Church. For this he will be simply ignored, despised, and even labeled an apostate by his critics.

Luke and salvation history (H. Conzelmann, E. Haenchen, and P. Vielhauer)

Bultmann's disciples are to be credited with major redactional critical studies on the synoptics: Willi Marxsen on Mark, Günther Bornkamm on Matthew, and Hans Conzelmann on Luke. Of these three, it is Conzelmann who is clearly the most sympathetic to the ideas of Bultmann and, in fact, elaborates his master's views. Scholars since Conzelmann have often had a love/hate reaction to him, but all agree that of him "it may justifiably be said that he almost singlehandedly changed the whole tenor of Lucan studies."[17] His work is explicitly a redaction study. He considers Luke's work in its present form without concern for the sources of historical value of the material. He describes his work as follows:

> The first phase in the collection of the traditional material (up to the composition of Mark's Gospel and the Q sayings) has been clarified by Form Criticism. Now a second phase has to be distinguished, in which the kerygma is not simply transmitted and received, but itself becomes the subject of reflection. This is what happens with Luke. This new stage is seen both in the critical attitude to tradition as well as in the positive formation of a new picture of history out of those already current, like stones used as parts of a new mosaic.[18]

According to Conzelmann, the delay of the Second Coming led Luke to substitute for primitive eschatology a salvation/history approach, in which the life of Jesus became "the middle of time." He supported this with a detailed examination of Luke's editorial contributions. He showed how Luke's modification of Mark and Q, his use of episodes in different contexts, the use of history and geography for theological purposes, and the total structure of Luke's two volumes, all point in the same direction. Luke's theology gives us a vision of time in three stages: (1) the Old Testament and expectancy; (2) the life of Jesus that ends in the passover mystery localized in Jerusalem; and (3) the period of the Chruch with an unknown end when the means of salvation are again localized.[19] In Conzelmann's understanding this view is totally Luke's and is not characteristic of early Christianity. Conzelmann claims that Luke de-eschatologized the Christ event, integrated the institutional Church into salvation history, and gave rise to a different way of living Christian life.

E. Haenchen limits himself to Acts rather than taking both volumes together. In large measure he agrees with Conzelmann's presentation. Speaking of Luke the Historian, he says, "It was his familiarity with the theological situation, and his understanding of what it required, that led Luke to turn historian and write a historical work in two volumes."[20] This historical work is again seen to have a clearly identified scheme which is Luke's work and not primitive. It is a picture in historical form which justifies the Church's mission to the Gentiles and legitimizes the Christian religion for Rome.[21]

This theology is on the redactional level and "everything that might interfere with its straightforward movement is smoothed out or omitted."[22] According to Haenchen, this does not correspond to the actual development of the early Church. The picture is created by Luke and sustained by his modifications and creation of edifying stories to fill out the picture.[23]

Having studied Luke's editorial work, Conzelmann and Haenchen have strong criticism for Luke's interpretation of the Good News, and these accusations can be summarized as follows: (1) Luke ignores the expectation of the imminent coming of the kingdom of God, consequently denying the right to ask about the time of the end. (2) Luke does not understand the death of Jesus as a saving event. (3) With Luke, the apostolic tradition gains an absolute significance, and Luke is seen as a proponent of early catholicism. (4) By means of legitimate apostolic succession, Luke offers guarantees for the reliability of faith. (5) Luke misunderstands the primitive *kerygma* by portraying the Jesus event as concluded in the past.[24]

These two major authors and their supporters believe that Luke gives an answer to the problem of the delayed Second Coming. For Luke the delay is not accidental, but a necessary part of God's plan. He then integrates the current period of the Church into God's plan, and this results in great emphasis on the Church. While the period of Jesus is the middle of time, Luke stresses the present period of the Church. His response is pastorally motivated and reasonably consistently presented, but according to Conzelmann and Haenchen, Luke has lost the essential emphasis on Jesus and the immediate eschatological challenge of the primitive *kerygma.*

Luke - historian and theologian (F.F. Bruce, I. Howard Marshall)
There has been profound and extensive disagreement with the positions of the redactional critics so far mentioned. Never widely accepted outside of Germany, they are now opposed within Germany itself. Wilckens comments

> At the present time the method called redaction-criticism is luring us into a one-sided concentration on the work of the editors. It does not ask with sufficient rigor where their personal achievements fit into the early Christian history of tradition . . Not everything characteristic of Luke's writing is originally Lucan![25]

While Conzelmann and Haenchen have been praised for the excellence and thoroughness of their work, the feeling persists that they and their supporters often appear one-sided in their explanations, perhaps approaching their tasks with philosophical, theological, and denominational prejudice, and lack rigor in their research. The following criticisms have arisen: the failure to deal sufficiently with Luke and Acts as a whole jeopardizes their work from the start; rejection of Luke 1-2 is unjustified;[26] the continued use of Paul as a measuring rod of scripture's value opens up the serious problem of selective use of the canon; the unquestioned denial of history's value for faith seems to color prejudicially these authors' view of Luke. As Ulrich Wilckens points out, there seems a lack of effort to tie up Luke's thought with early tradition; many convictions are insufficiently proved, and opposing scriptural documentation is ignored.[27]

Authors continue to express their dissatisfaction of Conzelmann and others. Although Conzelmann sees the historical centrality of the Christ event as a Lucan fabrication, O. Cullmann finds this characteristic of early Christianity.[28] J. Munck asks why Dibelius and Haenchen must presume that no preaching about the apostles in the early Church exists, and why they must then presume the edifying accounts to be created. Can the historical not be edifying?[29] C.H. Talbert disagrees with imposing modern distinctions between *kerygma* and history on Luke, who could not have viewed things in this way.[30] W. Gasque feels that philosophical views and theological concerns, linked to the lack of historical research, have colored the interpretations of the scholars mentioned. This opinion is shared by Wilckens, who states, "In contemporary German research on the book of Acts. . .exegetical observations and theological persuasions are intertwined."[31] W. Harrington, in his evaluation of H. Conzelmann, bluntly says, "All this is Heidegger, mediated through Bultmann; it is not Paul. . .or Jesus."[32]

A more moderate approach has been followed by British scholars F. F. Bruce and I. Howard Marshall. These critics do not see history and eschatology as opposites, seeing eschatology as bound up with history. History is seen as the means by which God achieves his saving purpose. Furthermore, they find no opposition between theology and history. The faith reflected upon in the former must be rooted in the latter. Faith cannot be indifferent to historical fact. Luke, however, is not mere chronicler. He is interested in presenting to future generations the call to salvation brought in Jesus and continually offered to us through the power of his Spirit. However, "It is not a man's motives in studying the past which determines whether the result is history; it is his diligence, accuracy and insight as an investigator."[33] Luke may not intend to be a historian, but desiring to root his evangelical call in the realities of the historical Jesus, he carefully investigates those events, and his work is reliable. Marshall concludes:

> Christian faith is dependent upon historically verifiable events. This was the view taken by Luke, and we have attempted to show that in adopting this view he was not taking up an individual point of view but that he was in agreement with the early church generally.[34]
>
> For the moment enough has been said to show that a blanket condemnation of Luke as a historian of the early church is uncalled for. We do not wish to make exaggerated claims for his reliability, nor to suggest that his views of the historian's task were identical with those of the modern historian. But it is unfair to suggest that he is a thoroughly tendentious and unreliable writer, freely rewriting the history of the early church in the interests of his own theology.[35]

For both Bruce and Marshall, Luke is a theologian. Their works are redactional in that they emphasize Luke's contribution to the composition of the text. For Bruce, Luke presents his audience with an explanation of their faith based on the acts of God, in Jesus and through his Spirit. Marshall sees Luke as the theologian of salvation.

Luke is acceptable to both writers as a theologian because his reflections and syntheses are based on reliable records. We cannot judge Luke as an historian in modern terms, but must evaluate his historical methods alongside those of his contemporaries.[36] Marshall in particular stresses Luke's role as an historian, and how this relates to Luke's theological convictions:

> Luke conceived his task as the writing of history and we shall fail to do justice to his work if we do not think of him as a historian. Modern research has emphasized that he was a theologian. The evidence which we have considered has shown that because he was a theologian he had to be a historian. His view of theology led him to write history.
>
> Luke was a historian because he was first and foremost an Evangelist: he knew that the faith which he wished to proclaim stands or falls with the history of Jesus and the early church.[37]

Luke Today?

C. H. Talbert, in a fine article on recent studies of the Gospel of Luke, says:

> Lukan studies in the last twenty years have been like shifting sands. At present, widespread agreement is difficult to find, except on the point that Conzelmann's synthesis is inadequate. Until the scholarly community can agree on a proper perspective for studying Luke-Acts, there is little likelihood that another synthesis will fare any better.[38]

Possibly this is true. However, I find several common convictions surfacing among the authors. First, there is the need to liberate Luke from the ideas of certain modern schools of theology in which exegetical observations and theological persuasions are often intertwined. Imposing existentialist interpretations on Luke's thought is unacceptable. Equally unacceptable are approaches based exclusively on theology of the word of God, which is sometimes called dialectical theology or the theology of crisis.[39] In this same connection the absolutizing of certain interpretations must be protested. There is a real danger of circular reasoning: some working hypotheses have been repeated so often that they have lost their hypothetical character.

Second, there is a need to consider new methods in our approach to Luke-Acts. Redaction criticism has resulted in isolating many themes in the author's compositional work. We now need something that will help us discern the unity of the evangelist's thought.[40] Perhaps structuralist interpretation and genre criticism will help.

Third, it is necessary to approach Lucan studies with common sense. Luke has, at times, been made into a philosophical, theological, and literary genius who seems unreal in the Church of the first century. It is probably nearer the mark to treat Luke as a preaching evangelist. Marshall does this, and Barrett has already done so.[41]

Fourth, Lucan studies are a good focal point for joint ecumenical efforts, for example in relation to the understanding of the nature of canonicity.

Fifth, it seems crucial that scholars return to discussion with Luke's primary texts, and not Luke filtered through schools of thought. Paul Minear comments on this problem: "I was amazed to observe how far such interpretations deviate from the text itself . . . It also warned me of the dangers of allowing the discussion with modern scholars to displace the dialogue with Luke himself."[42]

In this appendix we have seen the major developments in Lucan studies. It is true that we are still in "the shifting sands," but the future of Lucan studies lies in the direction of spirituality.

NOTES

INTRODUCTION

[1] A. Besnard, "Tendencies of Contemporary Spirituality," *Concilium*, 9 (1965), p. 26.

[2] Josef Sudbrack, "Spirituality," *Sacramentum Mundi*, Karl Rahner with Cornelius Ernst and Kevin Smyth, eds. (New York: Herder and Herder, 1970), VI, p. 151. See also C. Duquoc, "Theology and Spirituality," *Concilium*, 19 (1966), pp. 88-99.

[3] Document on Divine Revelation, Vatican Council II, 18:1; 25:1.

[4] Leo Scheffczyk, "Word of God," *Sacramentum Mundi*, VI, pp. 365-366.

[5] See Hans Urs von Balthasar, "The Gospel as Norm and Test of All Spirituality in the Church," *Concilium*, 9 (1965), pp. 14-17.

[6] Brevard Childs, *Biblical Theology in Crisis* (Philadelphia: Westminster Press, 1980), p. 100.

[7] See P. Schoonenberg, "Notes of a Systematic Theologian," *Concilium*, 70 (1971), p. 90.

[8] Childs, pp. 44-45.

[9] See J. N. Wijngaards, "Biblical Spirituality," *Scripture Bulletin*, 9 (1978), p. 9.

[10] See Sudbrack, p. 151.

CHAPTER ONE

[1] Early writings which state this include Irenaeus in his treatise, *Against Heresies* III, I, written about 178; *The Muratorian Canon* of authoritative books of scripture, written in Rome about 180-200; the so-called *Anti-Marcionite Prologue* dated around 180; Clement of Alexandria in *Stromateis*, V, 12 (c. 208-211); Tertullian in his *Adversus Marcionem*, IV, 2 (c. 207-208); Origen as quoted by Eusebius, and Eusebius himself in his *Historia Ecclesiastica*, III, 4, 24 (c. 311-325); and later Jerome in *De Viris Illustribus*, VII (c. 392).

[2] For additional biographical information on Luke gleaned from the early writings, see Joseph Kelly, "The Patristic Biography of Luke," *Bible Today*, No. 74 (1974), pp. 113-119.

[3] See A. von Harnack, *Luke the Physician* (New York: Williams and Norgate, 1909); W. K. Hobart, *The Medical Language of St. Luke* (Dublin: Hodges, Figgis and Co., 1882).

[4] See H. Cadbury, *The Making of Luke-Acts* (London: SPCK, 1968), p. 245; Richard Glover, "'Luke the Antiochene' and Acts," *New Testament Studies*, 11 (1964-65), pp. 97-106.

[5] See H. Cadbury, quoted by Ernst Haenchen, *The Acts of the Apostles* (Oxford: Blackwell, 1971), p. 14, note 6.

[6] Johannes Munck, *The Acts of the Apostles* (New York: Doubleday and Co., Inc.,1967), p. xxxiii.

[7] See I. Howard Marshall, *Luke: Historian and Theologian* (Grand Rapids: Zondervan, 1971), p. 220.

[8] Ernst Haenchen, "The Book of Acts as Source for the History of Early Christianity," in *Studies in Luke-Acts*, L. E. Keck and J. L. Martyn, eds. (New York: Abingdon Press, 1966), p. 272.

[9] See Haenchen, *Acts*, p. 72; also F. F. Bruce, *The Acts of the Apostles* (Grand Rapids: William B. Eerdmans Publishing Co., 1951), pp. 26-29.

[10] H. Conzelmann, "The Address of Paul on the Areopagus," in *Studies in Luke-Acts*, p. 218.

[11] See Vernon K. Robbins, "Prefaces in Greco-Roman Biography and Luke-Acts," *Perspectives in Religious Studies*, 6 (1979), pp. 100-108; John Drury, *Tradition and Design in Luke's Gospel* (Atlanta: John Knox Press, 1977), p. 50. Regarding the Septuagintal Greek used by Luke, I would agree with Johannes Munck and others that "they must be considered. . .as deliberate additions to the style of his work." See *Acts*, p. xxvii.

[12] See Cadbury, *Making of Luke-Acts*, ch. XVII: "Some Secular Interests"; and C. K. Barrett, *Luke the Historian in Recent Study* (Philadelphia: Fortress Press, 1970), pp. 15-19.

[13] See Barrett, *Luke the Historian*, pp. 9-12; Marshall, *Historian and Theologian*, chs. II and III; Bruce, *Acts*, pp. 15-18; Haenchen, "Acts as Source Material," p. 260.

[14] See C. H. Talbert, *Literary Patterns, Theological Themes and the Genre of Luke-Acts* (Missoula: Scholars Press, 1974), pp. 1-2.

[15] See J. Comblin, "La paix dans la théologie de saint Luc," *Ephêmerides Thêologicae Louvaniensis*, 32 (1956), pp. 439-460.

[16] See Bruce, *Acts*, pp. 34-40; Marshall, *Historian and Theologian*, p. 220; H. J. Cadbury, "'We' and 'I' Passages in Luke-Acts," *New Testament Studies*, 3 (1956-57), pp. 130-131. Cadbury suggests that Luke is not an eyewitness "from the beginning," but "for some time past" (Lk 1:3). Cadbury is convinced that the participle used by Luke indicates first hand knowledge, and means "to observe," not "to investigate."

[17] See Munck, *Acts*, pp. xlii-xliii; Haenchen, "Acts as Source Material," pp. 271-275; Cadbury, "'We' and 'I' Passages," pp. 129-130.

[18] See Haenchen, "Acts as Source Material," p. 264.

[19] Much has been written on this topic. I suggest B. Orchard, "The Problem of Acts and Galatians," *Catholic Biblical Quarterly*, 7 (1945), pp. 377-397; D. R. De Lacey, "Paul in Jerusalem," *New Testament Studies*,

20 (1973-74), pp. 82-86; P. Parker, "Once More, Acts and Galatians," *Journal of Biblical Literature*, 86 (1967), pp. 175-182.

[20] For more details and evaluation of the two portraits of Paul, see Haenchen, *Acts*, pp. 112-116; E. Goodenough, "The Perspective of Acts," in *Studies in Luke-Acts*, pp. 51-59.

[21] These four major differences are examined in detail by Paul Vielhauer, "On the Paulinism of Acts," in *Studies in Luke-Acts*, pp. 33-50. See also Günther Bornkamm, "The Missionary Stance of Paul in 1 Corinthians 9 and in Acts," in *Studies in Luke-Acts*, pp. 194-207; George MacRae, "'Whom Heaven Must Receive Until the Time': Reflections on the Christology of Acts," *Interpretation*, 27 (1973), pp. 151-165.

[22] See Vielhauer, p. 48.

[23] See Eckhard Plumacher, "The 'we-passages' in Acts," *Theology Digest*, 27 (1979), pp. 47-48.

[24] See Arland Hultgren, "Interpreting the Gospel of Luke," *Interpretation*, 30 (1976), p. 364; W. Gasque, "The Historical Value of the Book of Acts: An Essay in the History of New Testament Criticism," *Evangelical Quarterly*, 41 (1969), pp. 68-88.

[25] Ulrich Wilkens, "Interpreting Luke-Acts in a Period of Existentialist Theology," in *Studies in Luke-Acts*, p. 77. See also W. C. van Unnik, "Luke-Acts, A Storm Center in Contemporary Scholarship," in *Studies in Luke-Acts*, pp. 28-29.

[26] "Luke's Place in the Development of Early Christianity," in *Studies in Luke-Acts*, p. 305.

[27] See Peder Borgen, "From Paul to Luke," *Catholic Biblical Quarterly*, 31 (1969), pp. 169, 181-182.

[28] F. F. Bruce, "Is the Paul of Acts the Real Paul?" *Bulletin of the John Ryland Library*, 58 (1976), pp. 282-300. See also Drury, *Tradition*, p. 15; Joseph A. Fitzmyer, *The Gospel According to Luke*, I (New York: Doubleday and Co., Inc., 1981), pp. 47-51.

[29] See R. Zehnle, "The Salvific Character of Jesus' Death in Lucan Soteriology," *Theological Studies*, 30 (1969), pp. 443-444.

[30] A variation on this position was presented by Pierson Parker, "The 'Former Treatise' and the Date of Acts," *Journal of Biblical Literature*, 84 (1965), pp. 52-58. He accepts that Luke's gospel is dependent on Mark, and was therefore written after 64-70. Acts, on the other hand, ends before 64, predating the gospel. The "former treatise" is therefore Proto-Luke.

[31] Rome generally supported the national religon of a conquered nation. This national religion was the only *religio licita,* or lawful religion, of the country, and unlawful religions were persecuted. Several commentators, as we shall see, have suggested that Luke writes his two volumes as a defense of Christianity as the natural outgrowth of Judaism, and so a *religio licita*.

[32] See Bruce, *Acts*, pp. 11-13; Munck, *Acts*, pp. xlvii-xlviii; A. J. Matill, Jr., "The Date and Purpose of Luke-Acts: Rackham Reconsidered," *Catholic Biblical Quarterly*, 40 (1978), pp. 335-350; I. H. Marshall, "Recent Study of the Acts of the Apostles," *Expository Times*, 80 (1969), pp. 292-296; C. J. Hemer, "Luke the Historian," *Bulletin of the John Ryland Library*, 60 (1977), pp. 28-51.

[33] J. C. O'Neill, *The Theology of Acts in Its Historical Setting* (London: SPCK, 1961), pp. 1-58.

[34] For an evaluation of O'Neill, see H. Conzelmann, "Luke's Place in the Development of Early Christianity," in *Studies in Luke-Acts*, pp. 302-304.

[35] See J. Knox, "Acts and the Pauline Letter Corpus," in *Studies in Luke-Acts*, pp. 279-287. For an evaluation of Knox's position, see E. Wilshire, "Was Canonical Luke written in the Second Century?-A Continuing Discussion," *New Testament Studies*, 20 (1973-74), pp. 246-253.

[36] See Drury, *Tradition*, pp. 15-38; Henry Wansbrough, "St. Luke and Christian Ideals in an Affluent Society," *New Blackfriars*, 49 (1968), pp. 582-587; Paul Minear, "Jesus' audiences according to Luke," *Theology Digest*, 23 (1975), p. 256; A. W. Mosley, "Jesus' Audiences in the Gospels of St. Mark and St. Luke," *New Testament Studies*, 10 (1963-64), pp. 139-149.

[37] *Tradition*, p. 25.

CHAPTER TWO

[1] See the section on tendency criticism and redaction criticism in the appendix, "Studies of Luke-Acts."

[2] In support of some connection between Luke and John, read F. Lamar Cribbs, "St. Luke and the Johannine Tradition," *Journal of Biblical Literature*, 90 (1971), pp. 426-427: "The Lucan agreements with John. . . may have been due to Luke's familiarity with some form of the developing Johannine tradition or even to his acquaintance with an early draft of the original Gospel of John"; Pierson Parker, "Luke and the Fourth Evangelist," *New Testament Studies*, 9 (1962-63), p. 336: "The Fourth Evangelist must somewhere, some time, have been associated with Luke in the Christian missionary enterprise"; A. Feuillet in *Jésus et sa Mère* (Paris: Gabalda, 1974) also sees John as an intermediary between Mary and Luke.

[3] See E. P. Sanders, "The Argument from Order and the Relationship between Matthew and Luke," *New Testament Studies*, 15 (1968-69), p. 261; Drury, *Tradition*, chapter 6: "Using Matthew"; Fitzmyer, *Luke*, pp. 73-81.

[4] Munck, *Acts*, p. xxv, offers a variation: "Many are of the opinion that in his gospel, Luke is dependent on Mark. It is, however, more correct to

assume that Luke is dependent on oral tradition and also on the earliest written notes on parts of this tradition."

[5] For arguments in support of the Proto-Luke hypothesis, read G. B. Caird, *St Luke*, Pelican New Testament Commentaries (Harmondsworth: Penguin, 1963), pp. 23-27.

[6] J. Dupont, *The Sources of the Acts* (New York: Herder and Herder, 1964), p. 166.

[7] It has often been suggested that the sources of Acts can be identified by linguistic analysis, and that the early Palestinian-based episodes, reflecting an Aramaic background, presume a translated Aramaic document. However, these early chapters are not translation Greek, and the Aramaisms are Septuagintisms. We have already seen how Luke uses Septuagintal Greek to create atmosphere and context in this section of Acts. See Haenchen, *Acts*, pp. 73-74.

[8] Eric Franklin, *Christ the Lord, A Study in the Purpose and Theology of Luke-Acts* (Philadelphia: Westminster Press, 1975), p. 79.

[9] See Drury, *Tradition*, pp. 46-81. Concerning Luke's skillful use of the liturgical readings of Jewish feasts, see J. Dupont, "Ascension du Christ et don de l'Esprit d'après Actes 2:33," in *Christ and Spirit in the New Testament*, B. Lindars and S. Smalley, eds. (Cambridge: University Press, 1973), pp. 219-228.

[10] H. J. Cadbury, "Four Features of Lucan Style," in *Studies in Luke-Acts*, p. 93.

[11] F. Danker, *Luke*, Proclamation Commentaries (Philadelphia: Fortress Press, 1976), pp. 98-100; also Haenchen, *Acts*, p. 79.

[12] See H. F. D. Sparks, "St. Luke's Transpositions," *New Testament Studies*, 3 (1956-57), pp. 219-223.

[13] H. C. Kee, F. W. Young and K. Froelich, *Understanding the New Testament* (Englewood Cliffs: Prentice Hall, 1973), p. 372.

[14] See Robbins, pp. 100-108.

[15] See Caird, *St. Luke*, p. 30.

[16] H. Flender, *St Luke: Theologian of Redemptive History* (Philadelphia: Fortress Press, 1967), p. 9.

[17] See H. Conzelmann, *The Theology of St. Luke* (New York: Harper and Row, 1960), Part II: "Luke's Eschatology."

[18] See the section on Conzelmann in Appendix, "Studies on Luke-Acts."

[19] See W. G. Kümmel, "Current Theological Accusations Against Luke," *Andover Newton Quarterly*, 16 (1975), pp. 131-145; C. H. Talbert, "Shifting Sands: The Recent Study of the Gospel of Luke," *Interpretation*, 30 (1976), pp. 381-395.

[20] Talbert, "Shifting Sands," p. 386.

[21] See Francois Bovon, "Recent Trends in Lucan Studies," *Theology Digest*, 25(1977), p. 220.

[22] Marshall, *Historian and Theologian*, p. 46.

[23] Marshall, *Historian and Theologian*, p. 52.

[24] J. Dupont, "Apologetic Use of the Old Testament," in *The Salvation of the Gentiles* (New York: Paulist Press, 1979), p. 157.

[25] See Robbins, p. 100.

[26] B. S. Easton, *The Purpose of Acts* (London: SPCK and The Sheldon Press, 1936), considers Luke wrote to defend Christianity as a *religio licita*. See Munck, *Acts*, pp. lxxx-lxxxiv.

[27] See H. Schuster, "Pastoral Theology," in *Sacramentum Mundi* (New York: Herder and Herder, 1969), IV, pp. 365-368.

[28] Each of these topics will be dealt with later.

[29] H. F. Wickings, "The Nativity Stories and Docetism," *New Testament Studies*, 23 (1976-77), pp. 457-460; see C. H. Talbert, "Anti-Gnostic Tendency in Lucan Christology," *New Testament Studies*, 14 (1967-68), pp. 259-271.

[30] See Chapter 7 on Universal Salvation.

[31] Dupont, "Conversion in the Acts of the Apostles," in *Salvation of the Gentiles*, pp. 61-84.

[32] Conzelmann, *Theology*, p. 13.

[33] Paul Minear, "Dear Theo The Kerygmatic Intention and Claim of the Book of Acts," *Interpretation*, 27 (1973), p. 147.

CHAPTER THREE

[1] Minear, "Dear Theo," p. 134.

[2] Franklin, *Christ the Lord*, p. 145.

[3] See John Navone, "Three Aspects of Lucan Theology of History," *Biblical Theology Bulletin*, 3 (1973), p. 127. "Now" is used 3 times in Matthew and Mark, but 39 times in Luke-Acts. "Today," used 9 times in Matthew and Mark, appears 19 times in Luke-Acts.

[4] I would disagree with J. Munck, *Acts*, p. lv: "The purpose of Luke's two part work must be determined without regard . . . to the title. The Acts of the Apostles (added to Acts at a later date), with its associations concerning the genre of the book." I believe that people's reactions were important. The early Church saw this as describing the great acts of apostolic people.

[5] Paul Minear, "Luke's Use of the Birth Stories," in *Studies in Luke-Acts*, pp. 121-124; Marshall, *Historian and Theologian*, p. 97; H. H. Oliver, "The Lucan Birth Stories and the Purpose of Luke-Acts," *New Testament Studies*, 10 (1963-64), p. 203.

[6] See N. Turner, "The Relations of Luke I and II to Hebraic Sources and to the Rest of Luke-Acts," *New Testament Studies*, 2 (1955-56), pp. 100-109; M. D. Goulder and M. L. Sanderson, "St. Luke's Genesis," *Journal of Theological Studies*, 8 (1957), pp. 12-30; P. Winter considers these

chapters a translation from a Hebrew source: "Some Observations on the Language in the Birth and Infancy Stories of the Third Gospel," *New Testament Studies*, 1 (1954-55), pp. 111-121.

[7] See S. Muñoz Iglesias, "Los Evangelios de la Infancia y las infancias de los heroes," *Estudios Biblicos*, 16 (1957), pp. 5-36.

[8] Franklin, *Christ the Lord*, p. 80. See L. Legrand, "L'arrière-plan néotestamentaire de Luc 1,35," *Revue Biblique*, 70 (1963), pp. 161-192; Oliver, p. 223; W. B. Tatum, "The Epoch of Israel: Luke I-II and the Theological Plan of Luke-Acts," *New Testament Studies*, 13 (1966-67), pp. 184-195.

[9] Elements of the passion are anticipated in the presentation story. See R. Brown, "The Presentation of Jesus (Luke 2:22-40)," *Worship*, 51 (1977), pp. 2-11.

[10] Oliver, p. 221. See also R. Brown, "The Finding of the Boy Jesus in the Temple, A Third Christmas Story," *Worship*, 51 (1977), pp. 474-485.

[11] In some ways the names of the people in the infancy narratives are the message: Zechariah = God has remembered; Elizabeth = God is fullness; John = God is gracious; Mary = the beloved; Joseph = God gathers together; Jesus = Salvation.

[12] See Drury, *Tradition*, p. 98.

[13] See C. H. Talbert, "The Lukan Presentation of Jesus' Ministry in Galilee, Luke 4:31-9:50," *Review and Expositor*, 64 (1967), pp. 485-497.

[14] See P. H. Menoud, "Jésus et ses témoins; Remarques sur l'unité de l'oeuvre du Luc," *Eglise et Théologie*, 23 (1960), pp. 7-20; F. Stagg, "The Unhindered Gospel," *Review and Expositor*, 71 (1974), pp. 451-462.

[15] See F. V. Filson, "Live Issues in the Acts," *Biblical Research*, 9 (1964), pp. 26-37; R. F. O'Toole, "Why Did Luke Write Acts (Lk-Acts)?" *Biblical Theology Bulletin*, 7 (1977), p. 66.

[16] See J. J. Kilgallen, "Acts: Literary and Theological Turning Points," *Biblical Theology Bulletin*, 7 (1977), pp. 177-180.

[17] For a good synthesis, see Fitzmyer, "The Current State of Lucan Studies," in *Luke*, pp. 3-29; and R. F. O'Toole, "Why Did Luke Write Acts?" pp. 66-76.

[18] For a synthesis of some problems facing Luke's Church, see E. Earle Ellis, *The Gospel of Luke*, New Century Bible (Geenwood, SC.: Attic Press, 1974), pp. 61-62.

[19] A. R. C. Leaney, *The Gospel According to St. Luke* (London: Adam and Charles Black, 1966), p. 5.

[20] See Munck, *Acts*, p. lviii; Caird, *St. Luke*, p. 14; Goodenough, "The Perspective of Acts," p. 58.

[21] Cadbury, *Making of Luke-Acts*, p. 316.

[22] Danker, *Luke*, p. 104.

[23] Franklin, *Christ the Lord*, p. 114.

[24] See Hultgren, pp. 353-365.

[25] See M. 0. Tolbert, "Contemporary Issues in the Book of Acts," *Review and Expositor*, 71 (1974), pp. 521-531.

[26] Haenchen, *Acts*, p. 100; also Dupont, *Salvation of the Gentiles*, pp. 11-34. For an opposing opinion, see J. Gamba, "Praeoccupatio Universalistica in Evangelio S. Lucae," *Verbum Domini*, 40 (1962), pp. 131-135.

[27] See Talbert, *Literary Patterns*, p. 106.

[28] See Bruce, *Acts*, pp. 29-34; Drury, *Tradition*, p. 31.

[29] Hultgren, p. 365.

[30] Marshall, *Historian and Theologian*, p. 92.

[31] See A. George, "L'Emploi chez Luc du vocabulaire de salut," *New Testament Studies*, 23 (1976-77), pp. 308-320.

CHAPTER FOUR

[1] See C. F. Moule, "The Christology of Acts," *Studies in Luke-Acts*, L. E. Keck and J. L. Martyn, eds. (New York: Abingdon Press, 1966), pp. 159-185.

[2] See C. H. Talbert, "Anti-Gnostic Tendency," pp. 259-271.

[3] The word "Lord" is used to describe Jesus and the Father. On a few occasions it is not clear who is intended. The Father is referred to as "Lord" in at least the following cases: Lk 1:6, 9, 11, 15, 16, 17, 25, 28, 32, 38, 45, 46, 58, 66, 68, 76; 2:9, 15, 22, 23, 24, 26; 3:4; 4:8, 12, 19, 5:17; 10:2, 21, 27; 19:38; Acts 2: 20, 21, 25, 34, 39; 3:20, 22; 4:26; 8:22, 24, 25; 10:4; 11:8; 12:11, 17, 23; 13:10, 11; 15:17, 18; 21:14; 22:8; 26:15.

[4] John Navone, *Themes of St. Luke* (Rome: Gregorian University Press, 1970), p. 100. See also Conzelmann, *Theology*, p. 151, who gives the following examples: "foreknowledge" (Acts 2:23), "foretold" (Acts 3:18; 7:52), "heralded" (Acts 13:24), "predestines" (Acts 3:20; 22:14; 26:16).

[5] Navone, *Themes*, p. 100; see also Marshall, *Historian and Theologian*, p. 106.

[6] See Zehnle, p. 427: "The life of Jesus is presented above all as a life lived in complete conformity with the will of God."

[7] See Paul Achtemeier, "The Lucan Perspective on the Miracles of Jesus: A Preliminary Sketch," *Journal of Biblical Literature*, 94 (1975), pp. 552-553.

[8] *Theology*, p. 176.

[9] See Danker, *Luke*, chapters 2 and 3.

[10] Drury, p. 9. For similar views see Paul Hinnebusch, "Jesus, the New Elijah in St. Luke," *Bible Today*, 6 (1968), pp. 2175-2182.

[11] *Theology*, p. 174.

[12] R. Martin, "Salvation and Discipleship in Luke's Gospel," *Interpretation*, 30 (1976), pp. 366-380; Jacques Dupont, *Salvation of the Gentiles*, pp. 11-33, emphasizes a similar position.

[13] See Franklin, *Christ the Lord*, pp. 114-115, and chapters 3 and 4.

[14] See A. George, "La royauté de Jésus selon l'évangile de Luc," *Science Ecclésiastique*, 14 (1962), pp. 57-69.

[15] See Moule, pp. 159-166.

[16] G. W. H. Lampe, "The Lucan Portrait of Christ," *New Testament Studies*, 2 (1955-56), p. 171.

[17] See Oliver, p. 222.

[18] See Paul Hinnebusch, "In My Father's House - About My Father's Business (Luke 2:49)," *Bible Today*, 4 (1966), p. 1893.

[19] See Hultgren, pp. 358-359.

[20] Jesus performs the following miracles in Luke: the healing of Simon's mother-in-law (4:39), the sick at sundown (4:40), a leper (5:12), a paralysed man (5:18), the man with a withered hand (6:6), the centurion's son (7:2), many who needed him (7:21), Jairus's daughter (8:41), the woman with a hemorrage (8:43), an unnamed person (9:11), the convulsive boy (9:38), the dumb man (11:14), the crippled woman (13:11), the man with dropsy (14:2), ten lepers (17:12), and the servant of the high priest (22:51).

[21] See A. George, "Son of God in Luke," *Theology Digest*, 15 (1967), pp. 128-133.

[22] See Schulyer Brown, *Apostasy and Perseverance in the Theology of Luke* (Rome: Pontifical Biblical Institute, 1969), p. 133.

[23] Franklin, *Christ the Lord*, p. 68.

[24] See Navone, *Themes*, p. 136; Hinnebusch, "Jesus, the New Elijah," pp. 2175-2182.

[25] See George, "La royauté," pp. 57-69.

[26] Lk 5:24; 6:5, 22; 7:34; 9:22, 26, 44, 58; 11:30; 12:8, 10, 40; 17:22, 24, 30; 18:8, 31; 19:10; 21:27, 36; 22:22, 48, 69; 24:7.

[27] Lk 1:43; 2:11; 5:8, 12; 6:46; 7:6, 13, 19; 9:54, 59, 61; 10:1, 39, 40, 41; 11:1; 12:41, 42; 13:23, 35; 17:5, 6, 37; 18:6; 19:8, 31, 34; 22:38, 49.

[28] See George, "Son of God," pp. 128-133. Jesus is called "Son" by God: Lk 1:32, 35; 3:22; 9:35; Jesus is called "Son" by Satan: Lk 4:3, 9, 41; 8:28; Jesus uses the word "Son": Lk 10:22; 20:13; 22:70; Jesus implies this relationship when he speaks of the Father: Lk 2:49; 10:22; 22:29; 24:49.

[29] *Theology*, pp. 170-174.

[30] See Caird, *St. Luke*, p. 38; Navone, *Themes*, p. 153.

[31] See Richard Hiers, "The Problem of the Delay of the Parousia in Luke-Acts," *New Testament Studies*, 20 (1974-75), pp. 145-155.

[32] See H. P. Owen, "Stephen's Vision in Acts VII 55-56," *New Testament Studies*, 1 (1954-55), pp. 224-225. The author sees Luke as depicting Christ's career with the six action words used in the text.

[33] The following speak of subordinationism and adoptionism in Luke: Conzelmann, *Theology*, p. 173; Drury, *Tradition*, p. 123; Wilckens, "Interpreting Luke-Acts," p. 62.

[34] See S. S. Smalley, "The Christology of Acts," *Expository Times*, 73 (1962), pp. 358-362; George, "Son of God," pp. 131-132

[35] See Talbert, *Literary Patterns*, p. 142; "Anti-Gnostic Tendency," p. 271.

[36] See Zehnle, p. 432.

[37] See Lampe, p. 171.

[38] Acts 2:36; 3:18, 20; 5:42; 8:5; 9:22; 17:3; 18:5, 28; 26:23.

[39] Acts 1:6, 21; 2:36; 4:33; 5:14; 7:59, 60; 8:16; 9:1, 5, 10, 11, 13, 15, 17, 27, 28, 35, 42; 10:36; 11:17, 20, 21, 23, 24; 12:23; 13:49; 14:3, 23; 15:11, 26; 16:31-32; 18:8, 9, 25; 19:10, 13, 17, 20; 20:19, 21, 24, 35; 21:13; 22:10, 19; 23:11; 28:31.

[40] MacRae, p. 154; see also J. A. T. Robinson, "The Most Primitive Christianity of All?" *Journal of Theological Studies*, 7 (1956), pp. 177-189.

[41] See Navone, *Themes*, p. 154: "The word ,power, (dunamis) is also Lucan. It is found 10 times in his Gospel and 7 times in Acts; whereas, it appears only 3 times in Matthew and 2 times in Mark."

[42] Navone, *Themes*, pp. 59-60.

[43] Marshall, *Historian and Theologian*, p. 200.

[44] See Leonard Doohan, "Apostolic Prayer", *Review for Religious*, 33 (1974), pp. 785-789

[45] See Jacques Dupont, "Ascension du Christ et don de l'Esprit d'après Actes 2:33," pp. 219-228

[46] Luke modifies Mark where failures of the disciples is suggested, so he omits Mk 14:50 and adds "exhausted with grief" in Lk 22:45.

[47] See John Holland, "Impressed Unbelievers as Witnesses to Christ (Luke 4:22a)," *Journal of Biblical Literature*, 98 (1979), pp. 219-229

[48] See Dupont, "Conversion," pp. 74-76.

[49] See MacRae, pp. 151-165; R. F. O'Toole, "Luke's Understanding of Jesus' Resurrection-Ascension-Exaltation," *Biblical Theology Bulletin*, 9 (1979), pp. 112-114.

[50] F. F. Bruce, "The Holy Spirit in the Acts of the Apostles," *Interpretation*, 27 (1973), p. 173.

CHAPTER FIVE

[1] See Hultgren, "Interpreting," pp. 362-363, where the author addresses the Lucan interest in city life. See also Cadbury, *Making of Luke-Acts*, pp. 246-249.

[2] See Kee, Young, Froelich, p. 370.

[3] See R. Spivey and D. Moody Smith, *Anatomy of the New Testament* (New York: Macmillan, 1974), p. 254.

[4] See Lampe, p. 173.

[5] See Ben F. Meyer, "The Initial Self-Understanding of the Church," *Catholic Biblical Quarterly*, 27 (1965), pp. 35-42.

[6] Verses 15-26 would seem to be a later insertion. The text flows naturally and more logically from 1:14 to 2:1.

[7] See Dupont, "The First Christian Pentecost," in *The Salvation of the Gentiles*, pp. 35-59.

[8] Conzelmann, *Theology*, p. 146.

[9] Lampe, pp. 173-174.

[10] See Dupont, "Community of Goods in the Early Church," in *The Salvation of the Gentiles*, pp. 85 - 102.

[11] It must be stated that all were Jews. However, Luke's intention seems to be to give the story a universalist flavor.

[12] See R. H. Smith, "The Eschatology of Acts and Contemporary Exegesis," *Concordia Theological Monthly*, 29 (1958), pp. 641-663.

[13] See S. G. Wilson, "Lucan Eschatology," *New Testament Studies*, 16 (1969-70), pp. 330-347. The author identifies the following as referring to an imminent expectation: Lk 10:9-11; 12:38-40; 12:54 - 13:9; 18:8; 21:32.

[14] P. A. Stempvoort, "The Interpretation of the Ascension in Luke and Acts," *New Testament Studies*, 5 (1958-59), p. 42.

[15] See S. Brown, *Apostasy*, p. 73. The author gives 36 such references.

[16] Stempvoort, p. 39.

[17] S. Brown, *Apostasy*, p. 130; also Jerome Kodell, "The Word of God Grew. The Ecclesial Tendency of Logos in Acts 1,7; 12,24; 19,20," *Biblica*, 55 (1974), pp. 512-519.

[18] See Lars Hartman, "Into the Name of Jesus," *New Testament Studies*, 20 (1973-74), pp. 432-440.

[19] See Paul Bernadicou, "Christian Community According to Luke," *Worship*, 44 (1970), p. 213.

[20] S. Brown, *Apostasy*, p. 119.

[21] See Kodell, "Word of God," p. 505.

[22] See Carlo Martini, "L'esclusione dalla communità del popolo di Dio e il nuovo Israele secondo Atti 3,23," *Biblica*, 50 (1969), pp. 1-14. Regarding the identification of Word and community, see Kodell, "The Word of God," p. 511.

[23] See F. Bovon, "L'importance des Médiations dans le Projet Théologique de Luc," *New Testament Studies*, 21 (1974-75), pp. 26-28.

[24] See W. F. J. Ryan, "The Church as the Servant of God in Acts," *Scripture*, 15 (1963), pp. 110-115.

[25] "This process of ecclesialization may be observed within Acts itself in connection with the giving of the Spirit. At first this took place with complete spontaneity (2,4; 4,31; 10,44), independently of any churchly rite or office; later the Spirit is communicated by the apostles (8,17) or their duly constituted envoys (19,6)." S. Brown, *Apostasy*, p. 131.

[26] See Jerome Kodell, "Luke's Use of Laos, 'People,' Especially in the Jerusalem Narrative, (Lk 19,28 - 24,53)," *Catholic Biblical Quarterly*, 31 (1969), pp. 327-343.

[27] Hultgren, "Interpreting," p. 363.

[28] Joseph Fitzmyer, "Jewish Community in Acts in Light of the Qumran Scrolls," in *Studies in Luke-Acts*, p. 247.

[29] Franklin, *Christ the Lord*, pp. 169-170. See also Hultgren, p. 359.

[30] Marshall, *Historian and Theologian*, p. 214.

[31] See Joseph Lienhard, "Acts 6:1-6: A Redactional View," *Catholic Biblical Quarterly*, 37 (1975), pp. 228-236.

[32] See R. Brown, Karl P. Donfried, John Reumann, eds. *Peter in the New Testament* (New York: Paulist Press, 1973), pp. 39-56.

[33] I would accept the explanation given in R. Brown, namely that we are here dealing with a combination of two sources. The first describes a council which was a provincial meeting of the Church governed by James. The second was a meeting of the whole Church, in which Peter takes the leading role. Luke has combined these two.

[34] Kodell, "Word of God," p. 514.

[35] See Navone, *Themes*, p. 30; "The Lucan Banquet Community," *Bible Today*, 8 (1970), p. 155.

[36] See P. Minear, "Some Glimpses of Luke's Sacramental Theology," *Worship*, 44 (1970), pp. 322-331.

[37] See Dupont, "Community of Goods in the Early Church," pp. 85-102.

[38] See Robert Karris, "Poor and Rich: The Lukan Sitz im Leben," in *Perspectives on Luke-Acts*, C. H. Talbert, ed. (Danville, VA.: Association of Baptist Professors of Religion, 1978), pp. 112-125; also Wansbrough, pp. 582-587.

[39] S. Brown, *Apostasy*, p. 107.

[40] S. Brown, p. 105.

[41] See Karris, pp. 124-125.

[42] I refer the reader to a complete list of references in J. Navone, *Themes*, p. 71. He begins by saying: "Many expressions in Luke-Acts indicate joy: *makarios* and *makarizo* (blessed and to bless), *chara* and *chairein* (joy and to rejoice), *doksa* and *dokazein* (glory and to glorify), *agalliasis* and *agalliao* (exurberant joy and to rejoice exuberantly), *ainein* (to praise), *eulogein* (to bless), *eirene* (peace), *euphrainein* (to gladden or to feast), *megaluno* (to magnify), and *skirtao* (to leap for joy)."

CHAPTER SIX

[1] See Mark Sheridan, "Disciples and Discipleship in Matthew and Luke," *Biblical Theology Bulletin*, 3 (1973), pp. 235-255.

[2] See S. Brown, *Apostasy*, p. 82, where the author gives these references: Lk 5:14, 25; 8:39; 9:60; 19:32; 22:13.

[3] See A. Feuillet, "Le récit lucanien de l'agonie de Géthsemani (Lc xxii, 39-46)," *New Testament Studies*, 22 (1975-76), pp. 399-400.

[4] For general studies on conversion in Luke, see F. X. Hezel, "Conversion and Repentance in Lucan Theology," *Bible Today*, 6 (1968), pp. 2596-2602; R. Michiels, "La conception lucannienne de la conversion," *Ephémerides Théologicae Louvaniensis*, 41 (1965), pp. 42-78.

[5] "Conversion" is used 10 times in Lucan writings and 5 times in the rest of the New Testament. "Repentance" is used 23 times by Luke and 30 times in all the other New Testament books. For a good summary of repentance and conversion, see Fitzmyer, *Luke*, pp. 237-239.

[6] In this part I follow the excellent study of Dupont, "Conversion in the Acts of the Apostles," in *Salvation of the Gentiles*, pp. 61-84.

[7] In the following references, "believing" and "believers" mean the same as becoming or being a Christian: Lk 8:12, 13; Acts 2:44; 4:4, 32; 5:14; 6:7; 8:13; 11:21; 13:12, 39, 48; 14:1; 15:7; 17:12, 34; 18:8, 27; 19:2, 18; 21:20, 25. See Brown, *Apostasy*, p. 40.

[8] See Navone, *Themes*, p. 203: "The disciples' complaint about the exorcist, 'because he was not following us' (Mk 9:38), is changed in the Lucan account to 'because he does not follow *with* us' (9:49). In the Marcan account, the Baptist announces 'Someone is following me. . .' (1:7); Luke changes this to say that Jesus 'came after' (3:16)."

[9] See Navone, *Themes*, pp. 66-67, where he analyses the movement-words used of Jesus in this section of the narrative, which all add to the general description of the journey.

[10] Conzelmann, *Theology*, p. 62.

[11] Conzelmann, *Theology*, p. 47.

[12] See D. Gill, "Observations on the Lukan Travel Narrative and Some Related Passages," *Harvard Theological Review*, 63 (1970), pp. 214-221.

[13] Navone, "Lucan Joy," *Scripture*, 20 (1968), pp. 49-62.

[14] See Joseph Blenkinsopp, "The Church's Mission in St. Luke," *Clergy Review*, 50 (1965), p. 698.

[15] See S. Brown, *Apostasy*, pp. 131-145.

[16] "Since the journey of Jesus to Jerusalem in Luke is arranged in a chiastic pattern, it would be in line with the Lucan stylistic tendency to find Paul's journey which ends in Jerusalem arranged in a similar way. Close examination of Acts 15:1-21:26 reveals that this is exactly what the author of Luke-Acts has done." Talbert, *Literary Patterns*, p. 56.

[17] J. D'Arc, "Catechesis on the Road to Emmaus," *Lumen Vitae*, 32 (1977), p. 154.

[18] See R. Brown, *New Testament Essays* (New York: Doubleday and Co., Inc., 1968, pp. 275-320.

[19] The verb is present imperative, indicating continuity in the asking and seeking.

[20] See S. Brown, *Apostasy*, pp. 98-113.

[21] John Kealy, *Luke's Gospel Today* (Denville, NJ.: Dimension Books, 1979), p. 327.

[22] Wilfrid Harrington, *The Gospel According to St. Luke* (New York: Newman Press, 1967), p. 201.

[23] See Benjamin J. Hubbard, "The Role of the Commissioning Accounts in Acts," in *Perspectives on Luke-Acts*, C. H. Talbert, ed., pp. 187-198. Hubbard gives the following commissioning accounts: Lk 24:1-9, 36-53; Acts 1:1-14; 5:17-21a; 8:26-30; 9:1-9, 10-19; 10:1-8, 9-23, 30-33; 11:4-12; 12:6-12; 13:1-3; 16:8-10; 18:7-11; 22:6-11, 12-16, 17-21; 23:11; 26:12-20; 27:21-26.

[24]See Navone, *Themes*, p. 182: "'Now' occurs 14 times in the Third Gospel and 25 times in Acts; whereas, in Matthew and Mark it occurs only 3 times."

[25] Franklin, *Christ the Lord*, p. 71.

[26] "Today" occurs 11 times in Luke and 11 times in Acts, but only 9 times in the other synoptics.

CHAPTER SEVEN

[1] Kee, Young, Froelich, p. 383.

[2] J. D. Crossan, "Parable and Example in the Teaching of Jesus," *New Testament Studies*, 18 (1971-72), p. 295.

[3] See C. H. Cave, "Lazarus and the Lukan Deuteronomy," *New Testament Studies*, 15 (1968-69), pp. 319-325. Cave suggests that Lazarus represents Eliezar, the Gentile heir to Abraham, and that poor Lazarus inherits instead of Abraham's son.

[4] See Flender, pp. 9-10.

[5] "Men and women" occurs several times in Acts: 2:17-18; 5:12-16; 8:3, 12; 9:2; 17:12; 22:4, but only six times in the rest of the Bible.

[6] C. H. H. Scobie, "The Origins and Development of Samaritan Christianity," *New Testament Studies*, 19 (1972-73), pp. 396-397.

[7] Drury, *Tradition*, p. 110: "The injunction that each man should have a sword recalls Nehemiah 4:18 'each of the builders had his sword girded at his side while he built.' Like the rebuilding of Jerusalem the building of the Church will go forward through adversity."

[8] "Savior" (Soter) is used twice in Acts, but nowhere else in the synoptics; "To save" (Sozein) is used 17 times in Luke and 13 times in Acts (15 times in Mt, 14 times in Mk, 6 times in Jn); "Salvation" (Soteria) is used 4 times in Luke and 6 times in Acts, but nowhere else in the synoptics; "Salvation" (Soterion) is used twice in Luke and once in Acts, but only once more in the rest of the New Testament (Eph 6:17).

[9] See Marshall, *Historian and Theologian*, p. 93.

[10] Navone, *Themes*, p. 145: "Because there is a question of purely physical salvation, Luke avoids *Sozein*; he reserves this verb for the expression of Jesus' soteriological significance in a context which is more directly related to faith (pistis)."

[11] Marshall, *Historian and Theologian*, p. 95.

[12] See Zehnle, pp. 420-444.

[13] See Dupont, *Salvation of the Gentiles*, pp. 11-33.

[14] See P. H. Menoud, "Le plan des Actes des Apôtres," *New Testament Studies*, 1 (1954-55), pp. 44-51.

APPENDIX

[1] See Haenchen, *Acts*, pp. 1-14.

[2] Ellis, p. 37.

[3] See Haenchen, *Acts*, pp. 17-19.

[4] See chapter seven, which deals with universal salvation and the Gentile mission.

[5] See A. von Harnack, *Luke the Physician* (London: Williams and Norgate, 1909); *The Acts of the Apostles* (London: Williams and Norgate, 1909); *The Date of the Acts and of the Synoptic Gospels* (London: Williams and Norgate, 1911).

[6] See W. M. Ramsay, *St. Paul the Traveller and the Roman Citizen* (London: Hodder and Stoughton, 1905); *The Cities of St. Paul* (London: Hodder and Stoughton, 1907).

[7] See B. H. Streeter, *The Four Gospels: A Study of Origins, Treating of the Manuscript Tradition, Sources, Authorship and Dates* (London: Macmillan, 1924).

[8] For an excellent survey on critical research regarding the sources of Acts, see Haenchen, *Acts*, pp. 24-34.

[9] See Edgar V. McKnight, *What is Form Criticism?* (Philadelphia: Fortress press, 1969), pp. 13-15.

[10] See M. Dibelius, *From Tradition to Gospel* (New York: Scribner's Sons, 1965), R. Bultmann, *History of the Synoptic Tradition* (New York: Harper and Row, 1963).

[11] See Lawrence J. McGinley, *From Criticism of the Synoptic Healing Narratives-A Study in the Theories of Martin Dibelius and Rudolf Bultmann* (Woodstock: Woodstock College Press, 1944).

[12] Dibelius, p. 3.

[13] Bultmann, pp. 365, 367.

[14] Edgar Krentz, *The Historical-Critical Method* (Philadelphia: Fortress Press, 1975), p. 51.

[15] Norman Perrrin, *What is Redaction Criticism?* (Philadelphia: Fortress Press, 1969), p. 1.

[16] Perrin, p. 21.

[17] Perrin, pp. 29-30. See also Marshall, *Historian and Theologian*, p. 13.

[18] Conzelmann, *Theology*, p. 12.

[19] Conzelmann, *Theology*, pp. 16-17.

[20] Haenchen, *Acts*, pp. 98-99.

[21] Haenchen, *Acts*, pp. 98-103.

[22] Haenchen, *Acts*, p. 99.

[23] See Haenchen, "Acts as Source Material," *Studies in Luke-Acts*, pp. 258-278.

[24] See Kümmel, pp. 131-145.

[25] Wilckens, p. 65.

[26] See Minear, "Birth Stories," p. 111.

[27] See the article by Kümmel, in which he challenges the value of the major accusations underlying the positions of Bultmann, Käsemann, Conzelmann, and Haenchen.

[28] See Oscar Cullman, *Christ and Time* (Philadelphia: Westminster Press, 1964), p. 137.

[29] Munck, *Acts*, p. xxxviii.

[30] C. H. Talbert, "The Redactional Critical Quest for Luke the Theologian," *Perspectives in Religious Studies*, 2 (1970), pp. 171-222.

[31] See Wilckens, p. 60. W. W. Gasque, "The Historical Value of the Book of Acts. The Perspective of British Scholarship," *Theologische Zeitschrift*, 28 (1972), pp. 177-196. Regarding the three-fold division of salvation history, see Minear, "Birth Stories," p. 122: "They should also make clear how much weight Conzelmann places upon Luke 16:16, in establishing the pivot. It must be said that rarely has a scholar placed so much weight on so dubious an interpretaion of so difficult a logion."

[32] W. Harrington, "New Testament Theology. Two Recent Approaches." *Biblical Theology Bulletin*, 1 (1971), p. 184.

[33] Marshall, *Historian and Theologian*, pp. 47-48.

[34] Marshall, *Historian and Theologian*, p. 52.

[35] Marshall, *Historian and Theologian*, p. 75.

[36] Marshall, *Historian and Theologian*, pp. 54-57 and 69-76.

[37] Marshall, *Historian and Theologian*, p. 52. A similar view is expressed by van Unnik, p. 23.

[38] Talbert, "Shifting Sands," p. 395.

[39] See Wilckens, pp. 70-76.

[40] See Talbert, "Shifting Sands," p. 394. Drury, *Tradition*, p. 44, suggests that the next step in criticism is the study of midrash to situate the study in the matrix of contemporary theological storytelling.

[41] See Barrett, *Luke Historian* (Philadelphia: Fortress Press, 1970). Barrett speaks of Luke as a historian but actually treats Luke as a preacher.

[42] "Dear Theo," p. 131.

BIBLIOGRAPHY

Achtemeier, Paul. "The Lucan Perspective on the Miracles of Jesus: a Preliminary Sketch." *Journal of Biblical Literature*, 94 (1975), pp. 547-562.

Balthasar, Hans Urs von. "The Gospel As Norm and Test of All Spirituality in the Church." *Concilium*, 9 (1965), pp. 7-23.

Barrett, C. K. *Luke the Historian in Recent Study* . Philadelphia: Fortress Press, 1970.

Bernadicou, Paul. "Christian Community According to Luke." *Worship*, 44 (1970), pp. 205-219.

Besnard, Albert-Marie. "Tendencies of Contemporary Spirituality." *Concilium*, 9 (1965), pp. 25-44.

Blenkinsopp, Joseph. "The Church's Mission in St. Luke." *Clergy Review*, 50 (1965), pp. 698-704.

Borgen, Peder. "From Paul to Luke." *Catholic Biblical Quarterly*, 31 (1969), pp. 168-182.

Bornkamm, Günther. "The Missionary Stance of Paul in 1 Corinthians 9 and in Acts." *Studies in Luke-Acts*. L. E. Keck and J. L. Martyn, eds. New York: Abingdon Press, 1966, pp. 194-207.

Bovon, F. "L'Importance des Médiations dans le Projet Théologique de Luc." *New Testament Studies*, 21 (1974-75), pp. 23-39.

--- "Recent Trends in Lucan Studies." *Theology Digest*, 25 (1977), pp. 217-224.

Brown, Raymond, E. *New Testament Essays*. New York: Doubleday and Co., Inc., 1968.

--- "The Presentation of Jesus (Luke 2:22-40)." *Worship*, 51 (1977), pp. 2-11.

--- "The Finding of the Boy Jesus in the Temple: A Third Christmas Story." *Worship*, 51 (1977), pp. 474-485.

--- Karl P. Donfried, John Reumann, eds. *Peter in the New Testament*. New York: Paulist Press, 1973.

Brown, Schuyler. *Apostasy and Perseverance in the Theology of Luke*. Rome: Pontifical Biblical Institute, 1969.

Bruce, F. F. *The Acts of the Apostles*. Grand Rapids, Michigan: William B. Eerdmands Publishing Co., 1951.

--- "The Holy Spirit in the Acts of the Apostles." *Interpretation*, 27 (1973), pp. 166-183.

--- "Is the Paul of Acts the Real Paul?" *Bulletin of the John Ryland Library*, 58 (1976), pp. 282-300.

Bultmann, Rudolf. *Theology of the New Testament*. New York: Scribner's Sons, 1951.

--- *History of the Synoptic Tradition*. New York: Harper and Row, 1963.

Cadbury, H. J. "'We' and 'I' Passages in Luke-Acts." *New Testament Studies*, 3 (1956-57), pp. 128-132.

--- "Four Features of Lucan Style." *Studies in Luke-Acts*. L. E. Keck and J. L. Martyn, eds. New York: Abingdon Press, 1966, pp. 87-102.

--- *The Making of Luke-Acts*. London: SPCK, 1968.

Caird, G. B. *St. Luke*. Pelican New Testament Commentaries. Harmondsworth: Penguin, 1963.

Cave, C. H. "Lazarus and the Lukan Deuteronomy." *New Testament Studies*, 15 (1968-69), pp. 319-325.

Childs, Brevard. *Biblical Theology in Crisis*. Philadelphia: Westminster Press, 1980.

Comblin, J. "La paix dans la thêologie de saint Luc." *Ephêmerides Thêologicae Louvaniensis*, 32 (1956), pp. 439-460.

Conzelmann, Hans. *The Theology of St. Luke*. New York: Harper and Row, 1960.

--- "The Address of Paul on the Areopagus." *Studies in Luke-Acts*. L. E. Keck and J. L. Martyn, eds. New York: Abingdon Press, 1966, pp. 217-230.

--- "Luke's Place in the Development of Early Christianity." *Studies in Luke-Acts* L. E. Keck and J. L. Martyn, eds. New York: Abingdon Press, 1966, pp. 298-316.

Cribbs, F. Lamar. "St. Luke and the Johannine Tradition." *Journal of Biblical Literature*, 90 (1971), pp. 422-450.

Crossan, J. D. "Parable and Example in the Teaching of Jesus." *New Testament Studies*, 18 (1971-72), pp. 285-307.

Cullmann, Oscar. *Christ and Time*. Philadelphia: Fortress Press, 1964.

Danker, F. *Luke*. Proclamation Commentaries. Philadelphia: Fortress Press, 1976.

D'Arc, J. "Catechesis on the Road to Emmaus." *Lumen Vitae*, 32 (1977), pp. 143-156.

De Lacey, D. R. "Paul in Jerusalem." *New Testament Studies*, 20 (1973-74), pp. 82-86.

Dibelius, Martin. *From Tradition to Gospel*. New York: Scribner's Sons, 1965; orig. 1919.

"Dogmatic Constitution on Divine Revelation." *Documents of Vatican II*. Walter Abbott, ed. New York: Guild Press, 1966, pp. 111-128.

Doohan, Leonard. "Apostolic Prayer." *Review for Religious*, 33 (1974), pp. 785-789.

Drury, John. *Tradition and Design in Luke's Gospel*. Atlanta: John Knox Press, 1977.

Dupont, Jacques. *The Sources of the Acts*. New York: Herder and Herder, 1964.

--- "Ascension du Christ et don de l'Esprit d'après Actes 2:33." *Christ and Spirit in the New Testament*. B. Lindars and S. Smalley eds. Cambridge: University Press, 1973, pp. 219-228.

--- *The Salvation of the Gentiles.* New York: Paulist Press, 1979.
Duquoc, C. "Theology and Spirituality." *Concilium*, 19 (1966), pp. 88-99.
Easton, B. S. *The Purpose of the Acts.* London: SPCK, and The Sheldon Press, 1936.
Ellis, E. Earle. *The Gospel of Luke.* 1926; rev. ed. Greenwood, SC.:Attic Press, 1974.
Feuillet, A. *Jésus et sa Mère.* Paris: Gabalda, 1974.
--- "Le récit lucanien de l'agonie de Géthsemani (Lc xxii 39-46)." *New Testament Studies*, 22 (1975-76), pp. 397-417.
Filson, F. V. "Live Issues in the Acts." *Biblical Research*, 9 (1964), pp. 26-37.
Fitzmyer, Joseph. "Jewish Christianity in Acts in Light of the Qumran Scrolls." *Studies in Luke-Acts.* L. E. Keck and J. L. Martyn, eds. New York: Abingdon Press, 1966, pp. 233-257.
--- *The Gospel According to Luke.* Vol. I. New York: Doubleday and Co., Inc., 1981.
Flender, Helmut. *St. Luke: Theologian of Redemptive History.* Philadelphia: Fortress Press, 1967.
Franklin, Eric. *Christ the Lord: A Study in the Purpose and Theology of Luke-Acts.* Philadelphia: Westminster Press, 1975.
Gamba, J. "Praeoccupatio Universalistica in Evangelio S. Lucae," *Verbum Domini*, 40 (1962), pp. 131-135.
Gasque, W. W. "The Historical Value of the Book of Acts: An Essay in the History of New Testament Criticism." *Evangelical Quarterly*, 41 (1969), pp. 68-88.
--- "The Historical Value of the Book of Acts: The Perspective of British Scholarship." *Theologische Zeitschrift*, 28 (1972), pp. 177-196.
George, A. "La royauté de Jésus selon l'évangile de Luc." *Science Ecclésiastique*, 14 (1962), pp. 57-69.
--- "Son of God in Luke." *Theology Digest*, 15 (1967), pp. 128-133.
--- "L'Emploi chez Luc du vocabulaire de salut." *New Testament Studies*, 23 (1976-77), pp. 308-320.
Gill, D. "Observations on the Lukan Travel Narrative and Some Related Passages." *Harvard Theological Review*, 63 (1970), pp. 199-221.
Glover, Richard. "'Luke the Antiochene' and Acts." *New Testament Studies*, 11 (1964-65), pp. 97-106.
Goodenough, Edwin R. "The Perspective of Acts." *Studies in Luke-Acts.* L. E. Keck and J. L. Martyn, eds. New York: Abingdon Press, 1966, pp. 51-59.
Goulder, M. D. and M. L. Sanderson. "St. Luke's Genesis." *Journal of Theological Studies*, 8 (1957), pp. 12-30.
Haenchen, Ernst. "The Book of Acts as Source Material for the History of Early Christianity." *Studies in Luke-Acts.* L. E. Keck and J. L. Martyn, eds. New York: Abingdon Press, 1966, pp. 258-278.

--- *The Acts of the Apostles.* Oxford: Blackwell, 1971.

Hamel, E. "L'Usage de l'Escriture Sainte en théologie morale." *Gregorianum*, 47 (1966), pp. 53-85.

Harnack, Adolf von. *Luke the Physician.* London: Williams and Norgate, 1909.

--- *The Acts of the Apostles*, London: Williams and Norgate, 1909

--- *The Date of the Acts and of the Synoptic Gospels.* London: Williams and Norgate, 1911.

Harrington, Wilfrid. *The Gospel According to St. Luke.* New York: Newman Press, 1967.

--- "New Testament Theology: Two Recent Approaches." *Biblical Theology Bulletin*, 1 (1971), pp. 171-189.

Hartman, Lars. "Into the Name of Jesus." *New Testament Studies*, 20 (1973-74), pp. 432-440.

Hemer, C. J. "Luke the Historian." *Bulletin of the John Ryland Library*, 60 (1977), pp. 28-51.

Hezel, F. X. "Conversion and Repentance in Lucan Theology." *Bible Today*, 6 (1968), pp. 2596-2602.

Hiers, Richard. "The Problem of the Delay of the Parousia in Luke-Acts." *New Testament Studies*, 20 (1974-75), pp. 145-155.

Hinnebusch, Paul. "In My Father's House-About My Father's Business." *Bible Today*, 4 (1966), pp. 1893-1899.

--- "Jesus, the New Elijah, in St. Luke." *Bible Today*, 5 (1967), pp. 2175-2182 and 6 (1967), pp. 2237-2244.

Hobart, W. K. *The Medical Language of St. Luke.* Dublin: Hodges, Figgis and Co., 1882.

Holland, John. "Impressed Unbelievers as Witnesses to Christ (Luke 4:22a)." *Journal of Biblical Literature*, 98 (1979), pp. 219-229.

Hubbard, Benjamin. "The Role of the Commissioning Accounts in Acts." *Perspectives on Luke-Acts.* C. H. Talbert, ed. Danville, VA.: Association of Baptist Professors of Religion, 1978.

Hultgren, Arland. "Interpreting the Gospel of Luke." *Interpretation*, 30 (1976), pp. 353-365.

Karris, Robert J. "Poor and Rich: The Lukan Sitz im Leben." *Perspectives on Luke-Acts.* C. H. Talbert, ed. Danville, VA.: Association of Baptist Professors of Religion, 1978, pp. 112-125.

Kealy, John. *Luke's Gospel Today.* Denville, NJ.: Dimension Books, 1979.

Keck, L. E. and J. L. Martyn, eds. *Studies in Luke-Acts.* New York: Abingdon Press, 1966.

Kee, H. C., F. W. Young, and K. Froelich. *Understanding the New Testament.* 3rd. ed. Englewood Cliffs, NJ.: Prentice Hall, 1973.

Kelly, J. F. "The Patristic Biography of Luke." *Bible Today*, 12 (1974), pp. 113-119.

Kilgallen, J. J. "Acts: Literary and Theological Turning Points." *Biblical Theology Bulletin*, 7 (1977), pp. 177-180.

Knox, J. "Acts and the Pauline Letter Corpus." *Studies in Luke-Acts*, L. E. Keck and J. L. Martyn, eds. New York: Abingdon Press, 1966, pp. 279-287.

Kodell, Jerome. "Luke's Use of Laos, 'People,' Especially in the Jerusalem Narrative (Lk 19,28 - 24,53)." *Catholic Biblical Quarterly*, 31 (1969), pp. 327-343.

--- "The Word of God Grew. The Ecclesial Tendency of Logos in Acts 1,7; 12,24; 19,20." *Biblica*, 55 (1974), pp. 505-519.

Krentz, Edgar. *The Historical-Critical Method*. Philadelphia: Fortress Press, 1975.

Kümmel, W. G. "Current Theological Accusations Against Luke." *Andover Newton Quarterly*, 16 (1975), pp. 131-145.

Lampe, G. W. H. "The Lucan Portrait of Christ." *New Testament Studies*, 2 (1955-56), pp. 160-175.

Leaney, A. R. C. *The Gospel According to St. Luke*. Londom: Adam and Charles Black, 1966.

Legrand, L. "L'arrière-plan néotestamentaire de Luc 1,35," *Revue Biblique*, 70 (1963), pp. 161-192.

Lienhard, Joseph. "Acts 6:1-6: A Redactional View." *Catholic Biblical Quarterly*, 37 (1975), pp. 228-236.

MacRae, George. "'Whom Heaven Must Receive Until the Time': Reflections on the Christology of Acts." *Interpretation*, 27 (1973), pp. 151-165.

Marshall, I. Howard. "Recent Study of the Acts of the Apostles." *Expository Times*, 80 (1969), pp. 292-296.

--- *Luke: Historian and Theologian*. Grand Rapids, MI.: Zondervan, 1971.

Martin, Ralph. "Salvation and Discipleship in Luke's Gospel." *Interpretation*, 30 (1976), pp. 366-380.

Martini, Carlo. "L'esclusione dalla communità del popolo di Dio e il nuovo Israele secondo Atti 3, 23." *Biblica*, 50 (1968), pp. 1-14.

Mattill, A. J. Jr. "The Date and Purpose of Luke-Acts: Rackham Reconsidered." *Catholic Biblical Quarterly*, 40 (1978), pp. 335-350.

McGinley, Lawrence J. *Form Criticism of the Synoptic Healing Narratives-A Study in the Theories of Martin Dibelius and Rudolf Bultmann*. Woodstock: Woodstock College Press, 1944.

McKnight, Edgar V. *What is Form Criticism?* Philadelphia: Fortress Press, 1969.

Menoud, P. H. "Jésus et ses témoins. Remarques sur l'unité de l'oeuvre du Luc." *Eglise et Théologie*, 23 (1960), pp. 7-20.

--- "Le plan des Actes des Apôtres." *New Testament Studies*, 1 (1954-55), pp. 44-51.

Meyer, Ben. F. "The Initial Self-Understanding of the Church." *Catholic Biblical Quarterly*, 27 (1965), pp. 35-42.

Michiels, R. "La conception lucanienne de la conversion." *Ephêmerides Théologicae Louvaniensis*, 41 (1965), pp. 42-78.

Minear, Paul. S. "Luke's Use of the Birth Stories." *Studies in Luke-Acts*. L. E. Keck and J. L. Martyn, eds. New York: Abingdon Press, 1966, pp. 111-130.

--- "Some Glimpses of Luke's Sacramental Theology." *Worship*, 44 (1970), pp. 322-331.

--- "Dear Theo: The Kerygmatic Intention and Claim of the Book of Acts." *Interpretation*, 27 (1973), pp. 131-150.

--- "Jesus' audiences according to Luke." *Theology Digest*, 23 (1975), pp. 256-264.

Mosley, A. W. "Jesus' Audiences in the Gospels of St. Mark and St. Luke." *New Testament Studies*, 10 (1963-64), pp. 139-149.

Moule, C. F. "The Christology of Acts." *Studies in Luke-Acts*. L. E. Keck and J. L. Martyn, eds. New York: Abingdon Press, 1966, pp. 159-185.

Munck, Johannes. *The Acts of the Apostles* New York: Doubleday and Co., Inc., 1967.

Muñoz Iglesias, S. "Los Evangelios de la Infancia y las infancias de los heroes," *Estudios Biblicos*, 16 (1957), pp. 5-36.

Navone, John. "Lucan Joy." *Scripture*, 20 (1968), pp. 49-62.

--- *Themes of St. Luke*. Rome: Gregorian University Press, 1970.

--- "The Lucan Banquet Community." *Bible Today*, 8 (1970), pp. 155-161.

--- "Three Aspects of the Lucan Theology of History." *Biblical Theology Bulletin*, 3 (1973), pp. 115-132.

Oliver, H. H. "The Lucan Birth Stories and the Purpose of Luke-Acts." *New Testament Studies*, 10 (1963-64), pp. 202-226.

O'Neill, J. C. *Theology of Acts in Its Historical Setting*. London: SPCK, 1961.

Orchard, B. "The Problem of Acts and Galatians." *Catholic Biblical Quarterly*, 7 (1945), pp. 377-397.

O'Toole, R. F. "Why Did Luke Write Acts (Lk-Acts)?" *Biblical Theology Bulletin*, 7 (1977), pp. 66-76.

--- "Luke's Understanding of Jesus' Resurection-Ascension-Exaltation." *Biblical Theology Bulletin*, 9 (1979), pp. 106-114.

Owen, H. P. "Stephen's Vision in Acts VII:55-56." *New Testament Studies*, 1 (1954-55), pp. 224-226.

Parker, Pierson. "Luke and the Fourth Evangelist." *New Testament Studies*, 9 (1962-63), pp. 317-336.

--- "The 'Former Treatise' and the Date of Acts." *Journal of Biblical Literature*, 84 (1965), pp. 52-58.

--- "Once More, Acts and Galatians." *Journal of Biblical LIterature*, 86 (1967), pp. 175-182.

Perrin, Norman. *What is Redaction Criticism?* Philadelphia: Fortress Press, 1969.

Plumacher, Eckhard. "The 'We-passages' in Acts." *Theology Digest*, 27 (1979), pp. 47-48.

Ramsay, W. M. *St. Paul the Traveller and the Roman Citizen*. London: Hodder and Stoughton, 1905.

--- *The Cities of St. Paul*. London: Hodder and Stoughton, 1907.

Robbins, Vernon K. "Prefaces in Greco-Roman Biography and Luke-Acts." *Perspectives in Religious Studies*, 6 (1979), pp. 94-108.

Robsinson, J. A. T. "The Most Primitive Christianity of All?" *Journal of Theological Studies*, 7 (1956), pp. 177-189.

Ryan, W. F. J. "The Church as the Servant of God in Acts." *Scripture*, 15 (1963), pp. 110-115.

Sanders, E. P. "The Argument from Order and the Relationship between Mathew and Luke." *New Testament Studies*, 15 (1968-69), pp. 249-261.

Scheffczyk, Leo. "Word of God." *Sacramentum Mundi*, VI. Karl Rahner with Cornelius Ernst and Kevin Smyth, eds. New York: Herder and Herder, 1970, pp. 362-368.

Schoonenberg, Piet. "Notes of a Systematic Theologian." *Concilium*, 70 (1971), pp. 90-97.

Schuster, Heinz. "Pastoral Theology," *Sacramentum Mundi*, IV. Karl Rahner with Cornelius Ernst and Kevin Smyth, eds. New York: Herder and Herder, 1969, pp. 365-368.

Scobie, Charles H. H. "The Origins and Development of Samaritan Christianity." *New Testament Studies*, 19 (1972-73), pp. 390-414.

Sheridan, Mark. "Disciple and Discipleship in Matthew and Luke." *Biblical Theology Bulletin*, 3 (1973), pp. 235-255.

Smalley, S. S. "The Christology of Acts." *Expository Times*, 73 (1962), pp. 358-362.

Smith, R. H. "The Eschatology of Acts and Contemporary Exegesis." *Concordia Theological Monthly*, 29 (1958), pp. 641-663.

Sparks, H. F. D. "St Luke's Transpositions." *New Testament Studies*, 3 (1956-57), pp. 219-223.

Spivey, R. and D. Moody Smith. *Anatomy of the New Testaments.* New York: MacMillan, 1974.

Stagg, F. "The Unhindered Gospel." *Review and Expositor*, 71 (1974), pp. 451-462.

Stempvoort, P. A. "The Interpretation of the Ascension in Luke and Acts." *New Testament Studies*, 5 (1958-59), pp. 30-42.

Streeter, B. H. *The Four Gospels: A Study of Origins, Treating of the Manuscript Tradition, Sources, Authorship, and Dates.* London: Macmillan, 1924.

Sudbrack, Josef. "Spirituality." *Sacramentum Mundi*, VI. Karl Rahner with Cornelius Ernst and Kevin Smyth eds. New York: Herder and Herder, 1970, pp. 147-153.

Talbert, C. H. "An Anti-Gnostic Tendency in Lukan Christology." *New Testament Studies*, 14 (1967-68), pp. 259-271.

--- "The Lucan Presentation of Jesus' Ministry in Galilee, Luke 4:31 - 9:50." *Review and Expositor*, 64 (1967), pp. 485-497.

--- "The Redactional Critical Quest for Luke the Theologian." *Perspectives in Religious Studies*, 2 (1970), pp. 171-222.

--- *Literary Patterns, Theological Themes and the Genre of Luke-Acts.* Missoula, MT.: Scholars' Press, 1974.

--- "Shifting Sands: The Recent Study of the Gospel of Luke." *Interpretation*, 30 (1976), pp. 381-395.

Tatum, W. Barnes. "The Epoch of Israel: Luke I-II and the Theological Plan of Luke-Acts." *New Testament Studies*, 13 (1966-67), pp. 184-195.

Tolbert, M. 0. "Contemporary Issues in the Book of Acts." *Review and Expositor*, 71 (1974), pp 521-531.

Turner, N. "The Relation of Luke I and II to Hebraic Sources and to the Rest of Luke-Acts." *New Testament Studies*, 2 (1955-56), pp. 100-109.

Unnik, W. C. van. "Luke-Acts, A Storm Center in Contemporary Scholarship." *Studies in Luke-Acts.* L. E. Keck and J. L. Martyn, eds. New York: Abingdon Press, 1966, pp. 15-32.

Vielhauer, Paul. "On the Paulinism of Acts." *Studies in Luke-Acts*, L. E. Keck and J. L. Martyn, eds. New York: Abingdon Press, 1966, pp. 33-50.

Wansbrough, Henry. "St. Luke and Christian Ideals in an Affluent Scoiety." *New Blackfriars*, 49 (1968), pp. 582-587.

Wickings, H. F. "The Nativity Stories and Docetism." *New Testament Studies*, 23 (1976-77), pp. 457-460.

Wijngaards, J. N. "Biblical Spirituality." *Scripture Bulletin*, 9 (1978), pp. 9-14.

Wilckens, Ulrich. "Interpreting Luke-Acts in a Period of Existentialist Theology." *Studies in Luke-Acts.* L. E. Keck and J. L. Martyn, eds. New York: Abingdon Press, 1966, pp. 60-83.

Wilshire, L. E. "Was Canonical Luke written in the Second Century?- A Continuing Discussion." *New Testament Studies*, 20 (1973-74), pp. 246-253.

Wilson, S. G. "Lukan Eschatology." *New Testament Studies*, 16 (1969-70), pp. 330-347.

Winter, Paul. "Some Observations on the Language in the Birth and Infancy Stories of the Third Gospel." *New Testament Studies*, 1 (1954-55), pp. 111-121.

Zehnle, Richard. "The Salvific Character of Jesus' Death in Lucan Soteriology." *Theological Studies*, 30 (1969), pp. 420-444.

Index of Subjects

Index of Authors

Index of Scripture References

Luke (*continued*)

Luke (*continued*)

Luke (*continued*)

Luke (*continued*)

Luke (*continued)*

Luke (*continued*)

Luke (*continued*)

Luke (*continued*)

Acts (*continued*)

Acts (*continued*)

Acts (*continued*)

Acts (*continued*)

Acts (*continued*)

Acts (*continued*)

Tape cassettes by Leonard Doohan on "The Spirituality of Luke/Acts" are available by writing to:

Other Books by Bear & Company

MATTHEW: Spirituality for the 80's and 90's ($9.95)
Leonard Doohan

WESTERN SPIRITUALITY: Historical Roots, Ecumenical Routes ($11.95)
Matthew Fox

WHEE! WE, WEE ALL THE WAY HOME: A Guide to a Sensual, Prophetic Spirituality ($8.95)
Matthew Fox

ORIGINAL BLESSING: A Primer in Creation Spirituality ($10.95)
Matthew Fox

CRY OF THE ENVIRONMENT:
Rebuilding the Christian Creation Tradition ($14.95)
Philip N. Joranson and Ken Butigan, editors

THE CAPTAIN AMERICA COMPLEX: Spirituality and Politics in Our Own Times ($8.95)
Robert Jewett
Introduction by William Sloane Coffin

THE UNIVERSE IS A GREEN DRAGON: A Cosmic Creation Story ($8.95)
Brian Swimme

Contact your local bookseller or write:

Bear & Company, Inc.
PO Drawer 2860
Santa Fe, NM 87504